Stats to Go

A guide to statistics for hospitality, leisure and tourism

John Buglear

BUTTERWORTH
HEINEMANN

OXFORD AUCKLAND BOSTON JOHANNESBURG MELBOURNE NEW DELHI

Butterworth-Heinemann
Linacre House, Jordan Hill, Oxford OX2 8DP
225 Wildwood Avenue, Woburn, MA 01801-2041
A division of Reed Educational and Professional Publishing Ltd

℞ A member of the Reed Elsevier plc group

First published 2000

British Library Cataloguing in Publication Data
Buglear, John
　Stats to go
　1 Tourist trade – Statistical methods　　2 Hospitality
　industry – Statistical methods
　I Title
　338.4'7910015195

ISBN 0 7506 4556 3

Composition by Genesis Typesetting, Rochester, Kent
Printed and bound in Great Britain

FOR EVERY TITLE THAT WE PUBLISH, BUTTERWORTH-HEINEMANN
WILL PAY FOR BTCV TO PLANT AND CARE FOR A TREE.

Contents

Preface

This book is intended to equip students and others interested in the hospitality and tourism industries with an understanding of Statistics. As the sub-title implies, this is a guide to using Statistics rather than a specialist Statistics textbook. The book provides an accessible insight into the use of a variety of statistical techniques. These techniques are discussed and demonstrated using worked examples set in hospitality and tourism contexts.

The book aims to encourage readers to use computer software to carry out statistical work. It provides guidance on the use of MINITAB* and the statistical aspects of Excel. As a consequence the use of statistical tables has been kept to a minimum.

Solutions to review questions are included. These are intended to help students monitor their own progress and make the book an effective basis for independent learning.

*MINITAB is a registered trademark of Minitab Inc., 3081 Enterprise Drive, State College, PA 16801, USA. http://www.minitab.com

Acknowledgements

The author would like to thank Allison for her creative ideas and critical evaluation, Max and Tom for their forbearance, and his colleague Jan Lincoln for her assistance.

Starting out

'Statistics!' – 'Do you want to know a statistic?'

'Eighty-two per cent of students who say they can't understand a book on statistics haven't tried reading it . . .
. . . so don't stop here!'

Chapter Objectives

This chapter will help you:

- To understand why the ability to deal with numbers is important.
- To see how this book can help you develop that ability.
- To prepare effectively to study Statistics.

In this chapter you will find:

- A discussion of the importance of numbers to hospitality and tourism businesses.
- A description of the approach and style used in this book.
- An introduction to key words.
- Guidance on basic numerical skills you will need to use.
- Advice on technological support.

1.1 Numbers in the hospitality and tourism industries

This book is about analysing numbers. But why should analysing numbers matter to someone studying hospitality or tourism? How relevant can it be for someone planning to build a career in hospitality or tourism?

To understand this, and to appreciate why the study of numbers is built into your course, consider how the hospitality and tourism sector has changed in the course of a generation. The set of organizations that operate in the sector and the products they offer have changed dramatically.

If you look at films or read novels that reflect the lives people led twenty or thirty years ago, you will notice the changes. Almost all licensed premises were male-oriented places that provided a fairly narrow range of beverages and no hot food. At work people ate food chosen from a limited range of traditional fare in a workplace canteen. Fish and chips was the staple fast food and dining out was an infrequent pleasure for most people. For those who did dine out, the limits of exotic eating amounted to Chinese or Indian restaurants. Holidays were taken once a year, largely within the UK. Often families would return to the same resort, sometimes the very same place to stay, year after year. The fun-lovers could go to holiday camps, the very adventurous impressed their neighbours by going to Spain. Apart from the journeys of travelling salesmen, business travel hardly existed. People who made it to retirement age lived on modest pensions and travelled little, except to see relatives. For children there were beaches, parks and funfairs.

How strange all that seems, how very different things are today. We have a wide variety of licensed premises where managers and owners try to create an ambience and offer food and beverages to appeal to target market segments. The workplace canteen with its own kitchens has all but disappeared, instead contractors deliver a wide range of sandwiches and cook-chill food to work-based outlets. The phrase 'fast food', unknown a generation ago has become very big business, compared to which the traditional fish and chip shop seems like a cottage industry. The centre of even a modest-sized town provides a cosmopolitan selection of restaurants. The cuisine of Thailand, Mexico, Italy, the USA and Japan is usually only a short distance away. The popularity of food from exotic places of course reflects the transformation in the holiday market. A long-haul holiday is likely to be one of several holidays taken during a year. A shopping weekend in New York is no longer purely a bizarre indulgence of the super-rich. Business travel has become a major market with specialist operators. Retired people are often the most avid travellers, transforming the off-season business for many resorts. As far as children are concerned, the emergence of the theme park and the all-weather activity centre means that holiday decisions for many families are more overtly child-driven.

These are fundamental and far-reaching changes. Experts may disagree about the factors that have caused them, but as a result of them the business environment faced by hospitality and tourism organizations has altered profoundly, and will almost certainly continue to do so.

A further source of uncertainty for the hospitality and tourism sector is the fact that its products are typically considered luxury goods and services that are purchased from discretionary income. Demand for them is therefore highly sensitive to consumer confidence and taste. A family facing the loss of an income may well halve its consumption of clothing but is likely to abandon the idea of going on holiday completely.

How do organizations cope with this degree of change? The answer, in some cases, is that they don't. Many of the companies that dominated the sector a generation ago no longer exist. They became history because they failed to respond to the changing market. Others survived and some small operations thrived, becoming market-leaders within the lifetimes of their founders.

Although luck and the good fortune of happening to be in the right market place with the right product may have played a part, to succeed in a changing environment an organization needs to recognize the changes and anticipate the consequences for its operations. How can it do that? By constantly studying its markets and monitoring its operations. This means counting and measuring key factors, in other words gathering numerical facts, or statistics.

In every organization there is a flow of numbers which are either deliberately collected or arise from the regular interactions with customers, suppliers and other significant organizations. These figures in themselves cannot tell the organization what is going on in the market or how it is performing. One of the responsibilities of management is to ensure that such figures are used, which means they have to be processed and analysed. The patterns that emerge from this analysis provide information that enables managers to understand the situation they face and base their decisions on that understanding.

The ability to analyse figures and interpret the results is therefore considered a key management skill. Look at recruitment advertisements for management posts and you will see that employers attach great importance to 'numerical skills' and 'problem-solving'.

If you want to build a successful management career these are skills that you have to acquire sooner or later. Your course will provide you with the opportunity of developing them. Make the most of that opportunity and you will have a cutting-edge skill that will pay dividends for you in the future.

Hospitality, Leisure & Tourism Series

1.2 How this book is organized

This book will help you deal with the numerical parts of your course. How you use it depends on how you approach the study of numbers you are about to start. It can be a crutch to help you limp through what may seem like an unwelcome revisit to the sums of schooldays, or it can be a springboard that will help you accumulate a key investment for your future – the skill of numeracy.

This book may influence your attitude to studying numbers, but it cannot decide it. The attitude you take is something for you to develop, but whether this book is to be a crutch or a springboard for you, it is intended to be a guide which will provide support for the numerical work you will undertake throughout your course.

The first five chapters of the book (including this one) deal with topics that you are likely to meet during the first stage of your course. They deal largely with *descriptive* techniques, that is methods that will enable you to arrange or analyse data in a way that helps *describe* the situation being studied.

Chapters 6–9 cover topics that you may meet at a later stage of your course. They deal with *inferential* techniques, that is methods that enable you to make *inferences* or draw conclusions about an issue in general based on the study of a comparatively modest amount of data.

The final chapter is designed to help you tackle numerical aspects of the final-year project or dissertation you will probably be asked to write.

The book will introduce you to a variety of analytical techniques that together constitute a 'tool-kit' of methods that can be used to investigate situations and help solve problems. Like any other tool-kit, the key to using it properly is to know not only what each tool does, but to know how and when to use it. The book will help you develop this ability by illustrating the application of the methods described using contexts taken from the hospitality and tourism sectors.

Each technique will be explained and demonstrated. Any calculations will be explained in words before symbols are used to represent the process.

Being able to apply a technique, to produce the correct result from a calculation, is important, especially if you find 'learning by doing' useful, but it is by no means the end of the story. It is even more important to be able to interpret the results that the technique has enabled you to produce and to communicate the meaning of those results. In your future career you may be asked to apply techniques of analysis but you are much more likely to need to be able to explain results, perhaps to judge whether appropriate techniques have been used to produce them. The book therefore provides you with not only a description of each technique and an illustration of its use, but also a discussion of the types of results you could get, and what each of them would mean.

At the end of Chapters 1–9 there are a set of review questions that you can use to confirm your understanding of the methods and ideas featured in each chapter. You can find answers to these questions at the back of the book.

1.3 Taking the first steps

There are two key preliminary tasks that are worth investing a little time and effort on getting to grips with from the very beginning. The first is to understand a few key words which may be completely new to you, or whose meanings in the context of this subject are unfamiliar to you. The second is to review a set of basic arithmetical operations, which are involved in the use of some of the methods demonstrated further on in the book. Being clear about these basics from the start will mean you avoid unnecessary confusion later on.

You will find that the terms explained below are used many times in this book. They are the first words in a technical vocabulary that will become familiar to you as you proceed. As you will find with other subjects you study or interests that you have outside college, there are specialist words and phrases to comprehend, but once you have grasped their meaning you will get used to using them as a matter of course.

1.3.1 The key words you need to know

- *Data* A plural noun (the singular form is *datum*) which means a set of known or given things, facts. Note that data can be numerical (e.g. age of people) or non-numerical (e.g. gender of people).

- *statistics* Without a capital letter, i.e. in its lower case form, this means a set of numerical data or figures that have been collected systematically.

- *Statistics* With a capital letter this is a proper noun that means the study of statistics, the set of methods and theories that can be used to arrange, analyse and interpret numerical data.

- *A variable* A quantity that varies, the opposite of a constant. For example the number of rooms sold in a hotel is a variable, whereas the number of hours in a day is a constant. In the expressions that we will use to summarize methods a capital letter, usually X or Y, will be used to represent a variable.

- *Value* A specific amount that it is possible for a variable to be. For example the number of rooms sold in a 100-bedroom hotel

Hospitality, Leisure & Tourism Series

could be 53 or 68 or 93. These are all possible values of the variable 'number of rooms sold'.

- *Observation* or *observed value* A value of a variable that has actually occurred, i.e. been counted or measured. For example if hotel staff sell 75 rooms for a particular night that is an observation or observed value of the variable 'number of rooms sold'.

  An observation is represented by the lower case of the letter used to represent the variable; for instance 'x' represents a single observed value of the variable 'X'. A small numerical suffix is added to distinguish particular observations in a set; x_1 would represent the first observed value, x_2 the second and so on.

- *Random* This adjective refers to something that occurs in an unplanned way. A *random* variable is a variable whose observed values arise by chance. The sales of bottled beer in a pub are a variable which is random, whereas the number of days in a month is a variable which is not random, i.e. its observed values are pre-determined.

- *Distribution* The pattern exhibited by the observed values of a variable when they are arranged in order of magnitude. A *theoretical* distribution is one that has been deduced, rather than compiled from observed values.

- *Population* Generally this means the total number of persons residing in a defined area at a given time. In Statistics a *population* is the complete set of things we want to investigate. These may be human such as all the people who have visited a theme park, or inanimate such as the flights made by an aircraft.

- *Sample* A subset of the population, that is a smaller number of items picked from the population. A *random sample* is a sample whose components have been chosen in a random way, that is on the basis that any single item in the population has no more or less chance than any other to be included in the sample.

1.3.2 The basic numerical skills you need

Addition and subtraction • • •

Addition, represented by the plus sign '+', is the process of putting two or more numbers together to make a sum or total. As long as the numbers being added together are positive, i.e. more than zero, the resulting total grows as more numbers are added.

Example 1.1

A member of staff at a 'drive-through' conducts four operations in the course of serving a customer. If these tasks take 10, 12, 7 and 8 seconds, what is the total time that will elapse between the time a customer arrives at the order point and the time they can depart from the service point?

You can get the answer by adding together the times taken for the four operations.

Total time = 10 + 12 + 7 + 8 = 37 seconds

Because Statistics often involves combining observations, the arithmetical process of addition is a process you will come across in the context of several techniques dealt with later in the book.

Although you are probably already familiar with addition, you may not have encountered the symbol called 'sigma', which is used in Statistics to represent it. Sigma is the capital letter S from the Greek alphabet, written as 'Σ'. It is the letter s because s is the first letter of the word 'sum'. It is a Greek letter because at the time that much of the theory that makes up the subject of Statistics as we know it today was developed, the so-called 'classical' languages of the ancient world were taught in the schools and universities. The Greek language, with its particular alphabet, therefore provided the pioneers of Statistics, and other fledgling disciplines, with a ready source of distinctive symbols.

The symbol Σ (sigma) stands for 'the sum of' when it is used in Statistical expressions, for example:

Σx means 'the sum of a set of observed values of the variable X'

Sometimes it is necessary to specify precisely which observed values of X are to be added together. To show this, the letter 'i' is used to count the observations, for example:

$\sum_{i=1}^{4} x$ means 'the sum of the first to the fourth observations of the variable X'

The expression '$i = 1$' below the sigma tells us to start the addition with the first observed value of x and the '4' above the sigma sign tells us to finish the addition with the fourth observed value.

Hospitality, Leisure & Tourism Series

Example 1.2

In the situation described in Example 1.1, we could show that the total time taken to serve a customer in the drive-through facility (which we could represent by 'T') is the sum of the time taken to perform four tasks by using the expression:

$$T = \sum_{i=1}^{4} t = t_1 + t_2 + t_3 + t_4 = 10 + 12 + 7 + 8 = 37$$

If it is necessary to indicate that all of a set of observations should be added together and the exact number of observations is not known, we use the letter 'n' to represent the last observation in the set, so:

$$\sum_{i=1}^{n} x$$ means 'the sum of the first to the last observations of the variable X'

As you proceed with your study of the subject, you will find that the letter 'n' is used throughout Statistics to represent the number of observations in a set.

At first these types of symbol may appear strange to you, but it is worth learning to recognize and use them, they can become very useful shorthand forms which will save you space and time in future work.

Subtraction, represented by the minus sign '–', is the process of subtracting or 'taking away' one or more numbers from another. As long as the numbers being subtracted are positive, i.e. more than zero, the result reduces as more numbers are subtracted.

Example 1.3

The gross weekly pay of a tour guide is £200. If her stoppages are £28 tax, £9 National Insurance, and £52 accommodation charge, what is her weekly take-home pay?

You can get the answer by subtracting the stoppages from the gross wage.

Take-home pay $= £200 - £28 - £9 - £52 = £111$

An alternative approach to this operation is to add the stoppages first and then subtract the total stoppages from the gross pay. This would be represented in the following way:

Take home pay = £200 − (£28 + £9 + £52) = £111

The round brackets dictate that the operation shown within them must be carried out first. They are used to indicate priority.

You may well find addition and subtraction fairly easy, but there are cases where they are not so straightforward; first, when negative numbers are involved, and second when the operation involves numbers measured in awkward units, e.g. minutes and hours.

Addition and subtraction may give you some difficulty if negative numbers are involved. If a negative number is added to a total, it reduces the total.

Example 1.4

A customer's hotel bill consists of the following items: a room charge of £60, £25 for an evening meal, £8 for Minibar items, and a £10 discount for using a promotional voucher. What is the total amount that should be on the bill?

The answer can be shown as:

Total amount = £60 + £25 + £8 + (−£10) = £83

You can see that round brackets have been used, both to highlight the fact that there is a negative number in the sequence and to indicate that it must be dealt with first. This means deciding how to tackle the apparently contradictory '+ −' sequence of symbols. In fact the minus sign overrides the plus sign, so adding a number is therefore the same as subtracting a number. The arithmetical expression used to find the total amount in Example 1.4 has exactly the same result as the following expression, which combines addition and subtraction:

Total amount = £60 + £25 + £8 − £10 = £83

But what do you do if you have to subtract a negative number? In fact subtracting a negative number produces the same result as adding a positive number.

Example 1.5

The sharp-eyed Front Office Manager in the hotel mentioned in Example 1.4 spots that the voucher is out of date.. What effect will this have on the total amount of the bill?

They would have to take away the reduction from the previous total, so now:

Total amount = £83 – (–£10) = £93

You get exactly the same result if you simply add the amount concerned, £10.

You may find it helpful to imagine the two minus signs 'cancelling each other out' to leave you with an addition. Alternatively it may help to think that taking away a negative is always positive.

Addition and subtraction involving time is something many people find difficult because time is measured in hours made up of 60 minutes, and minutes made up of 60 seconds, rather than nice, neat numerical parcels of ten. The use of the 24-hour clock on top of all this seems to phase most people completely.

Example 1.6

A business traveller drives for 12 minutes to reach her local railway station where she boards a train that takes 33 minutes to reach its London terminus. It takes her 24 minutes by tube to reach another London terminus, where she boards another train. After a journey that takes 1 hour 5 minutes to reaches her station, from where she takes a 10-minute taxi ride to her destination. What is the total journey time?

To get the answer we can express all the times mentioned, including the figure for the second train journey, in minutes.

Total journey time = 12 + 33 + 24 + 65 + 10 = 144

The answer may not be satisfactory in this form. To convert it into hours and minutes we need to find how many units of 60 minutes there are in 144 minutes. The answer is 2, so the total journey time is 2 hours (120 of the total number of minutes) and 24 minutes (the number of minutes left over when 120 is subtracted from 144).

Example 1.7

If the traveller described in Example 1.6 begins her journey at 11 am in the morning, what time will she arrive at her destination, and how would this time be expressed using the 24-hour clock?

To get the answer, work in hours first, then minutes.

Arrival time = 11 + 2 hours = 1pm

+ 24 minutes = 1.24pm

To express this using the 24-hour clock, add 12 to the number of hours, because the arrival time is after midday.

Arrival time = 1.24 + 12 = 13.24

But what if the traveller started her journey later than expected, at 11.45, what time would she arrive? This is a little more complicated because the departure time and total journey time are measured in both hours and minutes. To find the answer we can start by adding the hours:

11 + 2 = 13

then add the minutes together:

45 + 24 = 69

Since this amount of minutes is longer than an hour, we have to express it in hour and minutes, and add the result to the sum of the hours:

69 minutes = 1 hour and 9 minutes

13 + 1 = 14 hours

+ 9 minutes = 14.09, or 2.09 pm

Multiplication and division • • •

Multiplication, or 'times-ing', represented either by the 'times' sign '×' or the asterisk '*', is the process of multiplying two or more numbers together to make a product. If the number is multiplied by a number greater than one, the resulting product will be greater than the original number.

Example 1.8

A holidaymaker wishes to convert £240 into US dollars. If the rate advertised at the bureau de change is $1.60 to the pound, how many dollars will his pounds buy?

You can get the answer by multiplying the total number of pounds by the exchange rate.

Dollars he can buy = £240 × 1.60 = $384

In this case the number of dollars is greater than the number of pounds, the product represents a numerical increase. But if you multiply a number by another number that is less than one, you will get a product that is lower than your first number.

Example 1.9

A business traveller returning from Oslo has 3200 Norwegian krone that she wishes to change into pounds. If the rate available at a bureau de change is £0.08 per krone, how many pounds will she get for her krone?

To get the answer, multiply the total number of krone by the exchange rate.

Pounds she can buy = Kr3200 × 0.08 = £256

If you have to multiply a positive number by a negative number, the product will be negative. However if you multiply two negative number together, the product will be positive:

$$3 \times (-2) = -6 \quad \text{but} \quad (-3) \times (-2) = 6$$

Division, or finding how many times one amount 'goes into' another, is the process of dividing one number by another. It is represented either by the forward slash '/' or the sign '÷'. If you divide a number by another number that is greater than one, the result will be smaller than the original number.

Example 1.10

The 48 guests attending a function are to be offered a glass of wine on arrival. If the contents of one bottle of wine will fill three and a half glasses, how many bottles will be required?

We can obtain the answer by dividing the number of guests by the number of glassfuls per bottle.

Number of bottles = 48/3.5 = 13.714 (to 3 decimal places)

Something to note in Example 1.10 is that although we can get a very precise result, in this case specified to three places of numbers after the decimal point, in the situation described the figure would be rounded up to the nearest whole number, 14.

If you divide a number by another number that is less than one, the result will be larger than the original number.

Example 1.11

A visitor to Britain sees a sign saying 'Airport 7 miles'. She asks you how far that is in kilometres.

A kilometre is equivalent to 0.62 of a mile (to 2 decimal places), so to reply to her question you need to find how many times 0.62 will 'go' into 7, that is you must divide 7 by 0.62.

Kilometres to the airport = 7/0.62 = 11.29   (to 2 decimal places)

Squaring and square rooting ● ● ●

Squaring, or taking the square of a number is the process of multiplying a number by itself. The process is represented by the number with a superscript showing the number two, for example the square of three, or three squared would be written 3^2 which tells us to multiply three by three.

If the number you want to square is more than one, the result will be larger than the number itself, for instance the square of three is nine. However if the number you want to square is less than one, the result will be smaller than the number itself, for example the square of a half is a quarter.

Example 1.12

The floor covering of the dance space in a live music venue has to be replaced. If the dance floor is 4.2 metres long by 4.2 metres wide, how much new floor covering will be needed?

To find an area multiply the length by the width. In this case because the area is a square, that is the length and width are the same, we need only take the square of 4.2.

Floor area = 4.2^2 = 17.64 square metres

Squaring a positive number will always give you a positive result. But because multiplying one negative number by another always gives you a positive product, squaring a negative number will always give you a positive result as well.

So: $3^2 = 9$ and $(-3)^2 = 9$

The fact that we always get a positive result when we square a negative number is worth remembering because it plays a vital role in several statistical techniques that you will meet.

Square rooting, or taking the square root of a number is the process of working out what number squared would produce a particular number. It is represented by the radical or 'tick' sign, $\sqrt{\ }$, so the square root of 9 would be shown as $\sqrt{9}$. The result of $\sqrt{9}$ is 3 because the number 3 multiplied by itself gives you 9.

Example 1.13

A new ornamental garden featuring a square lawn area is to be laid out at a conference centre. If there are 160 square metres of turf available, what will the dimensions of the lawn be?

You can find the answer by taking the square root of 160:

Lawn area $= \sqrt{160} = 12.65$ (to 2 decimal places)

The lawn would be 12.65 metres long by 12.65 metres wide.

Fractions, proportions and percentages • • •

Fractions, proportions and percentages sound very different, but they are only different ways of doing the same thing; expressing a part of something in relation to the whole. If, for example, water constitutes 100 g of 500 g of ham, this could be explained as either:

water constitutes one-fifth of the weight of this product

Or water constitutes 0.2 of the weight of this product

Or water constitutes 20 per cent of the weight of this product

One-fifth is the fraction, 0.2 is the proportion, and 20 per cent is the percentage. They are different ways of saying the same thing because there are five-fifths in one, five lots of 0.2 in one, and five lots of 20 per cent in 100 per cent. You should bear in mind that each of them is a number less than one, including the percentage, which doesn't look as if it is less than one.

It is easier to use percentages if you understand that the literal meaning of 'per cent' is per hundred. (The word 'cent' originally meant one hundred; a Roman centurion was an officer in the Roman army in charge of one hundred men.) This will especially help when you have to perform arithmetical operations using percentages.

Example 1.14

The proprietor of a souvenir shop located in the old part of a famous European city makes a deal with a tour guide. In return for the tour guide escorting parties of tourists to the shop the proprietor will give the tour guide 40 per cent of the profit the shop makes from the money the tourists spend. If the profit margin on the souvenirs is 60 per cent and the first group of tourists spends £735, how much money will the tour guide get?

The shop receives a profit of 60 per cent of £735, and the tour guide should receive 40 per cent of the 60 per cent of £735, so:

Guide's share $= 40/100 \times 60/100 \times £735 = £176.40$

Notice that in Example 1.14 the percentages appear in the expression as amounts per hundred.

Rounding and approximation

You may find it easy to manipulate figures in your head, or you may find such a skill impossible and marvel at those who possess it. The truth is that anyone can learn how to carry out mental arithmetic, the tricks are to round the numbers involved so that they are easier to deal with, and to use approximation to get a ballpark result which can be refined with a little more effort.

People who find it easy to work out numerical problems in their head often use rounding and approximation intuitively, that is without thinking about it. In fact you may already round certain numbers as a matter of course. If someone asks how old you are, you would say '18' or '21' as appropriate, you wouldn't say '18 years, 3 months and 10 days' or '21.63 years'. Automatically you round down to the nearest completed year of your age. If you want to check how much money you have you probably look at the notes and pound coins in your purse or pocket and make an approximation. Only if you are particularly concerned about how much there is, or have time on your hands, are you likely to count every penny.

Rounding and approximation are therefore not entirely new concepts to you. If you can apply them systematically in your numerical work you will develop a skill which will give you a better 'feel' for numbers, enable you to spot mistakes and think numerically 'on your feet'.

Example 1.15

You walk into a fast food restaurant which is so empty that there is a member of staff waiting to take your order. You know what you want but you don't know how much it will cost. As you give your order your eyes take in the prices of the items you want: one burger £1.49, another burger £1.69, one portion of fries 89p, one cold drink 79p, one hot drink 59p. You want to work out roughly how much it will be so you can decide whether to count up your change or get out a note.

If you want a really quick answer, round up each item to the nearest pound.

Approximate total cost = £2 + £2 + £1 + £1 + £1 = £7

Because we have rounded every figure up, this result will be an overestimate, so we can be certain that the total cost will be no more than this, but it is a rather crude estimate. You could get a more accurate approximation if you rounded each figure to the nearest ten pence.

Approximate total cost = £1.50 + £1.70 + £0.90 + £0.80 + £0.60 = £5.50

Each of the five figures used here is rounded up by one penny, so you can get the exact total by taking five pence away from £5.50, which comes to £5.45.

1.4 Technological support

Although the subject of Statistics is about numbers, the amount of time you will spend actually performing calculations during your study of the subject can be minimized by using readily available technology, specifically a suitable calculator and appropriate computer software.

If you do not already have a calculator you really need to get one. It is an essential tool for the numerical aspects of your course, and probably some of the not so numerical parts of it as well. To be of use to you in statistical work the calculator you have must have a square root function, and it really is worth spending a little more money to get one with statistical functions. Sometimes such calculators are described as having a 'statistical mode' or an 'SD' (standard deviation) mode. Whatever it is called by the manufacturer, if you have a calculator that can perform statistical operations it will assist you immensely.

When you have your calculator the first thing that you should do is to make sure you don't lose the instructions. Your calculator is a sophisticated scientific instrument that can do much more for you than you might imagine, but you can only find out how if you have the instructions. As a safeguard it is a good idea to keep a photocopy of them in a safe place.

You will most likely have access to a computer, perhaps at home but almost certainly at your place of study. Because today computers are used so widely to send messages and to access internet facilities, it is easy to forget that computers were originally developed as machines to process data.

The computers we have today still possess that capability. With the right software the machine you use should become an invaluable aid to you in carrying out statistical work. It will do most of the laborious calculations for you, leaving you free to concentrate on learning how to understand and interpret the results.

This reflects how you are likely to be involved in using Statistics later in your career; it is your perception and interpretation of results that will be important, rather than whether you can compete with a computer to do the calculations. Of course it is important to be able to understand how the computer has arrived at the results, but let the machine do the hard work for you.

So, what is the right software? There are two types of software that can help you with statistical tasks: statistical packages and spreadsheet packages.

Statistical packages such as MINITAB (which has been used to produce the diagrams and results for this book), Splus, and SPSS offer a full range of statistical functions and can carry out just about all of the techniques you are likely to meet during your studies. The authors of packages of this type are usually qualified in Statistics.

Spreadsheet packages such as Excel are intended primarily for accounting work and offer a more limited range of statistical functions, but nonetheless can perform the majority of methods you will probably need to use.

Although these two types of package offer different ranges of functions and different styles of output, they have become increasingly similar in some respects. The data storage layouts in statistical packages have become more like spreadsheets; numbers are usually stored in the rows and columns of a 'spreadsheet' in Excel, and in the rows and columns of a 'worksheet' in MINITAB. The statistical output generated by spreadsheet packages looks more like that produced using a statistical package.

Example 1.16

What are the relevant commands to use in a spreadsheet package and/or a statistical package to store the costs of the items listed in Example 1.15, and to produce the total cost of the order?

Using Excel:

- Enter the first value in Cell A1 then press **Enter**.

- Enter the next value in Cell A2, press **Enter**, and repeat until all the values are stored in Cells A1 to A5 and the cursor is resting in Cell A6.

- Click on the **Autosum** button (labelled Σ) that is located amongst the toolbars at the top of the screen. The message '=SUM(A1:A5)' will appear in Cell A6.

- Press the **Enter** key. The figure that now appears in Cell A6 should be 5.45, the total cost of the items.

Using MINITAB:

- Enter the first value in Row 1 of Column 1 (C1) of the worksheet that occupies the lower half of the screen, and then press **Enter**.

- Enter the next value in Row 2 of C1, press **Enter**, and repeat until all the values are stored in Rows 1 to 5 of C1.

- Click on the **Calc** (Calculations) menu at the top of the screen.

- Click on **Column Statistics** in the **Calc** pull-down menu.

- In the Command Window that appears select **Sum**, click on the box beside **Input variable**, type C1 in the box and click the **OK** button. A message telling you that the sum of C1 is 5.45 appears in the session window that occupies the upper half of the screen.

If you have a choice, learn how to use the statistical package at your disposal. If you have time, learn to use both the statistical package and the statistical functions of the spreadsheet package. After all, in the course of your career the software you use will evolve and you will need to adapt to it, so why not get used to learning how to use a variety of software while you are studying?

If you have to choose between a spreadsheet and a statistical package, it may help to consider some of the pros and cons of each.

The advantages of a spreadsheet are:

- They are fairly straightforward to use.
- Basic calculations and diagrams can be produced quickly and easily.
- They are useful for more than statistical work, e.g. for accounting or manpower planning.

The disadvantages of a spreadsheet are:

- They can perform only a limited range of statistical tasks.
- The control you have over the composition of some output, particularly diagrams, is limited and tricky to manage.

The advantages of a dedicated statistical package are:

- They can carry out a comprehensive range of statistical operations.
- The methods they use and the output they produce are statistically meticulous.

The disadvantages of a dedicated statistical package are:

- They can be more difficult to learn to use.
- Transferring output into other software may be elaborate.

Because computer software is continually being upgraded and improved the disadvantages are being reduced and the advantages extended so check the latest available versions before making your decision.

Whatever package you use for your statistical work, don't expect to know how to use all its functions straight away. It is worth investing some time in learning how to get the best out of the software you use.

Any package should have a help facility, use it to search for advice. It is really an on-line user manual available at your fingertips! You will find that what you regard as awesome when you begin will very soon become familiar.

Review questions

1.1 Select which of the definitions listed below on the right match the words listed on the left:

(a) statistics   (i) something that occurs by chance
(b) Statistics   (ii) a subset of a population
(c) random   (iii) a complete set of things to study
(d) sample   (iv) a value of a variable that has occurred
(e) population   (v) a set of numerical data
(f) observation   (vi) the study of statistics

1.2 Match each of the symbols on the left to the definitions listed on the right:

(a) X (i) the number of observed values
(b) Σ (ii) the third in a set of observed values of the variable X
(c) x (iii) a variable

(d) n (iv) a single observed value of the variable X

(e) x_3 (v) the sum of

1.3 A till-roll from a cash register in a café-bar shows the following transactions:

Beverages	£4.85
Food	£2.65
Food	£8.54
Food	£7.20
Beverages	£2.36

If the variable X is defined as the money taken per transaction:

(a) Calculate $\sum_{i=1}^{n} x$, the total amount taken through the till.

(b) Calculate $\sum_{i=2}^{4} x$, and explain what the answer means.

1.4 You have to fly from London to Tashkent. The plane is due to depart at 21.30 and the airline insists that you check in two hours before take off. You estimate that it will take an hour and a half to drive to the airport and a further 20 minutes to make your way from the car park to the check-in desk.

(a) What time should you start your journey to the airport?

(b) The flight is scheduled to take 6 hours 45 minutes. Going through passport control and collecting your baggage should take an hour. If local time is five hours ahead of UK time, by what time should the person who is meeting you aim to be at the airport in Tashkent?

1.5 A tour operator is organizing a coach trip around Bavaria. She has two vehicles available in Munich that could be used. In most respects the vehicles are identical, so she will use the one that has the better fuel economy. According to the records the first vehicle, which has been used extensively in the UK, does 15 miles per gallon. The second one, used entirely within Germany has a recorded fuel efficiency figure of 20 litres of fuel per 100 kilometres travelled. Which coach should she use? (There are 4.546 litres in a gallon and 1.609 kilometres in a mile, to 3 decimal places.)

1.6 A pub manager wants to create a square paved area immediately outside the main bar of the pub. A builder offers him 175 one metre square paving slabs that were left over from another job, at a very competitive price. What are the dimensions of the largest paved area that could be laid using these slabs, assuming that the pub manager does not want any slabs cut?

1.7 During a stay at a hotel in the USA a business traveller orders two concert tickets from the front office. A member of staff telephones her in her room to tell her that the tickets have arrived and that they cost $33 each plus sales tax. If the sales tax is 12 per cent, what is the total cost of the tickets? How much is this in pounds if the prevailing exchange rate is $1.60 to the pound?

1.8 A visitor to Britain from Bahrain wants to buy some articles of clothing in a department store in London. He selects a man's jumper costing £29.99, a lady's cardigan that costs £34.99, and a pair of man's shoes for £49.99. A large sign in the store says that visitors from abroad can buy goods 'VAT-free'. The prevailing rate of VAT is 17.5 per cent. How much will he be charged for the things that he wants to buy?

1.9 The promotional brochure produced by a Health Club says that '75 per cent of our members are under 30, and 60 per cent of our members who are under 30 are female'. If the Club has 900 members, how many of them are women under 30?

CHAPTER 2

Presenting data

This chapter will help you:

- To recognize different types of data.
- To produce a variety of statistical diagrams.
- To interpret basic statistical diagrams.
- To know which diagrams are suitable for which types of data.

In this chapter you will find:

- A description of different data types.
- Diagrams to use for qualitative data.
- Diagrams to use for quantitative data.
- Diagrams to use for bivariate and time series analysis.
- Guidance on producing diagrams using computer software.

'A picture is worth a thousand words . . .'

This chapter is about using diagrams and charts to present or display data. The pictorial techniques you will meet are widely used in business documents and being able to understand what they mean is an important skill.

When you apply these techniques you will be presenting data in visual forms that will reveal patterns and sequences. You will be taking the first steps in transforming data (sometimes people talk of data as 'meaningless') into *information*, that is something that *informs*, you will be bringing meaning to the apparently meaningless.

There are many different diagrams and charts that can be used to do this, so it is important to know when to use them. Deciding which type of diagram to use from such a wide selection is not always straightforward, but picking the right one depends on the type of data you are dealing with. In the same way that a fork is an invaluable tool if you are eating spaghetti, but completely useless for consuming soup, a particular statistical diagram may be appropriate for some types of data and entirely inappropriate for others.

2.1 Types of data

The word *data* means a set of known facts. There are different types of data because there are different ways in which facts are gathered. Some data may exist because specific things have characteristics that have been categorized whereas other data may exist as a result of things being counted, or measured on some sort of scale.

Example 2.1

A restaurant is described in a review as 'attracting a wealthy clientele'.

To verify this we could use socio-economic definitions of class to *categorize* its customers, or we could *count* the number of homes owned by each customer, or we could *measure* the amount of land owned by each customer.

The first important distinction to make is between *qualitative* data and *quantitative* data. Qualitative data consists of categories or types of a characteristic or attribute. In Example 2.1 the socio-economic definitions, social class A, B, C1 and so on, would be qualitative data, whereas the numbers of houses or amount of income would be quantitative data. Any data that is based on characteristics or attributes is qualitative. Data that is based on counting or measuring is quantitative data.

The second important distinction to make is between the two different types of quantitative data: *discrete* and *continuous*. Discrete data is quantitative data that can take only a limited number of values because it is produced by counting in distinct or 'discrete' steps, or measuring against a scale made up of distinct steps.

There are three types of discrete data that you may have to deal with:

1 Data that can only take certain values because other values simply cannot occur, for example the number of children in parties of tourists. There could be 12 children in one group and 7 in another, but no group could have 9.3 children because there is no such thing as 0.3 of a child.
2 Data that take only certain values because those are the ones that have been established by long-standing custom and practice, for example licensed premises in the UK sell draught beer in whole and half pints. You could try asking for three-quarters of a pint, but the bar staff would no doubt insist that you purchase the smaller or larger quantity.
3 Data that only takes certain values because the people who have provided the data or the analysis have decided, for convenience, to round values that don't have to be discrete. This is what you are doing when you give your age to the last full year. Similarly, the temperatures given in weather reports are rounded to the nearest degree, and the distances on road signs are usually rounded to the nearest mile. Such data is discrete by discretion rather than by definition. It is really *continuous* data.

Discrete data often but not always consists of whole number values. The number of covers in a restaurant will always be a whole number, but shoe sizes include half sizes. In other cases, like the sizes of women's clothing, only some whole numbers occur.

The important thing to remember about discrete data is that there are gaps between the values that can occur, that is why it is sometimes referred to as *discontinuous* data. In contrast, continuous data consists of numerical values that are not restricted to specific numbers. Such data is called continuous because there are no gaps between feasible values. This is because measuring on a continuous scale such as distance or temperature yields continuous data.

The precision of continuous data is limited only by how precisely the quantities are measured. For instance we measure both cooking periods and athletic performances using the scale of time. In the first case a clock or a wristwatch is sufficiently accurate, but in the second case we would use a stopwatch or an even more sophisticated timing device.

Further on you will find the terms *discrete variable* and *continuous variable*. A discrete variable has discrete values whereas a continuous variable has continuous values.

Example 2.2

Airline staff are told to find out the following information when passengers arrive at the check-in desk:

- Class of travel – first, business or economy;
- Number in their party;
- Seat type preferred – window or aisle;
- Weight of baggage.

Which responses will be qualitative and which will be quantitative?

The class of travel and seat type are qualitative, the number in the party and the weight of baggage are quantitative.

Which quantitative responses will be discrete and which will be continuous?

The number in the party is discrete; the weight of baggage is continuous.

In most of your early statistical work you will probably be analysing data that consists of observed values of a single variable. However, you may need to analyse data that consists of observed values of two variables in order to find out if there is a connection between them. For instance we might want to ascertain whether the prices of hotel rooms are related to the rating given to hotels by a tourist guide.

Dealing with a single variable is known as *univariate* analysis, whereas dealing with two variables is known as *bivariate* analysis. The prefixes uni- and bi- in these words convey the same meaning as they do in some other pairs of words, for instance unilateral and bilateral.

2.2 Displaying qualitative data

Arranging and displaying qualitative data is quite straightforward as long as the number of categories of the characteristic being studied is relatively small. Even if there are a large number of categories, the task can be made easier by merging categories.

The easiest way you can present a set of qualitative data is to *tabulate* it, to arrange it in the form of a summary table. As well as being a useful way of displaying qualitative data, if you want to draw a diagram to portray the data, compiling such a table is an essential preliminary task.

A summary table consists of two parts, a list of categories of the characteristic, and the number of things that fall into each category, known as the *frequency* of the category.

Example 2.3

Suppose we want to find out how many of the different types of fast food outlets there are in a city centre.

We might survey the streets or consult a trade directory in order to compile a list of establishments, but the list itself may be too crude a form in which to present our results.

By listing the types of outlet and the number of each type of outlet we have found we could construct a summary table.

The number of fast food outlets by type of establishment

Type of establishment	Frequency	Relative frequency (%)
Sandwich bar	15	38.5
Fish and chip shop	8	20.5
Burger bar	6	15.4
Other	10	25.6
Total number of establishments	39	100.0

In Example 2.3 the establishment types are qualitative data. The 'Other' category, which might contain 10 completely different types of outlet, has been created in order to keep the summary table to manageable proportions.

Notice that for each category, the number of establishments as a percentage of the total, the *relative frequency* of each category, is listed on the right-hand side. This is to make it easier to communicate the contents; saying 38.5 per cent of the places were sandwich bars is more effective than saying 15/39ths of them were sandwich bars, although they are two different ways of saying the same thing.

You may want to use a summary table to present more than one attribute. Such a two-way tabulation is also known as a *contingency table* because it enables us to look for connections between the attributes, in other words to find out whether one attribute is *contingent* upon another.

Example 2.4

An adventure travel agency offers four types of holiday: activity cruise, bird watching, canoeing, and diving.

The following table shows the number of customers who bought a holiday from them.

Number of customers by type of holiday and gender

	Females	Males	Total
Activity cruise	68	43	111
Bird watching	32	81	113
Canoeing	84	60	144
Diving	52	89	141
Total	236	273	509

Whilst summary tables are perfectly adequate means of presenting qualitative data, it is possible to show qualitative data in a visually more dramatic way using a diagram.

A diagram is usually a much more effective way of communicating data because it is easier for the eye to digest than a table. This will be important when you have to include data in a report or presentation because you want your audience to focus their attention on what you are saying. They can do that more easily if they don't have to work too hard to understand the form in which you have presented your data.

There are three types of diagram that you can use to show qualitative data: *pictographs*, *pie charts* and *bar charts*. They are listed here in order of increasing sophistication.

A pictograph is no more than a simple adjustment of a summary table. The categories of the attribute are listed as they are in a summary table, but we use symbols to represent the number of things in each category. The symbols used are thematically linked to the nature of the data.

Example 2.5

The table below shows the number of flights to different categories of destination departing from a regional airport in a six-hour period.

Number of departures by type of destination

Type of destination	Departures
Domestic	2
Short-haul	2
Long-haul	1

Show this set of data in the form of a pictograph.

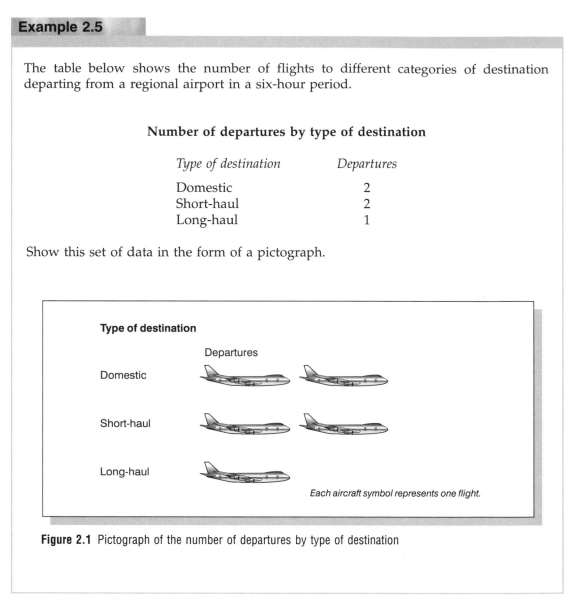

Figure 2.1 Pictograph of the number of departures by type of destination

A pictograph like Figure 2.1 can be an effective way of presenting a simple set of qualitative data. The symbols are a straightforward way of representing the number of things in each category and have the extra advantage of emphasizing the context of the data.

Unfortunately pictographs have several drawbacks which are likely to deter you from using them. Unless you are artistically gifted and can create appropriate images by hand, you will probably have to rely on computer software to produce them for you. Creating a pictograph by computer is a laborious process. Spreadsheet and statistical packages cannot produce a pictograph for you directly from data, so symbols have to be grafted alongside text in a word-processing or desktop publishing package.

You need to choose the symbol you use carefully. It should be easy to associate with the context of the data and not so elaborate that the symbols themselves become the centre of attention rather than the data they are supposed to represent.

You may occasionally spot a pictograph used in academic and business documents; you are more likely to see them used on television and in newspapers. Sadly, the computer graphics software at the disposal of reporters and editors is much more sophisticated than any that you are likely to have access to during your studies!

The second way of displaying qualitative data is much more commonly used than the pictograph, the pie chart.

A pie chart, like a pictograph is designed to show how many things belong to each category of an attribute. It does this by representing the entire set of data as a circle or 'pie' and dividing the circle into segments or 'slices'. Each segment represents a category, and the size of the segment reflects the number of things in the category.

Example 2.6

Present the data from Example 2.3 in the form of a pie chart.

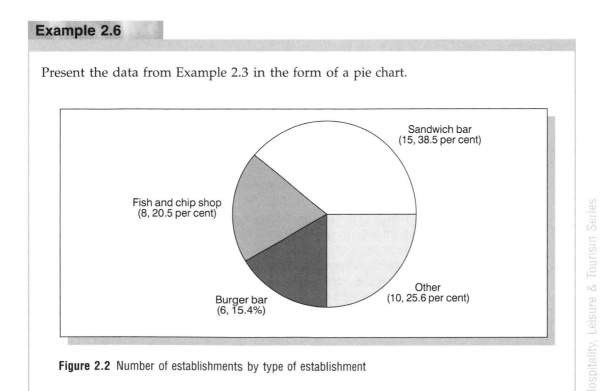

Figure 2.2 Number of establishments by type of establishment

You can produce a pie chart like Figure 2.2 using MINITAB. Put the categories in one column of the worksheet and their frequencies in another. Select **Pie Chart** from the **Graph** menu. When the **Pie Chart** command window appears select **Chart table** and specify the columns in which the categories and frequencies are stored. Click the **OK** button and the graphic will appear.

Alternatively you could store the categories and frequencies in an Excel spreadsheet then select **Chart** from the **Insert** menu. In the sequence of windows called **Chart Wizard** that appear, choose **Pie** as the type of chart and the default sub-type.

Just about every spreadsheet or statistical package can produce a pie chart for you, either from the original data or from a summary table. They will probably offer you a number of ways of embellishing the pie chart, e.g. colour and shading patterns, three-dimensional effect, exploded slices to emphasize particular segments.

With practice you will be able to use these options in creating pie charts, but don't overdo it. Remember that the pattern of the data is what you want to convey not your ability to use every possible gimmick the software offers.

Pie charts are so widely used and understood that it is very tempting to regard them as an almost universal means of displaying qualitative data. In many cases they are appropriate and effective, but in some situations they are not.

Because the role of a pie chart is to show how different components make up a whole, using one when we cannot or do not want to show the whole is inappropriate. In Example 2.6 it may be tempting to present the chart without the 'Other' category, but if we left it out we would not be presenting the whole.

One reason that people find pie charts easy to grasp is that the analogy of cutting up a pie is quite an obvious one. As long as the pie chart looks like a pie it works. However, if we construct a pie chart that has too many categories it can look more like a bicycle wheel than a pie, and confuses rather than clarifies the situation. If you have a lot of categories to present, say more than ten, either merge some of the categories in order to reduce the number of segments in the pie chart or consider other ways of presenting your data.

A third way of presenting qualitative data is to display it in the form of a bar chart. Like pie charts, bar charts are widely used, straightforward to interpret, and can be constructed using a spreadsheet or statistical package. However because there are several different varieties of bar charts, they are more flexible tools. By using a bar chart we can portray two- (or even three-) way tabulation in a single diagram.

The basic function of a bar chart is the same as the function of a pie chart, and for that matter a pictograph – to show the number or frequency of things in each of a succession of categories of an attribute. It does this by representing the frequencies as a series of bars. The height of each bar is in direct proportion to the frequency of the category: the taller the bar that represents a category, the more things there are in that category and vice versa.

Example 2.7

Produce a bar chart to show the data from Example 2.3.

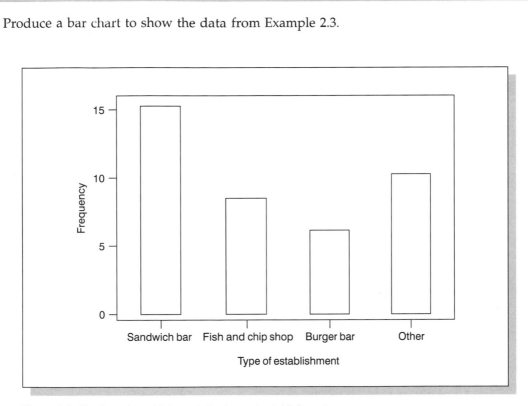

Figure 2.3 Number of establishments by type of establishment

You can produce a bar chart like Figure 2.3 using Excel. Store the summary table in a spreadsheet, select **Chart** from the **Insert** menu. In the **Chart Wizard** windows, choose **Column** as the type of chart (or **Bar** if you prefer a chart with horizontal bars).

To use MINITAB to produce your bar chart, store the summary table in two columns in the worksheet then select **Chart** from the **Graph** menu. You will need to put the column location of the frequencies in the **Y (measurement)** box and the location of the categories in the **X (category)** box then click on the **OK** button.

The type of bar chart shown in Figure 2.3 is called a *simple* bar chart because it represents only one attribute. If we had two attributes to display we might use a more sophisticated type of bar chart known as a *component* or *stack* bar chart.

Example 2.8

Produce a component bar chart to portray the data from Example 2.4

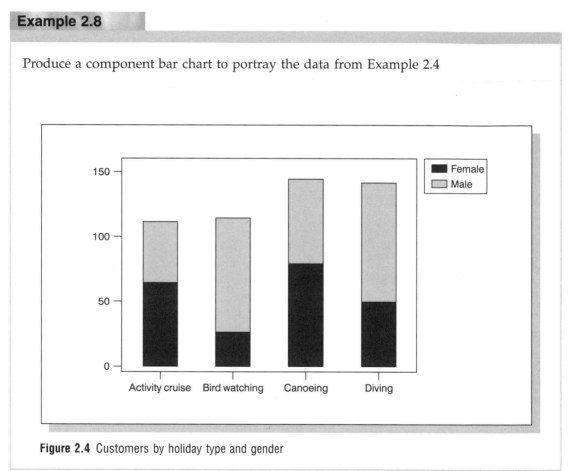

Figure 2.4 Customers by holiday type and gender

You can produce a component bar chart using MINITAB by following the same procedure as you would in order to produce a simple bar chart, but with some amendments. First, put the data in three columns: one for the category of holiday, a second for the number in each category, and a third for the gender.

The worksheet might look like this:

Type	Number	Gender
Activity cruise	68	Female
Bird watching	32	Female
Canoeing	84	Female
Diving	52	Female
Activity cruise	43	Male
Bird watching	81	Male
Canoeing	60	Male
Diving	89	Male

Because each holiday category has *two* numbers associated with it, every holiday type must appear *twice*. Because each gender category has *four* numbers associated with it, the gender categories appear *four times*.

To obtain the bar chart, choose **Chart** from the **Graph** menu. Type the column location of the frequencies in the **X (category)** box and the column location of the holiday types in the **Y (measurement)** box. Click the ▼ button by **For each** and choose **Group**. Put the column location of the genders below **Group variables** then click the **Options** button. Select **Stack** in the **Options** window and specify the column where the gender categories are stored in the box alongside **Stack**. Click the **OK** buttons on first the **Options** window then the **Chart** window.

To get this sort of diagram from Excel, put the holiday categories in one column of a spreadsheet, the numbers of females in a second and the number of males in a third. Select **Column** from **Chart Wizard** then pick the **Stacked Column** Chart sub-type.

This type of bar chart is known as a component bar chart because each bar is divided into parts or components. The alternative name for it, a stacked bar chart, reflects the process of stacking the components of each bar on top of one another.

A component bar chart is particularly useful if you want to emphasize the relative proportions of each category, in other words to show the balance within the categories of one attribute (in the case of Example 2.8 the type of holiday) between the categories of another attribute (gender). If you want to emphasize the absolute differences between the categories of one attribute within the categories of another you may prefer to use an alternative form of bar chart that is designed to portray a two-way tabulation, the *cluster* bar chart.

Example 2.9

Produce a cluster bar chart to show the data from Example 2.4.

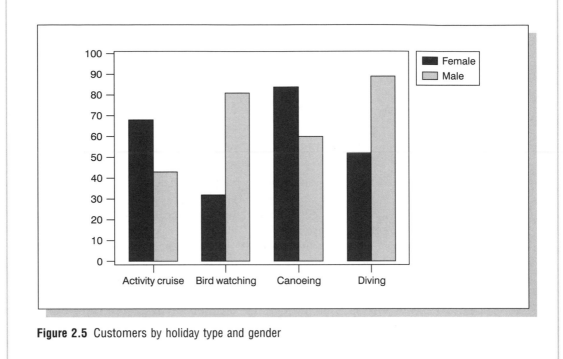

Figure 2.5 Customers by holiday type and gender

Excel will give you this type of bar chart if you put the summary table in a spreadsheet then select the **Clustered Column** chart sub-type from the **Chart Wizard** sequence.

To get the same sort of chart from MINITAB, follow the same procedure as you would for obtaining a component bar chart, but select **Cluster** instead of **Stack** in the **Options** window. Put the column location of the gender categories in the box alongside **Cluster**.

This type of bar chart is called a cluster bar chart because it uses a group or cluster of bars to show the composition of each category of one characteristic by categories of a second characteristic.

2.3 Displaying quantitative data

The nature of quantitative data is different to qualitative data and therefore the methods used to present quantitative data are rather different. However, the most appropriate ways of presenting some types of quantitative data are the same ones used to present qualitative data.

This applies to the analysis of a discrete quantitative variable that has very few feasible values. You simply treat the values as you would the categories of a characteristic. As a first step, tabulate the data to show how often each value occurs. When quantitative data is tabulated the resulting table is called a *frequency distribution* because it demonstrates how frequently each value in the distribution occurs. One you have compiled the frequency distribution you can use it to construct a bar chart or pie chart.

Example 2.10

The number of passengers in each of 20 cars boarding a ferry were:

2 3 5 2 4 2 4 4 4 3 2 5 3 2 3 4 4 3 2 4

These figures could be first tabulated and then presented in the form of a simple bar chart.

Number of passengers	Number of cars
2	6
3	5
4	7
5	2

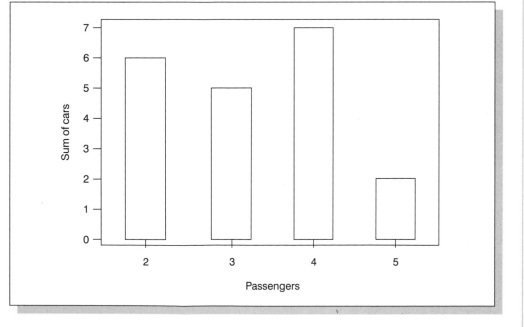

Figure 2.6 Number of cars by number of passengers

You can produce this type of chart in Excel by selecting **Insert/Chart/Chart Wizard** and **Column** as the type of chart. Alternatively you could select **Graph/Chart** in MINITAB then specify the column location of the number of cars in the **Y (measurement)** box and the column location of the number of passengers in the **X (category)** box.

2.3.1 Grouped frequency distributions

We can present the data in Example 2.10 in the form of a bar chart or a pie chart purely because there are only a very limited number of values so a bar can represent each value. Unfortunately this is not always the case, even with discrete quantitative data.

For instance, if Example 2.10 included minibuses, coaches and buses then the range of possible values would go up to 50 or so. If you try to use a simple bar chart to represent such a wide range, the bar chart would contain far too many bars to be of any use in communicating the data.

To get around this problem we can *group* the data into fewer categories or classes by compiling a *grouped frequency distribution*, which shows the frequency of observations in each class. Once the data is arranged in this way we can use a relatively simple diagram to portray it.

Example 2.11

A hotel guide lists 22 hotels in one town. The number of rooms in each hotel is:

50 14 25 8 10 33 52 12 45 15 7 5 98 13 31 52 6 75 17 22 12 64

Produce a grouped frequency distribution to present this set of data.

Number of rooms	Frequency
0–19	11
20–39	4
40–59	4
60–79	2
80–99	1

In order to compile a grouped frequency distribution you will need to exercise a little judgement because there are many sets of classes that could be used for a specific set of data. To help you, there are three rules:

1 Don't use classes that overlap.

2 Don't leave gaps between classes.

3 The first class must begin low enough to include the lowest observation and the last class must finish high enough to include the highest observation.

In Example 2.11 it would be wrong to use the classes 0–20, 20–40, 40–60 and so on because values on the very edge of the classes like 20 and 40, which may very well occur, could be put into either one, or even both, of two classes. Although there are numerical gaps between the classes that have been used in Example 2.11, they are not real gaps because no feasible value could fall into them. The first class finishes on 19 and the second begins on 20, but since the number of bedrooms is a discrete variable a value like 19.6, which would fall into the gap, simply will not occur. Since there are no observed values lower than zero or higher than 99, the third rule is satisfied.

We could sum up these rules by saying that anyone looking at a grouped frequency distribution should be in no doubt where each feasible value belongs. Every piece of data must have one and only one place for it to be. To avoid any ambiguity whatsoever you may like to use the phrase 'and under' in place of the hyphen between the beginning and end of each class. The classes in Example 2.11 could be rewritten as:

    0 and under 20

    20 and under 40

    and so on.

It is especially important to apply these rules when you are dealing with continuous quantitative data. Unless you decide to use 'and under' or a similar style of words, it is vital that the beginning and end of each class is specified to at least the same degree of precision as the data.

Example 2.12

Spot checks of the temperature in the meat fridge of a restaurant have produced the following figures (in degrees Celsius).

4.55 6.44 4.50 4.97 5.54 4.45 5.56 4.95 3.15 4.85 3.63 7.16 6.52 4.92 5.65

6.49 5.78 5.42 4.20 4.40 4.67 3.78 2.49 3.11 5.01 3.97 4.41 6.24 4.16 3.87

Arrange these figures in a grouped frequency distribution.

Temperature	Frequency
2.00–2.99	1
3.00–3.99	6
4.00–4.99	12
5.00–5.99	6
6.00–6.99	4
7.00–7.99	1

When you construct a grouped frequency distribution you will also need to decide how many classes to use and how wide they are. These are related issues: the fewer the number of classes the wider each one needs to be. It is a question of balance. You should avoid having a very few very wide classes because they will only convey a crude impression of the distribution. On the other hand if you have very many narrow classes you will be conveying too much detail. So, what is too few and what is too many? As a starting point, take the square root of the number of observations in the set of data. In Example 2.11 there are 22 observations. The square root of 22 is 4.69 which we round up to 5 because we can only have whole numbers of classes.

Once you have some idea of the number of classes, the width of the classes has to be decided. When you come to producing a diagram to represent a grouped frequency distribution you will find it helpful (but not essential) if all the classes have the same width.

The set of classes you use must cover all the observations from lowest to highest, so to help you decide the width of classes, subtract the lowest observation from the highest observation to give you the difference between the two, known as the *range* of values. Divide this by the number of classes you want to have and the result will be the minimum class width you must use. In Example 2.11 the range is 93 (98 minus 5) which, when divided by 5 gives 18.6. So if we want a set of five classes of equal width to cover the range from 5 to 98, each class must be at least 18.6 wide.

This number, 18.6, is not particularly 'neat', so to make our grouped frequency distribution easier to digest we can round it up. The most obvious number to take is 20, so 5 classes 20 units wide will be sufficient to cover the range. In fact because these classes will combine to cover a range of 100, whereas the range of our data is 93 we have some flexibility when it comes to deciding where the first class should start.

The first class must begin at or below the lowest observation in the set, in Example 2.11 this means it must start at 5 or below. Because 5 is a fairly 'neat' round number it would make a perfectly acceptable start for our first class, which would then be 5–24, the second class would be 25–44 and so on. But what if the first observed value was 3 or 7? Starting a set of classes with such a value would result in a grouped frequency distribution that would look rather ungainly. If we start the classes at a round number lower than the lowest value in the distribution, zero in Example 2.11, we can guarantee that the resulting set of classes will have 'neat' beginnings and ends.

2.3.2 Histograms

The best-known way of displaying a grouped frequency distribution is the *histogram*. This is a special type of bar chart where each bar or block represents the frequency of a class of values rather than the frequency of a single value.

Example 2.13

Construct a histogram to display the grouped frequency distribution in Example 2.11.

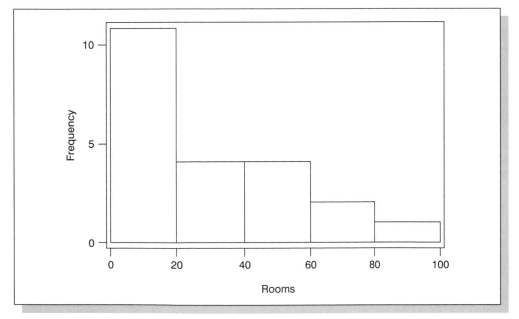

Figure 2.7 Hotels by number of rooms

Hospitality, Leisure & Tourism Series

You can use MINITAB to produce a histogram like Figure 2.7 by putting the raw data into one of the columns of the worksheet and selecting **Histogram** from the **Graph** menu. Specify the column location of the data in the command window that appears. Clicking on the **Options** button in the command window will allow you to choose how to arrange your classes if you are not satisfied with the diagram the package produces for you.

To plot a histogram using Excel, put the raw data into a column of the spreadsheet and select **Data Analysis** from the **Tools** menu. Click on **Histogram** in the list of techniques that appears in the command window. Specify the location of the data in **Input Range** and click on **Chart Output** to obtain your diagram. If you are not satisfied with the classes the package has used you can alter them by putting your choice of classes in a column of the spreadsheet and putting the column location in the **Bin Ranges** box in the command window. The word 'bin' is used as a synonym for class because putting observations into classes is the same sort of thing as sorting objects into different bins.

Producing an effective histogram is often a matter of trial and error so experiment to try and find the balance which best enables you to present the data.

A histogram is a visual tool that displays the pattern or distribution of observed values of a variable. The larger the size of the block that represents a class, the greater the number of values that has occurred in that class. Because the connection between the size of the blocks and the frequencies of the classes is the key feature of the diagram the scale along the vertical or 'Y' axis should start at zero.

As long as the classes are of the same width it is the height of the block alone that reflects the frequency of observed values in the class. If the classes have different widths it is important to ensure that the areas of the blocks are proportional to the frequencies of the classes.

Example 2.14

The ages of a random sample of guests staying at a hotel were recorded and the following grouped frequency distribution has been produced.

Age range	Frequency
Under 15	0
15 to 24	5
25 to 44	22
45 to 64	19
Over 64	7

Produce a histogram to depict this distribution.

You can see that not only do the classes have different widths, but the first and last do not have a numerical beginning and end, they are 'open-ended' classes. Before we can plot a histogram we need to 'close' these classes. In the case of the first class this is straightforward, we can simply express it as '0 to 14'. The last class poses more of a problem. If we knew the age of the oldest guest in the sample we could use that as the end of the class, but as we don't we have to select an arbitrary yet plausible end of the class. In keeping with the style of some of the other classes we could use '65 to 84'.

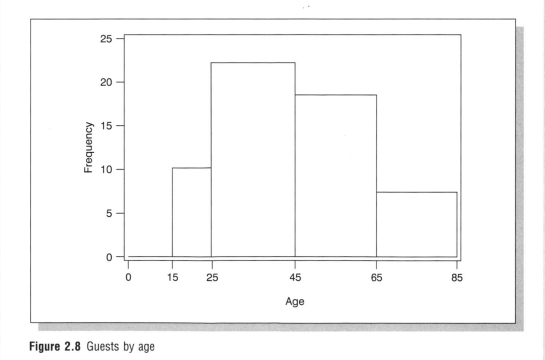

Figure 2.8 Guests by age

In Figure 2.8 the height of the block representing the '15 to 24' class is increased to reflect the fact that it is narrower than the other classes. The height of the block is ten although the frequency of the class is only five. The class is *half* the width of the classes above it so to keep the area in proportion to the frequency the height of the block is *doubled*.

The pattern of the distribution shown in Figure 2.8 is broadly balanced or *symmetrical*. There are two large blocks in the middle and smaller blocks to the left and right of the 'bulge'. From this we would conclude that the majority of observed values occur towards the middle of the age range, with only a few relatively young and old guests.

In contrast, if you look back at Figure 2.7, the histogram showing the numbers of bedrooms in a sample of hotels, you will see an asymmetrical or *skewed* pattern. The block on the left-hand side is the largest and the size of the blocks gets smaller to the right of it. It could be more accurately described as *right* or *positively* skewed. From Figure 2.7 we would conclude that the majority of hotels have a relatively small number of bedrooms and only a few hotels have a large number of bedrooms.

2.3.3 Stem and leaf displays

Histograms are well established and widely used effective diagrammatic means of presenting quantitative data. Until fairly recently they could be described as unrivalled. However there is now an alternative way of presenting quantitative data in visual form, the *stem and leaf display*. This is one of a number of newer techniques known collectively as *Exploratory Data Analysis* (EDA).

The role of a stem and leaf display is the same as the role of a histogram, namely to show the pattern of a distribution. But unlike a histogram a stem and leaf display is constructed using the data itself as building blocks, so as well as showing the pattern of a distribution it is also a list of the observations that make up that distribution.

The basis of a stem and leaf display is the structure of numbers, the fact that a number is made up of units, tens, hundreds and so on. For instance the number 45 is composed of two digits, the 4 tens and the 5 units. Using the analogy of a plant, the stem of the number 45 is the number on the left-hand side, 4 (the number of tens) and the leaf is the number on the right-hand side, 5 (the number of units). A stem on a plant can have different leaves, in the same way the numerical stem 4 can have different numerical leaves. The number 48 has the same stem as the number 45, but a different leaf, 8.

To produce a stem and leaf display for a set of data we have to list the set of stem digits that appear in the data and then record each observation by putting its leaf digit alongside its stem digit.

Hospitality, Leisure & Tourism Series

When we have done this for every observed value in the set of data the result is a series of 'stem lines' each of which consists of a stem digit and the leaf digits of all the observations sharing that particular stem. The final stage in the process is to arrange the leaf digits on each stem line in order of magnitude.

Example 2.15

The weekday rack rate (to the nearest £) for a single room in each of 25 hotels located in the South of England are:

$$59 \quad 36 \quad 25 \quad 19 \quad 50 \quad 23 \quad 33 \quad 28 \quad 20 \quad 50 \quad 58 \quad 41 \quad 48$$
$$64 \quad 18 \quad 45 \quad 55 \quad 21 \quad 34 \quad 35 \quad 65 \quad 54 \quad 31 \quad 17 \quad 45$$

Produce a stem and leaf display for this set of data.

Every number consists of two digits, so the tens are the stem digits. The first stem line will be for the stem digit 1, and the last one for the stem digit 6. The first stem line will have three leaf digits, the 7 from 17, the 8 from 18, and the 9 from 19. The second stem line, for the stem digit 2, will have five leaf digits, the 5 from 25, the 3 from 23, and so on.

Stem	Leaves
1	7 8 9
2	5 3 8 0 1
3	6 3 4 5 1
4	1 8 5 5
5	9 0 0 8 5 4
6	4 5

This is a stem and leaf display, but it is not yet finished. We need to rearrange the leaf digits so they are listed from the smallest to the largest.

Stem	Leaves
1	7 8 9
2	0 1 3 5 8
3	1 3 4 5 6
4	1 5 5 8
5	0 0 4 5 8 9
6	4 5

Leaf unit = 1.0

The message 'leaf unit = 1.0' that has been added to the final version of the stem and leaf display in Example 2.15 has the same role as the scale on the horizontal or 'X' axis of a histogram, it specifies the order of magnitude of the data. Without the message you might look at the display, note that the lowest value in the distribution has the stem digit 1 and the leaf digit 7, but the number could be 0.17, 1.7, 17, 170, 1700, or any other number with a 1 followed by a 7. It is only when you know that the leaf unit is one that you can be sure that, in this display the stem digit 1 and the leaf digit 7 represents the number 17.

You can produce a stem and leaf display using MINITAB. Select **Stem-and-Leaf** from the **Graph** menu and specify in the command window the column location of your data.

Although the stem and leaf display may look a little odd at first it is a tool that is well worth learning to use because of two clear advantages that it enjoys over a histogram: particular values can be highlighted and two distributions can be shown in one display. A histogram can't do the former because it consists of blocks rather than data. It is possible to plot a histogram showing two distributions but the result is cumbersome and you would do better to plot two separate histograms.

Example 2.16

Seven of the hotels whose single room prices are listed in Example 2.15 offer room service. Their prices appear in bold type.

> **59** **36** 25 19 50 23 33 28 20 50 **58** 41 **48**
>
> **64** 18 45 55 21 34 35 **65** **54** 31 17 45

The same means of distinguishing the prices of the hotels that offer room service can be incorporated into the stem and leaf display by putting the leaf digits representing the prices of those hotels in bold type.

Stem	Leaves
1	7 8 9
2	0 1 3 5 8
3	1 3 4 5 **6**
4	1 5 5 **8**
5	0 0 **4** 5 **8 9**
6	**4 5**

Leaf unit = 1.0

You can see from the display in Example 2.16 that the hotels offering room service are generally among the more expensive hotels.

To show two distributions in one stem and leaf display you simply list the leaf digits for one distribution to the left of the list of stem digits and the leaf digits for the other distribution to the right of the stem digits.

Example 2.17

The weekday rack rate (to the nearest £) for a single room in each of 28 hotels located in the North of England are:

40 27 25 24 30 35 22 18 25 19 19 31 36 39

34 16 21 45 20 33 30 18 26 27 16 56 29 34

Produce a stem and leaf display to show this set of data and the data in Example 2.15.

	North			South
	9 9 8 8 6 6	1		7 8 9
	9 7 7 6 5 5 4 2 1 0	2		0 1 3 5 8
	9 6 5 4 4 3 1 0 0	3		1 3 4 5 6
	5 0	4		1 5 5 8
	6	5		0 0 4 5 8 9
		6		4 5

Leaf unit = 1.0

By looking at the display in Example 2.17 you can see that the hotels in the North seem to be cheaper whereas those in the South appear to have a greater spread of prices.

2.3.4 Presenting two variables

The techniques for presenting quantitative data that you have met so far in this chapter have one thing in common; they are all designed to portray the observed values of one variable. They are sometimes described as tools of *univariate* analysis.

But what if we want to present the observed values of two variables in one diagram in order to illustrate a connection (or maybe a lack of connection) between them? In that case we need to use another type of graph, the *scatter diagram*, which is a tool of *bivariate*, that is two-variable, analysis. The word scatter is used because the intention of the diagram is to show how the observed values of one variable are distributed or *scattered* in relation to the observed values of another variable.

A set of bivariate data consists of two sets of observed values, a pair of values for each item or thing or person that has been studied. A scatter diagram is constructed by plotting a point for every pair of observed values in the set of data. The first value in the pair is plotted against one axis, the second value against the other axis. The result is a scatter of points that will form some pattern if there is a connection between the variables.

Typically when we plot a scatter diagram we do so because we have a specific theory about the possible connection between the two variables. We may believe that one variable depends in some way on the other variable. If this is the case we refer to one of the variables as the *dependent* variable whose values we think depend on the values of the other, which is called the *independent* variable. The dependent variable is known as the Y variable and its observed values are plotted against the Y, or vertical, axis. The independent variable is known as the X variable and its values are plotted against the X, or horizontal, axis.

Example 2.18

The maximum weekday rack rate, to the nearest £, for a double room and the total number of rooms of 13 hotels in a city centre are:

Rate	40	39	135	68	89	94	120	110	100	109	95	85	85
Rooms	13	59	5	27	130	73	201	108	167	72	22	19	96

Produce a scatter diagram to show whether the rate depends on the number of rooms.

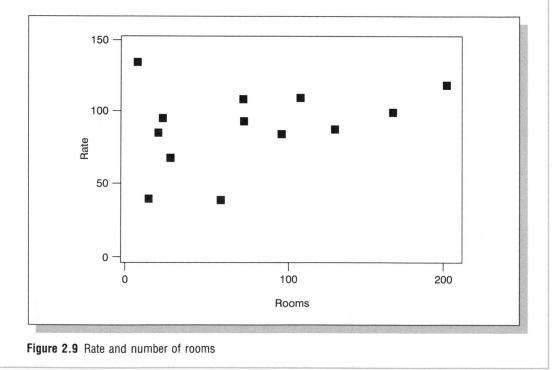

Figure 2.9 Rate and number of rooms

You can produce a scatter diagram using MINITAB by selecting **Plot** from the **Graph** menu and then specifying the column locations of the observed values of the Y and X variables in the appropriate boxes in the command window. In Excel select **XY(Scatter)** from the **Chart Wizard** menu and specify the cell locations of your data.

In Figure 2.9 you can see 13 points in the diagram, one for each of the 13 hotels in the set of data. Each point represents both the rate and the number of rooms for a particular hotel. The position of the point along the vertical or Y axis tells you the rate for the room and the position of the point along the horizontal or X axis tells you the number of rooms in the hotel. So, for instance, the point on the far right of the diagram represents the hotel that has a rate of £120 and 201 rooms.

The diagram shows us that there appears to be no clear connection between the rate and the number of rooms. Although we might have suspected that the bigger hotels are more expensive, the diagram does not bear this out. Indeed the most expensive hotel has the smallest number of rooms.

2.3.5 Presenting time series data

Sometimes we go about presenting two variables in a rather different way. This is when we need to present a *time series*, which is a set of bivariate data in which one of the variables is time. A time series is a set of data that consists of observations collected over a period, usually at regular intervals. Businesses of all kinds collect this sort of data as a matter of course, for instance weekly sales, monthly output, annual profit, so presenting time series data is important.

The type of graph used to portray time series data is a *time series* plot. It is similar in style to a scatter diagram in that each point represents a pair of observed values of two variables plotted against a pair of axes.

However there are some key differences. In a time series plot the time variable is always plotted on the horizontal, or X, axis which represents the passage of time from left (the first observation) to right (the last observation). The points that represent the data are usually joined up to emphasize the flow of time, whereas in a scatter diagram they are never joined up. The scale of the vertical, or Y, axis should begin at zero so that the fluctuations over time are not over-emphasized, whereas the scales on the axes of a scatter diagram do not need to start at zero.

Example 2.19

The number of licensed premises owned and operated by a company over a ten-year period is:

Year	1990	1991	1992	1993	1994	1995	1996	1997	1998	1999
Number of premises	4	7	15	38	112	149	371	371	508	422

Produce a time series chart to show this set of data.

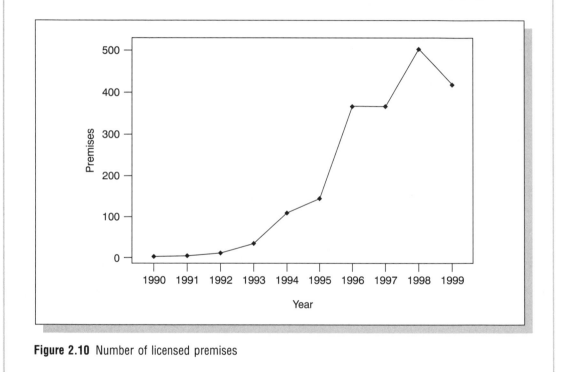

Figure 2.10 Number of licensed premises

You can produce a time series chart by selecting **Time Series Plot** from the **Graph** menu in MINITAB and then specifying the column location of the time series in the command window. The time scale along the axis will be plotted for you, but you need to specify the intervals of time and the first time period. For the data in Example 2.19 these are 'year' and '1990' respectively. In Excel you can obtain a simple plot by selecting the **Line** chart from the **Chart Wizard** sequence.

You can see from Figure 2.10 that in general this company has undergone a dramatic growth in its number of premises over this period. In other words there has been a strong upward *trend*, or basic movement. Plots of other time series might show a more fluctuating pattern, perhaps with *seasonal* variations, that is a recurrent pattern within each year, or *cyclical* variations, that is recurrent variations over periods of years.

Example 2.20

The number of passengers carried by a charter airline over two years is.

Year	Quarter			
	1	2	3	4
1	6375	21 958	29 640	10 283
2	6941	23 095	31 286	10 537

Produce a time series plot to show this set of data.

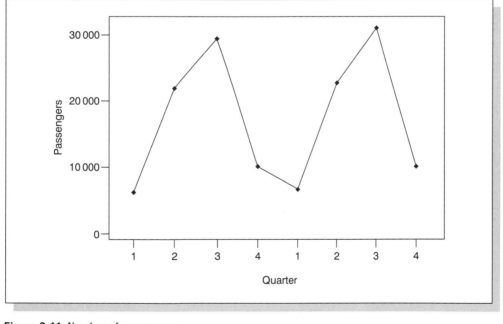

Figure 2.11 Number of passengers

You can tell by looking at Figure 2.11 that this airline carries far more passengers in the spring and summer months (Quarters 2 and 3) than it does in the autumn and winter months (Quarters 1 and 4), and that this pattern occurs in both years.

Review questions

2.1 Which of the variables below are:

(i) Qualitative;
(ii) Discrete quantitative;
(iii) Continuous quantitative.

(a) Calories in foodstuffs
(b) Alcohol content of wine
(c) The number of people visiting a theme park
(d) The types of room in a hotel
(e) The number of meals served in a restaurant
(f) Travel destinations

2.2 The table below gives the locations of holiday organized by the agency in Example 2.4 by type of holiday:

	Location	
	UK	Overseas
Activity cruise	36	75
Bird watching	79	34
Canoeing	49	95
Diving	59	82

Display the date in the tabulation using:

(a) A component bar chart;
(b) A cluster bar chart.

2.3 A restaurant receives 15 telephoned reservations. The number of diners involved in these reservations are:

4 2 4 2 4 2 2 6 2 2 3 4 2 2 4

Construct a simple bar chart to portray these figures.

2.4 Construct a histogram to display the data in Example 2.12. Does your diagram show that the distribution is symmetrical or skewed?

2.5 The time taken to serve each of 30 customers at one outlet of a fast food chain was recorded. The results (in seconds) were:

25 32 37 22 21 16 13 31 13 43
42 37 40 47 39 27 36 23 34 27
16 44 41 20 31 41 44 30 26 34

(a) Construct a stem and leaf display to show this set of data.
(b) The time taken to serve each of 30 customers at another outlet of the same fast food chain was

recorded. The results of this study (in seconds)
were:

```
18  20  20  18  22  27  32  37  30  35
33  27  17  34  16  26  33  16  15  21
22  21  34  25  28  26  31  18  40  39
```

Arrange this set of data on the other side of the stem
and leaf display you produced for (a). How does the
service in the second outlet compare with the service
in the first outlet?

2.6 On her return from a French city a business traveller
submits receipts for 18 meals consumed in a variety of
restaurants. The amounts involved, to the nearest franc,
are:

```
162  329  253  355  283  223  287  230  284
245  528  272  206  491  298  380  431  385
```

Use a stem and leaf display to present this set of data.

2.7 The amount of the bill paid by each of 11 customers in a
restaurant, and the size of the gratuity they left are:

Customer	Bill	Gratuity
1	£28.63	£2.50
2	£26.78	£2.00
3	£75.29	£5.00
4	£23.63	£2.70
5	£84.20	£6.50
6	£90.77	£6.80
7	£78.91	£6.00
8	£83.19	£8.24
9	£43.46	£3.26
10	£92.11	£8.00
11	£42.10	£3.16

Plot a scatter diagram to present this set of data. Assume
that the size of the gratuity depends on the amount of the
bill. Does your diagram suggest there is a strong
connection between the two variables?

2.8 On the tenth anniversary of the opening of a theme park
the manager releases the following figures to show how
the number of visitors per year (in thousands) has grown.

Year	1990	1991	1992	1993	1994	1995	1996	1997	1998	1999
Visitors	12	67	155	270	486	713	1102	1284	1229	1475

Construct a time series plot to portray this set of data.

Hospitality, Leisure & Tourism Series

2.9 A café-bar is open from 11.00 in the morning to 11.00 in the evening. The number of customers in the establishment has been counted at hourly intervals on two consecutive days.

Day	Time												
	11	12	1	2	3	4	5	6	7	8	9	10	11
1	4	18	63	55	30	14	28	47	59	82	135	166	152
2	0	16	71	60	41	17	19	38	51	93	158	182	176

Plot this time series and point out any regular patterns your diagram shows.

2.10 Select which of the statements listed below on the right-hand side describe the words listed on the left-hand side.

(a) histogram   (i) can only take a limited number of values

(b) time series   (ii) segments or slices represent categories

(c) pictograph   (iii) each plotted point represents a pair of values

(d) discrete data   (iv) separates parts of each observation

(e) stem and leaf   (v)   each block represents a class
    display

(f) scatter diagram   (vi) data collected at regular intervals over time

(g) pie chart   (vii) comprises a set of small pictures

Summarizing univariate data

This chapter will help you:

- To understand why summarizing data is important.
- To distinguish location and spread.
- To produce various methods of summarizing data.
- To interpret the different ways of summarizing data.
- To know when to use the different ways of summarizing data.

In this chapter you will find:

- A discussion of the different approaches to summarizing data.
- Measures of location.
- Measures of spread.
- Diagrams to display order statistics.
- Guidance on using computer software to produce summary measures.

'To put it in a nutshell . . .'

This chapter is about using figures known as *summary measures* to represent or *summarize* quantitative data. Because they are used to describe sets of data they are also called *descriptive measures*. The summary measures that you will come across are very effective and widely used methods of communicating the essence or gist of a set of observations in just one or two figures, particularly when it is important to compare two or more distributions. Knowing how to interpret them and when to use them will help you become a much more effective communicator and user of statistical information.

There are two basic ways of summarizing a set of data. The first is to use a figure to give some idea of what the values within a set of data are like. This is the idea of an average, something you are probably familiar with; you may have achieved an average mark, you may be of average build, etc.

The word average suggests a 'middle' or 'typical' level. An average is a representative figure that summarizes a whole set of numbers in a single figure. There are two other names for averages that you will meet. The first is the phrase *measures of location*, used because averages tell us where the data is positioned or *located* on the numerical scale, so they measure the location of the data. The second is the phrase *measures of central tendency*, used because averages provide us with some idea of the *centre* or middle of a set of data.

The second basic way of summarizing a set of data is to measure how widely the figures are spread out or dispersed. Summary measures that do this are therefore known as *measures of spread* or *measures of dispersion*. They are single figures that tell us how broadly a set of observations is scattered.

These two types of summary measures, measures of location and measures of spread are not alternatives; they are complementary to each other. That is, we don't use either a measure of location or a measure of spread to summarize a set of data. More often than not we use both a measure of location and a measure of spread to convey an overall impression of a set of data, in the same way that police suspects are described by both their height and their weight.

3.1 Measures of location

There are various averages, or measures of location, that you can use to summarize or describe a set of data. The simplest both to apply and to interpret is the mode.

3.1.1 The mode

The *mode*, or *modal value*, is the most frequently occurring value in a set of observations. You can find the mode of a set of data by simply inspecting the observations.

Example 3.1

The ages of the 15 staff working at a fast food restaurant are:

17 18 21 18 16 19 17 28 16 20 18 17 17 19 17

What is the mode?

The value 17 occurs more often (5 times) than any other value, so 17 is the mode.

If you want an average to represent a set of data that consists of a fairly small number of discrete values in which one value is clearly the most frequent, then the mode is a perfectly good way of describing the data. Looking at the data in Example 3.1 you can see that using the mode, and describing these workers as having an average age of 17, would give a useful impression of the data.

The mode is much less suitable if the data we want to summarize consists of a larger number of different values, especially if there is more than one value that occurs the same number of times.

Example 3.2

The ages of the 18 staff working in the restaurant at a motorway service station are:

39 17 44 22 39 45 40 37 31 33 39 28 32 32 31 31 37 42

What is the mode?

The values 31 and 39 each occur three times.

The data in Example 3.2 is *bimodal*; that is to say it has two modes. If another person aged 32 joined the workforce there would be three modes. The more modes there are, the less useful the mode is to use. Ideally we want a single figure as a measure of location to represent a set of data.

If you want to summarize a set of continuous data, using the mode is going to be even more inappropriate; usually continuous data consists of different values so every value would be a mode because it occurs as often as every other value. If two or more observations take exactly the same value it is something of a fluke.

3.1.2 The median

Whereas you can only use the mode for some types of data, the second type of average or measure of location, the *median*, can be used for any set of data.

The median is the middle observation in a set of data. We find the median by first arranging the data in order of magnitude, that is listed in order from the lowest to the highest values. Such a list is called an *array*. Each observation in an array may be represented by the letter 'x' and the position of the observation in the array is put in round brackets, for instance $x_{(3)}$ would be the third observation in the array and $x_{(n)}$ would be the last.

Example 3.3

Find the median of the data in Example 3.1.

Array   16 16 17 17 17 17 17 **18** 18 18 19 19 20 21 28

Since there are 15 observations, the middle one is the 8th, the first 18, which is shown in bold type. There are seven observations to the left of it in the array, and seven observations to the right of it.

You can find the exact position of the median in an array by taking the number of observations, represented by the letter n, adding one and then dividing by two.

$$\text{Median position} = (n + 1)/2$$

In Example 3.3 there are 15 observations, that is $n = 15$, so

$$\text{Median position} = (15 + 1)/2 = 16/2 = 8$$

The median is in the 8th position in the array, in other words the 8th highest value, 18. The median age of these workers is 18.

Example 3.4

Find the median of the data in Example 3.2.

Array 17 22 28 31 31 31 32 32 **33 37** 37 39 39 39 40 42 44 45

In this case there are 18 observations, that is $n = 18$, so:

Median position $= (18 + 1)/2 = 9.5$th

Although we can find a ninth observation and a tenth observation there is clearly no 9.5th observation. The median position of 9.5th means that the median lies half way between the 9th and 10th observations, 33 and 37, which appear in bold type in the array. To find the half way mark between these observations, add them together and divide by two.

Median $= (33 + 37)/2 = 35$

The median age of this group of workers is 35.

When we are dealing with an odd number of observations there will be a median, that is a value in the middle. However, if there are an even number of observations in a set of data there will be no single middle value, we always have to split the difference between the middle pair of observations.

3.1.3 The arithmetic mean

Although you have probably come across averages before, and you may already be familiar with the mode and the median, neither of them are likely to be the first thing to come to mind if someone asked you how to find the average of a set of data. Faced with such a task you might well say something about adding the observations together and then dividing by the number of observations there are.

This is what many people think of as 'the average', although actually it is one of several averages. We have already dealt with two of them, the mode and the median. This third average, or measure of location, is called the *mean* or more specifically the *arithmetic* mean in order to distinguish it from other types of mean. Like the median the arithmetic mean can be used with any set of quantitative data.

The procedure for finding the arithmetic mean involves calculation so you may find it more laborious than finding the mode, which only involves inspecting data, or finding the median, which only involves arranging data. You have to first get the sum of the observations and then divide by n, the number of observations in the set of data.

$$\text{Arithmetic mean} = \Sigma x / n$$

The symbol x is used here to represent an observed value of the variable X, so Σx represents the sum of the observed values of the variable X. The arithmetic mean of a sample is represented by the symbol $\bar{x}$, 'x-bar'. The arithmetic mean of a population is represented by the Greek letter μ, 'mu'.

The mean is one of several statistical measures you will meet which have two different symbols, one of which is Greek, to represent them. The Greek symbol is always used to denote the measure for the population. Rarely do we have the time and resources to calculate a measure for a whole population so almost invariably the ones we do calculate are for a sample.

Example 3.5

The lunch-time temperature in degrees Celsius in Miami on 23 days selected at random were:

26   22   22   26   26   23   23   19   26   22   26   26

28   27   32   31   18   29   27   30   33   28   27

Find the mean temperature.

The sum of the temperatures, $\Sigma x = 26 + 22 + 22 + \ldots + 28 + 27 = 597$

So $\Sigma x / n = 597/23 = 25.957$ which is the arithmetic mean.

You can use MINITAB to find a mean by choosing **Column Statistics** from the **Calc** menu. In the command window select **Mean** and specify the column location of your data in the box alongside **Input variable**. You can obtain the median and a variety of other measures using **Column Statistics**.

Alternatively, in Excel select **Data Analysis** from the **Tools** menu then choose **Descriptive Statistics** from the menu in the command window. Specify the cell locations of your data in the box alongside **Input Range** and tick **Summary statistics** which will give you a selection of representative figures including the mean, median and mode.

3.1.4 Choosing which measure of location to use

The whole point of using a measure of location is that it should convey an impression of a distribution in a single figure. If we need to communicate this to an audience it won't help if we quote the mode, median and mean and then invite our audience to please themselves which one to pick. It is important to use the right sort of average.

Picking which average to use might depend on a number of factors:

- The type of data we are dealing with;
- Whether the average needs to be easy to find;
- The shape of the distribution;
- Whether the average will be the basis for further work on the data.

As far as the type of data is concerned, unless you are dealing with fairly simple discrete data the mode is redundant. If you do have such data to analyse the mode may be worth considering particularly if it is important that your measure of location is a feasible value for the variable to take.

Example 3.6

A restaurant stocks 16 types of wine. The numbers of bottles of each type sold in one evening are:

    1   1   6   0   2   1   1   4   0   2   4   1   4   3   2   1

Find the mode, median and mean for this set of data.

The modal value is 1, which occurs six times.

Array   0   0   1   1   1   1   1   1   2   2   2   3   4   4   4   6

The median position is: $(16 + 1)/2 = 8.5$th position

So (8th value + 9th value)/2 $= (1 + 2)/2 = 1.5$

The arithmetic mean $= (0 + 0 + 1 + 1 + \ldots + 4 + 6)/16 = 33/16 = 2.0625$

In Example 3.6 it is only the mode that has a value that is both feasible and actually occurs, 1. Although the value of the median, 1.5 may be feasible if the restaurant sells wine by the half bottle, it is not one of the observed values. The value of the mean, 2.0625 is not feasible and therefore cannot be one of the observed values.

The only other reason you might prefer to use the mode rather than the other measures of location, assuming that you are dealing with discrete data made up of a relatively few different values, is that it is the easiest of the measures of location to find. All you need to do is to look at the data and count how many times the values occur. Often with the sort of simple data that the mode suits it is pretty obvious which value occurs most frequently and there is no need to count the frequency of each value.

There are more reasons for not using the mode than there are for using the mode. Firstly, it is not appropriate for some types of data. Secondly, there is no guarantee that there is only one mode, there may be two or more in a single distribution. Thirdly, only the observations that have the modal value 'count', the rest of the observations in the distribution are not taken into account at all. In contrast, when we calculate a mean we add all the values in the distribution together, none of them are excluded.

In many cases you will find that the choice of average boils down to either the median or the mean. The shape of the distribution is a factor that could well influence your choice. If you are dealing with a distribution that has a skewed rather than a symmetrical shape, the median is likely to be the more realistic and reliable measure of location to use.

Example 3.7

Produce a histogram to display the data from Example 3.6 and comment on the shape of the distribution.

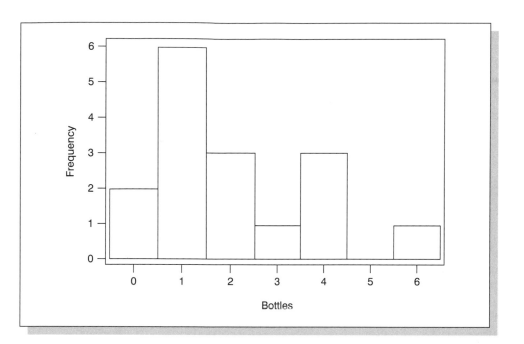

Figure 3.1 Wine sales

Figure 3.1 shows that the distribution of wine sales is skewed positively, the majority of the observations occur to the left of the distribution.

The median and mean for the data in Example 3.6 were 1.5 and 2.0625 respectively. There is quite a difference between them, especially when you consider that the difference between the lowest and highest values in the distribution is only 6. The difference between the median and the mean arises because the distribution is skewed.

When you find a median you concentrate on the middle of the distribution, you are not concerned with the observations to either side of the middle, so the pattern of the distribution at either end of the distribution does not have any effect on the median. In Example 3.6 it would not matter if the highest value in the distribution were 66 rather than 6, the median would still be 1.5. The value of the median is determined by how many observations lie to the left and right of it, not the values of those observations.

The mean on the other hand depends entirely on all of the values in the distribution, from the lowest to the highest, they all have to be added together in order to calculate the mean. If the highest value in the distribution were 66 rather than 6 it would make a considerable difference to the value of the mean (in fact it would increase to 5.8125).

Because calculating the mean involves adding all the observations together the value of the mean is sensitive to unusual values or outliers. Every observation is equal in the sense that it contributes 1 to the value of n, the number of observations. However if an observation is much lower than the rest, when it is added into the sum of the values it will contribute relatively little to the sum and make the value of the mean lower. If an observation is much higher than the rest, it will contribute disproportionately more to the sum and make the value of the mean higher.

Example 3.8

One of the observed values in the data in Example 3.6 has been recorded wrongly. The figure '6' should have been '2'. How does this affect the values of the mode, median and mean?

The mode is unaffected, the value '1' still occurs more frequently than the other values.

The median is unaffected because the 8th and 9th values will still be '1' and '2' respectively.

The mean will be affected because the sum of the observations will reduce by 4 to 31, so the mean is $31/16 = 1.9375$.

In Example 3.8 only one value was changed yet the mean drops from 2.0625 to 1.9375.

In a skewed distribution there are unusual values so if you use a mean to represent a skewed distribution you should bear in mind that it will be disproportionately influenced or 'distorted' by the relatively extreme values or outliers in the distribution. This is why the median for the data in Example 3.6 was 1.5 and the mean was 2.0625. The higher values in the distribution, the 6 and the 4s have in effect pulled the mean away from the median.

So, should you use the median or the mean to represent a skewed distribution? The answer is that the median is the more representative of the two. Look carefully at the values of the median and mean in relation to the figures in Example 3.6. The median, 1.5 is by definition in the middle of the distribution with eight observations below it and eight observations above it. The mean, 2.0625 in contrast has eleven observations below it and only five above it.

If you are dealing with a symmetrical distribution you will find that the mean is not susceptible to distortion because by definition there is roughly as much numerical 'ballast' to one side of the distribution as there is to the other. The mean and median of a symmetrical distribution will therefore be fairly close together.

Example 3.9

Produce a histogram to portray the data in Example 3.5. Find the median and compare it to the mean.

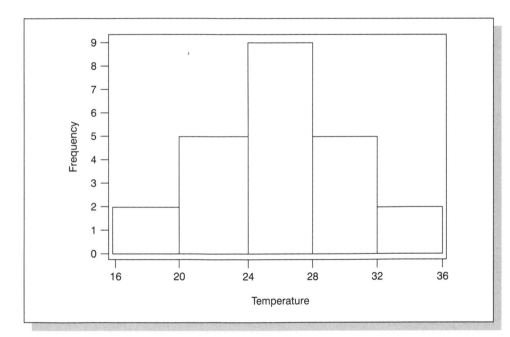

Figure 3.2 Temperatures (°Celsius) in Miami

There are 23 observations so the median is the (23 + 1)/2 = 12th observation.

Array   18   19   22   22   22   23   23   26   26   26   26   **26**   26
                27   27   27   28   28   29   30   31   32   33

The median is 26, which also happens to be the modal value. The median is very close in value to the mean, which was 25.957.

Hospitality, Leisure & Tourism Series

Figure 3.2 shows a much more symmetrical distribution than we saw in Figure 3.1. This symmetry has resulted in the mean and the median being very close together.

There is one further factor to consider when you need to choose a measure of location, and that is whether you will be using the result as the basis for further statistical analysis. If this were the case you would be well advised to use the mean because it has an extensive role within statistics as a representative measure, whereas the median does not.

You will find that choosing the right measure of location is not always straightforward. The conclusions from the discussion in this section are:

- Use a mode if your data is discrete and has only one mode.

- It is better to use a median if your data is skewed.

- In other cases use a mean.

3.1.5 Finding measures of location from classified data

You may find yourself in a situation where you would like to use a measure of location to represent a distribution but you only have the data in some classified form, perhaps a frequency distribution or a diagram. Perhaps the original data has been mislaid or discarded, or perhaps you want to develop work initiated by someone else and the original data is simply not available to you.

If the data is classified in the form of a stem and leaf display finding a measure of location from it is no problem since the display is also a list of the observed values in the distribution. Each observation is listed, but in a detached form so all you have to do is to put the stems and their leaves back together again to get the original data from which they were derived.

You can find the mode of a distribution from its stem and leaf display by looking for the most frequently occurring leaf digits grouped together on a stem line. Finding the median involves counting down (or up) to the middle value. To get the mean you would have to reassemble each observation in order to add them up.

Example 3.10

Construct a stem and leaf display to show the data in Example 3.5. Use the display to find the mode, median and mean of the distribution.

Stem and leaf of temperature $n = 23$

Leaf unit = 1.0

1	89
2	22233
2	666666777889
3	0123

The modal value is 26, the leaf digit '6' appears six times on the lower of the two stems lines for the stem digit '2'.

We know from the calculation $(23 +1)/2 = 12$ that the median is the 12th observation, which is also 26. To find it we can count from the top. The two leaf digits on the first stem line, which represent the observed values '18' and '19' are the 1st and 2nd observed values in the distribution in order of magnitude. The five leaf digits on the next stem line, the first of the two stem lines for the stem digit '2', are the 3rd to the 7th observed values in order of magnitude. The first leaf digit on the third stem line, the second of the two for the stem digit '2', is the 8th observed value, so if we count a further four values along that stem line we come to the 12th observation, the median value. The leaf digit that represents the median value in the display is shown in bold type.

To get the mean we have to put the observed values back together again and add 18, 19, 22, 22, etc.

In Example 3.10 you can see that we can get the same values for the mode, median and mean as we obtained from the original data because the stem and leaf display is constructed from the parts of the original data. Even if the stem and leaf display were made up of rounded versions of the original data we would get a very close approximation of the real values of the measures of location.

But what if you didn't have a stem and leaf display to work with? If you had a frequency distribution that gave the frequency, of every value in the distribution, or a bar chart that depicted the frequency distribution, you could still find the measures of location.

Example 3.11

Use Figure 3.1 to find the mode, median and mean of the distribution of restaurant wine sales.

Figure 3.1 shows the frequency with which each level of sales occurs, in the form of a bar. By checking the height of the bar against the vertical axis we can tell exactly how many times that quantity of bottles has been sold. We can put that information in the form of a frequency distribution.

Number of bottles sold	Frequency
0	2
1	6
2	3
3	1
4	3
5	0
6	1

We can see that the value '1' has occurred six times, more than any other level of sales, so the mode is 1.

The median position is $(16+1)/2 = 8.5$th. To find the median we have to find the 8th and 9th values and split the difference. We can find these observations by counting down the observations in each category, in the same way as we can with a stem and leaf display. The first row in the table contains two 0s, the 1st and 2nd observations in the distribution in order of magnitude. The second row contains the 3rd to the 8th observations, so the 8th observation is a '1'. The third row contains the 9th to the 11th observations, so the 9th observation is a '2'. The median is therefore half way between the 8th value, 1, and the 9th value, 2, that is 1.5.

To find the mean from the frequency distribution we could add each sales level into the sum the same number of times as its frequency. We add two '0's, six '1's and so on. There is a much more direct way of doing this involving multiplication, which is after all collective addition. We simply take each sales level and multiply it by its frequency, then add the products of this process together. If we use the letter 'x' to represent sales, and the letter 'f' to represent frequency we can describe this procedure as Σfx. Another way of representing n, the number of observations, is Σf, the sum of the frequencies, so the procedure of calculating the mean can be described as $\Sigma fx / \Sigma f$.

Number of bottles sold (x)	Frequency (f)	fx
0	2	0
1	6	6
2	3	6
3	1	3
4	3	12
5	0	0
6	1	6
	$\Sigma f = 16$	$\Sigma fx = 33$

The mean = $\Sigma fx / \Sigma f = 33/16 = 2.0625$.

You can see that the results obtained in Example 3.11 are exactly the same as the results found in Example 3.6 from the original data. This is possible because every value in the distribution is itself a category in the frequency distribution so we can tell exactly how many times it occurs.

But suppose you need to find measures of location for a distribution that is only available to you in the form of a grouped frequency distribution? The categories are not individual values but classes of values. We can't tell from it exactly how many times each value occurs, only the number of times each class of values occurs. From such limited information we can find measures of location but they will be approximations of the true values that we would get from the original data.

Because the data used to construct grouped frequency distributions usually includes many different values, hence the need to divide them into classes, finding an approximate value for the mode is a rather arbitrary exercise. It is almost always sufficient to identify the modal class, that is the class that contains most observations.

Example 3.12

Use Figure 3.2 to find the modal class, median and mean of the temperatures in Miami.

The grouped frequency distribution used to construct Figure 3.2 was:

Temperature	Frequency
16 and under 20	2
20 and under 24	5
24 and under 28	9
28 and under 32	5
32 and under 36	2

The modal class is '24 and under 28' because it contains more values, nine, than any other class.

To find a value for the median we first need to locate the class that contains the median value. There are 23 observations in the distribution so the median is the $(23 + 1)/2 = 12$th value in order of magnitude. Clearly the median value does not belong to the first class, '16 and under 20', which contains only the 1st and 2nd, the lowest observed values in the distribution. Neither does it belong to the second class, which contains the 3rd to the 7th values. The median is in the third class, which contains the 8th to the 16th values. But which one of the nine observations in the class is the median value? We know that the median will be the fifth observation in the median class but if we only have the grouped frequency we simply don't know what that observation is.

All we know is that it is at least 24 because that is where the median class begins so all nine observations in it are no lower than 24. We can approximate the median by assuming that all nine observations in the median class are distributed evenly through it. If that were the case the median would be 5/9ths the way along the median class.

So to get an approximate value for the median:

Begin at the start of the median class		24
Add 5/9ths of the width of the median class	$5/9 \times 4$	2.22
		26.22

which is not too far away from the real value we got from the original data, 26.

To obtain an approximate value for the mean from the grouped frequency distribution we apply the same frequency-based approach as we used in Example 3.11, but once again we have to get around the problem of not knowing the exact values of the observations in a class. In the absence of this knowledge we assume that all the observations in a class take, on average, the value in the middle of the class, known as the class midpoint. The set of class midpoints are then used as the values of the variables, x, that are contained in the distribution. So, for the purposes of calculating $\Sigma fx/\Sigma f$, the two observations in the first class are both assumed to have the value 18, that is the midpoint of the first class, '16 and under 20'.

Temperature	Midpoint (x)	Frequency (f)	fx
16 and under 20	18	2	36
20 and under 24	22	5	110
24 and under 28	26	9	234
28 and under 32	30	5	150
32 and under 36	34	2	68
		$\Sigma f = 23$	$\Sigma fx = 598$

The approximate value of the mean $= \Sigma fx/\Sigma f = 598/23 = 26$, which is very close to the actual value, 25.957.

3.2 Measures of spread

Just as there are several measures of location you can use to convey the central tendency of a distribution, there are several measures of spread you can use to convey the dispersion of a distribution. They are very often used alongside measures of location in order to give an overall impression of a distribution; where its middle is and how widely scattered the observations are around the middle. Indeed the two most important ones are closely linked to the median and the mean.

3.2.1 The range

The simplest measure of spread is the *range*. The range of a distribution is the difference between the lowest and the highest observations in the distribution, that is

$$\text{Range} = \text{highest observed value} - \text{lowest observed value}$$

$$= x_{(n)} - x_{(1)}$$

Although it is very easy to use and understand, and often a perfectly adequate method of measuring dispersion, it is not a wholly reliable or thorough way of doing it because it is based on only two observations. If, for instance you were asked to compare the spread in two different sets of data you may find that the ranges are very similar but the observations are spread out very differently.

Example 3.13

Two independent travel agencies each employ 9 people. The number of years' experience in the travel industry that the employees of these companies have is:

Agency A   0   4   4   5   7   8   10   11   15

Agency B   0   0   4   4   7   10   10   14   15

Find the range of each set of data and compare them.

Range (A) $= 15 - 0 = 15$

Range (B) $= 15 - 0 = 15$

The ranges are exactly the same, but this does not necessarily mean that the observations in the two distributions are spread out in exactly the same way.

If you compare Figure 3.3 and Figure 3.4 on page 70 you can see that the distribution of experience of the staff at Agency A has a much more pronounced centre whereas the distribution of experience of staff at Agency B has much more pronounced ends.

Although the ranges for the distributions in Example 3.13 are identical, the distributions show different levels of dispersion. The figures for Agency B are more widely spread or dispersed than the figures for Agency A.

Hospitality, Leisure & Tourism Series

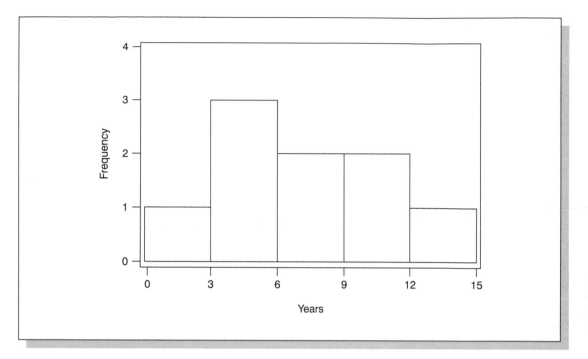

Figure 3.3 Experience (in years) of staff at Agency A

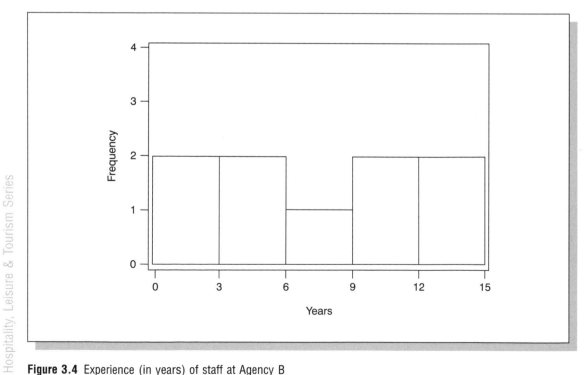

Figure 3.4 Experience (in years) of staff at Agency B

3.2.2 Quartiles and the semi-interquartile range

The second measure of location at our disposal is the *semi-interquartile range*, or SIQR for short. It is based on *quartiles*, which are a development from the idea of the median.

One way of looking at the median, or middle observation, of a distribution is to regard it as the point which separates the distribution into two equal halves, one consisting of the lower half of the observations and the other consisting of the upper half of the observations. The median, in effect, cuts the distribution in two.

If the median is a single cut that divides a distribution in two, the quartiles are a set of three separate points in a distribution that divide it into four equal quarters. The first, or lower quartile, known as Q1, is the point that separates the lowest quarter of the observations in a distribution from the rest. The second quartile is the median itself, it separates the lower two quarters (i.e. the lower half) of the observations in the distribution from the upper two quarters (i.e. the upper half). The third, or upper quartile, known as Q3, separates the highest quarter of observations in the distribution from the rest.

The median and the quartiles are known as *order statistics* because their values are determined by using the order or sequence of observations in a distribution. You may come across other order statistics such as *deciles*, which divide a distribution into tenths, and *percentiles*, which divide a distribution into hundredths.

You can find the quartiles of a distribution from an array or a stem and leaf display of the observations in the distribution. The quartile position is half way between the end of the distribution and the median, so it is defined in relation to the median position, which is $(n + 1)/2$, where n is the number of observations. You can find the approximate position of the quartiles by taking the median position, round it down to the nearest whole number if it is not a whole number, add one and divide by two, that is:

Quartile position = (median position + 1)/2

Once you know the quartile position you can find the lower quartile by counting up to the quartile position from the lowest observation and the upper quartile by counting down to the quartile position from the highest observation.

Example 3.14

The lunch-time temperature in degrees Celsius in Moscow on 23 days selected at random was:

–7 –10 –14 –3 –4 –2 0 1 –2 –10 –6 –4 4 21 19 24 5 8 13 11 21 25 28

Find the median and upper and lower quartiles for this distribution.

Array   –14 –10 –10 –7 –6 –4 –4 –3 –2 –2 0 1 4 5 8
                  11   13   19   21   21   24   25   28

The median position = (23 + 1)/2 = 12th position, so the median value is the value '1'. This suggests that half the time the temperature in Moscow is below one degree, and half the time it is above one degree.

The quartile position = (12 + 1)/2 = 6.5th position, that is midway between the 6th and 7th observations.

The lower quartile is half way between the observations 6th and 7th from the lowest, which are both –4, so the lower quartile is –4. This suggests that 25 per cent of the time the temperature in Moscow is below minus four.

The upper quartile is half way between the observations 6th and 7th from the highest, which are 19 and 13 respectively. The upper quartile is midway between these values, i.e. 16, which suggests that 25 per cent of the time the temperature in Moscow is above sixteen degrees.

If the upper quartile separates off the top quarter of the distribution and the lower quartile separates off the bottom quarter, the difference between the lower and upper quartiles is the range or span of the middle half of the observations in the distribution. This is called the *interquartile range*, which is the range between the quartiles. The semi-interquartile range (SIQR) is, as its name suggests, half the interquartile range, that is:

$$SIQR = (Q3 - Q1)/2$$

Example 3.15

Find the semi-interquartile range for the data in Example 3.14.

The lower quartile temperature was −4 and the upper quartile temperature, 16.

$$SIQR = (16 - (-4))/2 = (16 + 4)/2 = 20/2 = 10$$

The semi-interquartile range is a measure of spread. The larger the value of the SIQR, the more dispersed the observations in the distribution are.

Example 3.16

Find the SIQR of the data in Example 3.5 and compare this to the SIQR of the data in Example 3.14.

Array	18	19	22	22	22	23	23	26	26	26	26	26
	26	27	27	27	28	28	29	30	31	32	33	

There are 23 observations, so the median position is the $(23 + 1)/2 = $ 12th position.

The quartile position is the $(12 + 1)/2 = $ 6.5th position.

$$Q1 = (23 + 23)/2 = 23 \qquad Q3 = (28 + 28)/2 = 28 \qquad SIQR = (28 - 23)/2 = 2.5$$

The SIQR for the data from Miami (2.5) is far lower than the SIQR for the data from Moscow (10) indicating that there is far more variation in the temperature in Moscow. The temperatures in Miami are more consistent, as well as being warmer (compare the median value for Miami, 26, with the median value for Moscow, 1).

There is a diagram called a *boxplot*, which you might find a very useful way of displaying order statistics. In a boxplot the middle half of the values in a distribution is represented by a box, which has the lower quartile at one end and the upper quartile at the other. A line inside the box represents the median. The top and bottom quarters are represented by straight lines sometimes called 'whiskers' at each end of the box. A boxplot is a particularly useful way of comparing distributions.

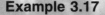

Example 3.17

Produce boxplots for the temperature data from Miami and Moscow.

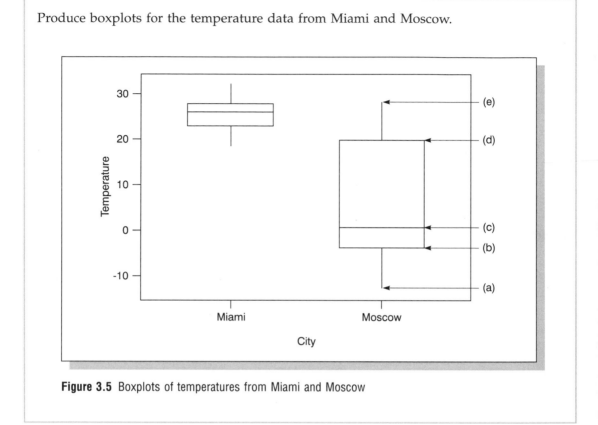

Figure 3.5 Boxplots of temperatures from Miami and Moscow

Look carefully at the boxplot to the right in Figure 3.5, which represents the temperatures in Moscow. The letter (a) indicates the position of the lowest observation, (b) indicates the position of the lower quartile, (c) is the median, (d) is the upper quartile, and (e) is the highest value.

In Figure 3.5 the diagram representing temperatures in Miami sits far higher than the diagram representing the temperatures in Moscow emphasizing the higher temperatures in Miami. The Miami box is also much more compact than the Moscow box, which reflects the greater variation in temperature in Moscow. The fact that the median line in the Moscow box is positioned low down within the box suggests that the middle half of the distribution is skewed. The quarter of observations between the median and the upper quartile are more widely spread than the quarter of observations between the median and the lower quartile.

A boxplot is particularly useful for identifying outliers, observed values that seem detached from the rest of the distribution. If you have outliers in a distribution it is important to check firstly that they have not been written down wrongly and secondly, assuming that they are accurately recorded, what reasons might explain such unusual observations.

Example 3.18

If the lowest value in the set of temperatures in Miami was wrongly recorded as 18 but was actually 8, how does the boxplot change?

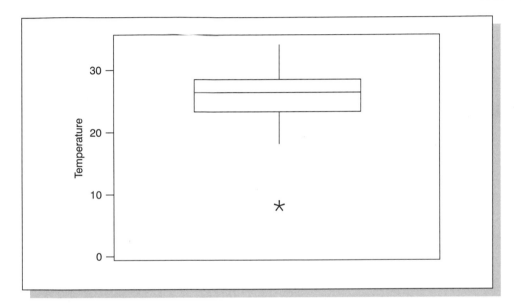

Figure 3.6 Temperatures in Miami

The lowest observation, 8, is now represented as an asterisk to emphasize its relative isolation from the rest of the observations.

You can produce a boxplot using MINITAB by selecting **Boxplot** from the **Graph** menu.

Quartiles and the SIQR are useful ways of measuring spread, and together with the median they are often the best way of summarizing skewed distributions. However like the range they focus on a very few observations in a distribution. So it is possible that the SIQR, like the range, cannot always detect dispersion.

Example 3.19

Find the SIQR for each of the two sets of data in Example 3.13.

There are nine observations in each distribution, so the median position is $(9 + 1)/2 = 5$th in both cases. The quartile position is $(5 + 1)/2 = 3$rd position.

Agency A	0 4 4 5 7	8	10	11	15
Agency B	0 0 4 4 7	10	10	14	15

In both cases the lower quartile is 4 and the upper quartile is 10, giving an SIQR of 3 for each distribution. Despite the identical SIQR results, Figures 3.3 and 3.4 clearly show that these distributions are not spread out in the same way.

3.2.3 The standard deviation

In order to avoid the shortcomings of the range and the SIQR we have to turn to a measure of spread that is based on including every observation rather than selecting just a few. That measure, the most important measure of spread in Statistics, is known as the *standard deviation*.

As the name suggests, the standard deviation is based on the idea of measuring the typical, or standard, amount of deviation, or difference, in a set of observations. But deviation from what? In fact the deviation from the arithmetic mean.

We find the standard deviation by first calculating the mean and then finding how far each observation is from it.

Example 3.20

Six public houses sell the following number of boxes of plain potato crisps in a particular week:

2 5 6 4 3 4

The mean, $\bar{x} = 24/6 = 4$

Observation (x)	Mean $(\bar{x})$	Deviation $(x - \bar{x})$
2	4	−2
5	4	1
6	4	2
4	4	0
3	4	−1
4	4	0

To get a single measure of spread from deviation figures like those in Example 3.20 it would be very convenient to add up the deviations and divide the sum of the deviations by the number of them to get a sort of 'average' deviation. Unfortunately, as you will find out if you try it with the deviations in Example 3.20, it doesn't work because the deviations add up to zero.

This will always happen because the mean is, in effect, the centre of gravity of a distribution. In the same way that the centre of gravity of an object has as much weight to one side as it does to the other, the mean has as much numerical 'weight' below it as it has above it. The result is that the deviations between the mean and the observations that are lower than the mean, which are always negative, cancel out the deviations between the mean and the observations that are higher than the mean, which are always positive. You can see in Example 3.20 that the negative deviations (−1 and −2) would be cancelled out by the positive deviations (1 and 2) if we added all the deviations together.

To get around this problem we square the deviations before adding them up, since any number squared is positive. The sum of the squared deviations, $\Sigma(x - \overline{x})^2$, is the basis of the standard deviation.

Example 3.21

Find the sum of the squared deviations, $\Sigma(x - \overline{x})^2$, from the mean for the data in Example 3.20.

Observation (x)	Mean ($\overline{x}$)	Deviation ($x - \overline{x}$)	Squared deviation ($x - \overline{x}$)^2
2	4	−2	4
5	4	1	1
6	4	2	4
4	4	0	0
3	4	−1	1
4	4	0	0

$\Sigma(x - \overline{x})^2 = 4 + 1 + 4 + 0 + 1 + 0 = 10$

Now we have a way of measuring total deviation it would be convenient to simply divide by the number of deviations that have been added together, which is the same as n, the number of observations. However, we actually divide the sum of the squared deviations by one less than n instead of n itself.

Any set of data starts off with the same number of *degrees of freedom* as it has observations, n. The implication is that if you wanted to specify all the figures in the set of data yourself you can do so freely. However, once you have found the mean you could only specify one less than the number of figures freely. The last one would have to be the only figure that combines with the ones you have specified to keep the mean the same, so you have 'lost' a degree of freedom. For instance if we know that the mean of a set of three figures is 5, and we suggest that 2 and 7 are the first two figures in the set, the third value has to be 6 in order that the mean is still 5. Choose any other value for the third figure and the mean will be different.

When we calculate a standard deviation we are using the mean, so we lose one degree of freedom, so the procedure that we use to calculate the standard deviation, s, of a sample involves dividing the sum of squared deviations by $(n - 1)$. The only exception is the rare occasion when we need to calculate the population standard deviation, σ (the lower case of the Greek letter s), in which case the sum of squared deviations is divided by n.

In later work you will find that a sample standard deviation can be used as an estimate of a population distribution. This can save time and money, but it can only be done if the sample standard deviation is calculated properly.

The final part of the procedure you follow to obtain a sample standard deviation is to take the square root of the sum of squared deviations divided by $(n - 1)$. You have to do this to get a figure that is in the same units as your original data. For instance, the squared deviation figures in Example 3.21 are in 'boxes of crisps squared'. It is much more useful to have a figure measured in boxes of crisps.

We can sum up the procedure that is used to obtain a sample standard deviation in the following expression:

$$s = \sqrt{\frac{\Sigma (x - \bar{x})^2}{(n - 1)}}$$

Example 3.22

Calculate the standard deviation for the data in Example 3.20.

The sum of squared deviations is 10 and the number of observations is 6, so the standard deviation of this sample is:

$$s = \sqrt{10/5} = \sqrt{2} = 1.414$$

The expression for the population standard deviation is:

$$\sigma = \sqrt{\Sigma(x - \bar{x})^2/n}$$

If you use either of these expressions to calculate the standard deviation of a set of data with many observations you will find the experience laborious. It really is a task that should be carried out with the aid of a calculator or computer software.

If you have a calculator with statistical functions look for a key with s or $x\sigma_{n-1}$ or σ_{xn-1} on or alongside it. Alternatively you can use the **Descriptive Statistics** facility in the **Data Analysis** option from the **Tools** menu in Excel, or choose **Standard deviation** from the **Column Statistics** option on the **Calc** menu in MINITAB.

In later statistical work you may encounter something called a *variance*. The variance is the square of the standard deviation. The expression for the variance looks like the expression for the standard deviation, in fact the only difference is that finding the variance does not involve taking a square root.

The sample variance:

$$s^2 = \Sigma(x - \bar{x})^2/(n - 1)$$

The population variance:

$$\sigma^2 = \Sigma(x - \bar{x})^2/n$$

The standard deviation is widely used with the mean to provide an overall summary or description of a distribution. Indeed for many distributions the mean and the standard deviation are the key defining characteristics or *parameters* of the distribution.

One of the reasons it has become such an important measure of spread is that it is a reliable way of detecting dispersion.

Example 3.23

Find the mean and the standard deviation of the data from Example 3.13 and compare the results for the two agencies.

Agency A   Mean = $(0 + 4 + 4 + 5 + 7 + 8 + 10 + 11 + 15)/9 = 7.11$

Experience (x)	Mean ($\bar{x}$)	($x - \bar{x}$)	($x - \bar{x}$)^2
0	7.11	−7.11	50.55
4	7.11	−3.11	9.67
4	7.11	−3.11	9.67
5	7.11	−2.11	4.45
7	7.11	−0.11	0.01
8	7.11	0.89	0.79
10	7.11	2.89	8.35
11	7.11	3.89	15.13
15	7.11	7.89	62.25

$$\Sigma(x - \bar{x})^2 = 160.87$$

$$s = \sqrt{\Sigma(x - \bar{x})^2/(n - 1)} = \sqrt{160.87/(9 - 1)}$$

$$= \sqrt{160.87/8} = \sqrt{20.11} = 4.48$$

Agency B   Mean = $(0 + 0 + 4 + 4 + 7 + 10 + 10 + 14 + 15)/9 = 7.11$

Experience (x)	Mean ($\bar{x}$)	($x - \bar{x}$)	($x - \bar{x}$)^2
0	7.11	−7.11	50.55
0	7.11	−7.11	50.55
4	7.11	−3.11	9.67
4	7.11	−3.11	9.67
7	7.11	−0.11	0.01
10	7.11	2.89	8.35
10	7.11	2.89	8.35
14	7.11	6.89	47.47
15	7.11	7.89	62.25

$$\Sigma(x - \bar{x})^2 = 246.87$$

$$s = \sqrt{\Sigma(x - \bar{x})^2/(n - 1)} = \sqrt{246.87/(9 - 1)}$$

$$= \sqrt{246.87/8} = \sqrt{30.86} = 5.56$$

The means are the same, 7.11, but the standard deviation for Agency B is higher than the standard deviation for Agency A, 5.56 compared to 4.48. The difference between the standard deviations reflects the contrasting spread that we could see in Figures 3.3 and 3.4.

The mean and standard deviation can be used to approximate the overall spread of observations in a distribution. Typically nearly all the observations will lie between the point three standard deviations below the mean and the point three standard deviations above the mean. Another way of saying this is to say that almost the entire distribution is located within three standard deviations of the mean. Another rule of thumb is that 90 per cent or so of a distribution will be within two standard deviations of the mean.

In further work you will find that the mean and the standard deviation can be used to define the positions of values in a distribution. For instance, if we have a distribution that has a mean of 4 and a standard deviation of 2 we could describe the value '8' as being two standard deviations above the mean. The value '1' could be described as being one and a half standard deviations below the mean.

Review questions

3.1 Select which of the statements on the right-hand side best define the words on the left-hand side:

(a) median   (i)   the square of the standard deviation
(b) range   (ii)   a diagram based on order statistics
(c) variance   (iii)   the most frequently occurring value
(d) boxplot   (iv)   the difference between the extreme observations
(e) SIQR   (v)   the middle value
(f) mode   (vi)   half the difference between the quartiles

3.2 The Information Office at an airport offers airport users a list of local hotels. The distance from the airport of each of the 25 hotels on the list is:

```
3  5  2  0  4  3  0  1  1  9  1  4  1
3  9  4  1  4  1  5  5  2  3  1  1
```

(a) Find the mode of this distribution.
(b) Find the median.
(c) Calculate the mean of the distribution and compare it to the mode. What can you conclude about the shape of the distribution?

3.3 The sole food and beverage facility at the football ground of non-league Dynamo Doriston has taken the following amounts (to the nearest £) during each of the 22 home fixtures played at the ground:

```
452  134  235  408  385  266  412  285  257
369  324  127  284  399  146  343  424  422
403  364  267  239
```

(a) Find the median.
(b) Find the quartiles and the semi-interquartile range.

3.4 The ground of the local rivals of Dynamo Doriston, Real Roshborough, also has a single food and beverage facility. The receipts during the 22 home fixtures of the same season (to the nearest £) were:

555 454 514 483 486 542 414 547 372
328 595 416 585 512 478 422 520 500
551 513 441 595

(a) Find the median.

(b) Find the semi-interquartile range.

How do their sales compare with those at Dynamo Doriston?

3.5 The times taken (in minutes) to clean and restock 6 hotel rooms by two housekeepers were:

Housekeeper A	Housekeeper B
29.0	26.6
21.8	16.3
25.5	23.2
23.4	17.1
16.6	16.7
20.0	17.1

Calculate (a) the mean and (b) the standard deviation for each set of times and use them to compare the performance of the chambermaids.

3.6 A survey of 100 customers was conducted at two fast food outlets, the 'Silly Burger' city centre restaurant and the 'Car Burger Eater' drive-in on a major commuter route. The incomes of the respondents were put into the following grouped frequency distributions:

Income (£'000)	Frequency (Silly Burger)	Frequency (Car Burger Eater)
0 and under 5	7	1
5 and under 10	20	8
10 and under 15	28	11
15 and under 20	22	20
20 and under 25	18	33
25 and under 30	4	16
30 and under 35	1	9
35 and under 40	0	2

Find approximate values of the median and mean for each distribution. What do your results tell you about the customers of the establishments?

3.7 A family visits the Goddo theme park on a busy public holiday, and go on 19 rides. The times (in minutes) that they have to wait for these rides are shown in the stem and leaf display below:

Stem Leaves

```
0    2 2 5 6 8 9
1    0 0 0 1 4 4 5 5 7
2    2 5
3    0
4    0
```

Leaf unit = 1.0

Find the values of the median and semi-interquartile range. Does the shape of this distribution mean that these are suitable summary measures to use?

3.8 The prices of a pint of ordinary bitter in each of 30 public houses in one city in the North of the UK and another city in the South of the UK were recorded and the following boxplots were produced to portray the two distributions.

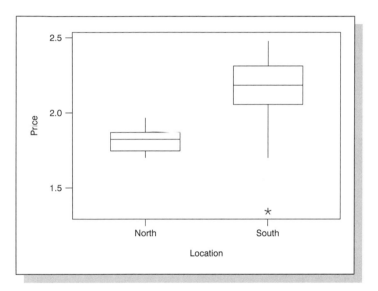

Look carefully at the figure and say whether each of the statements beneath is true or false:

(a) The lowest price is to be found in the North
(b) The SIQR for the figures from the South is larger
(c) There is one outlier, the lowest price in the South
(d) The middle half of the prices in the North are more symmetrically distributed
(e) The highest price in the North is lower than the first quartile price in the South
(f) The range of the prices in the South is smaller
(g) The upper quartile of prices in the North is about £1.85
(h) The median price in the South is about £2.40

CHAPTER 4

Summarizing bivariate data

This chapter will help you:

- To understand why summarizing bivariate data is important.
- To investigate the connection between two variables.
- To measure changes over time.
- To adjust figures for the effects of inflation.
- To analyse time series.
- To predict future values of time series.

In this chapter you will find:

- Measures of correlation.
- Simple linear regression analysis.
- Price indices.
- Analysis of the components of time series.
- Guidance on using computer software.

'Getting from A to B ... making the right connections.'

This chapter is about techniques that you can use to study the relationship between two variables. The type of data that these techniques are intended to analyse is called *bivariate* data because they consist of observed values of two variables. The techniques themselves make up what is known as bivariate analysis.

Bivariate analysis is of great importance to business. The results of this sort of analysis have indeed influenced the hospitality and tourism sectors considerably. When the relationship between the amount of alcohol in the blood system and reaction times was established, drink-driving laws were introduced. The analysis of survival rates of micro-organisms and temperature is crucial to the setting of appropriate standards in food storage and preparation. Marketing strategies of organizations in the tourism sector are often based on the analysis of consumer expenditure in relation to age or income. Sometimes time itself is an important variable; for instance the timing of advertising and promotional activities in the tourism industry is based on the analysis of consumer expenditure over time.

This chapter will introduce you to some of the techniques that companies and other organizations use to summarize bivariate data. The first set of techniques you will meet, *correlation* and *regression*, are general techniques that can be used with any bivariate data. The second set of techniques, which consists of price indices and basic time series analysis, are designed to summarize sets of bivariate data in which one of the variables is time.

4.1 Correlation and regression

Suppose you have a set of bivariate data that consists of observations of one variable, X, and the associated observations of another variable, Y, and you want to see if X and Y are related. For instance, the Y variable could be sales of ice cream per day and the X variable the daily temperature, and you want to investigate the connection between temperature and ice cream sales. In such a case correlation analysis enables us to assess whether there is a connection between the two variables and, if so, how strong that connection is.

If correlation analysis tells us there is a connection we can use regression analysis to identify the exact form of the relationship. It is essential to know this if you want to use the relationship to make predictions, for instance if we want to predict the demand for ice cream when the daily temperature is at a particular level.

The assumption that underpins bivariate analysis is that one variable depends on the other. The letter Y is used to represent the *dependent* variable, the one whose values are believed to depend on the other variable. This other variable, represented by the letter X is called the *independent* variable. The Y or dependent variable is sometimes known as the *response* because it is believed to respond to changes in the value of X. The X or independent variable is also known as the *predictor* because it might help us to predict the values of Y.

4.1.1 Correlation analysis

Correlation analysis is a way of investigating whether two variables are correlated, or connected with each other. We can study this to some extent by using a scatter diagram to portray the data, but such a diagram can only give us a visual 'feel' for the association between two variables, it doesn't actually measure the strength of the connection. So, although a scatter diagram is the thing you should begin with to carry out bivariate analysis, you need to calculate a *correlation coefficient* if you want a precise way of assessing how closely the variables are related.

The correlation coefficient is similar to the standard deviation in that it is based on the idea of dispersion or spread. The comparison isn't complete because bivariate data is spread out in two dimensions. If you look at a scatter diagram you will see that the points representing the data are scattered both vertically and horizontally.

The letter r is used to represent the correlation coefficient of sample data. Its Greek counterpart, the letter ρ (rho) is used to represent the correlation coefficient of population data. As is the case with other summary measures it is exceedingly unlikely that you will ever have to find the value of a population correlation coefficient because of the cost and practical difficulty of studying entire populations.

The correlation coefficient is a ratio; it compares the coordinated scatter to the total scatter. The coordinated scatter is the extent to which the observed values of one variable, X, vary in coordination with the observed values of a second variable, Y. We use the *covariance* of the values of X and Y, Cov_{XY} to measure the degree of coordinated scatter.

To calculate the covariance you have to multiply the amount that each x deviates from the mean of the X values, $\bar{x}$, by the amount that its corresponding y deviates from the mean of the Y values, $\bar{y}$. That is, for every pair of x and y observations you calculate:

$$(x - \bar{x})(y - \bar{y})$$

The result will be positive whenever the x and y values are both bigger than their means, because we will be multiplying two positive deviations together. It will also be positive if both the x

and y values are smaller than their means, because both deviations will be negative and the result of multiplying them together will be positive. The result will only be negative if one of the deviations is positive and the other negative.

The covariance is the total of the products from this process divided by n, the number of pairs of observations, minus one. We have to divide by $n-1$ because the use of the means in arriving at the deviations results in the loss of a degree of freedom.

$$\text{Cov}_{XY} = \Sigma(x - \overline{x})(y - \overline{y})/(n-1)$$

The covariance is positive if values of X below $\overline{x}$ tend to be associated with values of Y below $\overline{y}$, and values of X above $\overline{x}$ tend to be associated with values of Y above $\overline{y}$. In other words if high x values occur with high y values and low x values occur with low y values we will have a positive covariance. This suggests that there is a positive or *direct* relationship between X and Y, that is if X goes up we would expect Y to go up as well, and vice versa. If you compared the income of a sample of consumers with their expenditure on holidays you would expect to find a direct relationship.

The covariance is negative if values of X below $\overline{x}$ are associated with values of Y above $\overline{y}$, and vice versa. The low values of X occur with the high values of Y, and the high values of X occur with the low values of Y. This is a negative or *inverse* relationship. If you compared the prices of package holidays with demand for them you might expect to find an inverse relationship.

Example 4.1

A couple are planning a wedding and are looking for somewhere for the reception. They are considering six venues. The price per guest for the standard food and beverage package (in £s), and the distance in miles from the location of the ceremony are:

Price	18	20	25	27	28	32
Distance	8	6	5	2	2	1

Plot a scatter diagram and calculate the covariance.

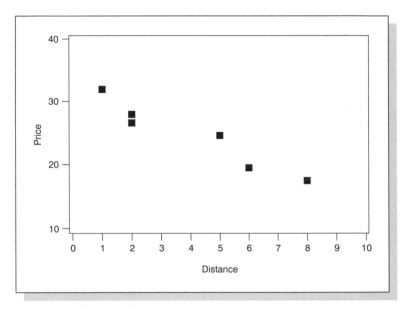

Figure 4.1 Price and distance

In Figure 4.1 price has been plotted on the Y, or vertical axis, and distance has been plotted on the X, or horizontal axis. We are assuming that price depends on distance rather than the other way round.

To calculate the covariance we need to calculate deviations from the mean for every x and y value.

$\bar{x} = (8 + 6 + 5 + 2 + 2 + 1)/6 = 24/6 = 4$

$\bar{y} = (18 + 20 + 25 + 27 + 28 + 32)/6 = 150/6 = 25$

Distance (x)	$\bar{x}$	$(x - \bar{x})$	Price (y)	$\bar{y}$	$(y - \bar{y})$	$(x - \bar{x})(y - \bar{y})$
8	4	4	18	25	−7	−28
6	4	2	20	25	−5	−10
5	4	1	25	25	0	0
2	4	−2	27	25	2	−4
2	4	−2	28	25	3	−6
1	4	−3	32	25	7	−21

$$\Sigma(x - \bar{x})(y - \bar{y}) = -69$$

Covariance $= \Sigma(x - \bar{x})(y - \bar{y})/(n - 1) = -69/5 = -13.8$

The other ingredient necessary to obtain a correlation coefficient is some measure of total scatter, some way of assessing the horizontal and vertical dispersion. We can do this by taking the standard deviation of the X values, which measures the horizontal spread, and multiplying by the standard deviation of the Y values, which measures the vertical spread.

The correlation coefficient, r, is the covariance of the X and Y values divided by the product of the two standard deviations.

$$r = \text{Cov}_{XY}/(s_x \times s_y)$$

There are two things to note about r at this stage:

1 It can be either positive or negative because the covariance can be positive or negative
2 It cannot be larger than 1 or −1 because the coordinated scatter, measured by the covariance, cannot be larger than the total scatter, measured by the product of the standard deviations.

Example 4.2

Calculate the correlation coefficient for the data in Example 4.1.

We need to calculate the sample standard deviation for X and Y.

Distance (x)	$\bar{x}$	$(x - \bar{x})$	$(x - \bar{x})^2$	Price (y)	$\bar{y}$	$(y - \bar{y})$	$(y - \bar{y})^2$
8	4	4	16	18	25	−7	49
6	4	2	4	20	25	−5	25
5	4	1	1	25	25	0	0
2	4	−2	4	27	25	2	4
2	4	−2	4	28	25	3	9
1	4	−3	9	32	25	7	49
			38				136

From Example 4.1, covariance $= -13.8$

Sample standard deviation of X, $S_X = \sqrt{\Sigma(x - \bar{x})^2/(n - 1)} = \sqrt{38/5} = 2.76$

Sample standard deviation of Y, $S_Y = \sqrt{\Sigma(y - \bar{y})^2/(n - 1)} = \sqrt{136/5} = 5.22$

Correlation coefficient, $r = (-13.8)/(2.76 \times 5.22) = -13.8/14.41 = -0.96$

As you can see calculating a correlation coefficient, even for a fairly simple set of data, is quite laborious. You can use MINITAB to produce a correlation coefficient by selecting **Basic Statistics** from the **Stat** menu. Choose **Correlation** from the sub-menu then give the column location of both sets of observations in the command window. In Excel you should select **Data Analysis** from the **Tools** menu, choose **Correlation** from the menu in the command window and specify the cell locations of your data.

What should we conclude from the results of Example 4.1? The scatter diagram shows that the points representing the data almost lie along a straight line, in other words there is a pronounced linear pattern. The diagram also shows that this linear pattern goes from the top left of the diagram to the bottom right, suggesting that the more expensive venues are closer to the location of the ceremony. This means there is an inverse relationship between the price and distance variables.

What does the correlation coefficient tell us? The fact that it is negative, −0.96, confirms that the relationship between price and distance is indeed an inverse one. The fact that it is very close to the maximum possible negative value that a correlation coefficient can take, −1 indicates that there is a strong association between the variables.

The correlation coefficient measures linear correlation, that is the extent to which there is a straight-line relationship between the variables. Every correlation coefficient will lie somewhere on the scale of possible values, that is between −1 and +1 inclusive.

A correlation coefficient of +1 tells us that there is a perfect positive linear association between the variables. If we plotted a scatter diagram of data that has such a relationship we would expect to find all the points lying in the form of an upward-sloping straight line. You can see this sort of pattern in Figure 4.2. A correlation coefficient of −1 means we have perfect negative correlation, which is illustrated in Figure 4.3.

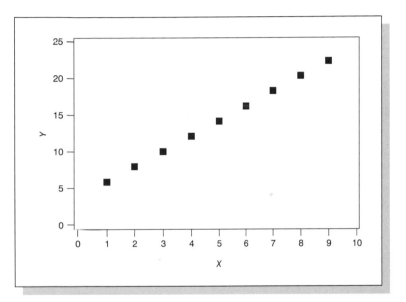

Figure 4.2
Perfect positive correlation

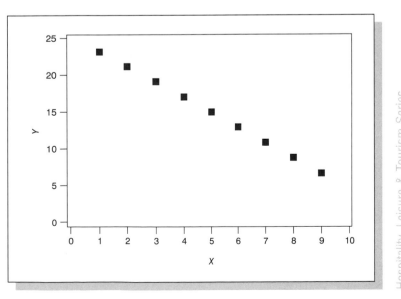

Figure 4.3
Perfect negative correlation

In practice you are unlikely to come across a correlation coefficient of +1 or –1, but you may well meet correlation coefficients that are positive and fairly close to +1 or negative and fairly close to –1. Such values reflect good positive and good negative correlation respectively. Figure 4.4 shows a set of data with a correlation coefficient of +0.9. You can see that although

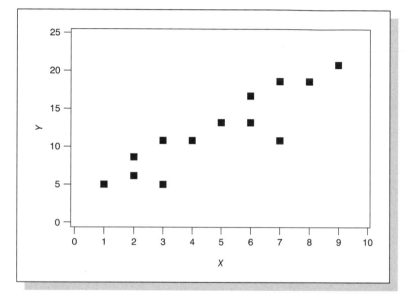

Figure 4.4
Good positive correlation

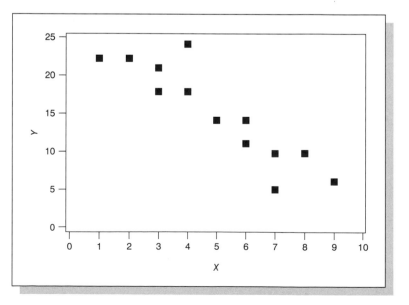

Figure 4.5
Good negative correlation

the points do not form a perfect straight line they form a pattern that is clearly linear and upward sloping.

Figure 4.5 portrays bivariate data that has a correlation coefficient of −0.9. In this case you can see a clear downward linear pattern.

The closer your correlation coefficient is to +1 the better the positive correlation. The closer it is to −1 the better the negative correlation. It follows that the nearer a correlation coefficient is to zero the weaker the connection between the two variables. Figure 4.6 shows a sample of observations of two variables with a correlation coefficient of −0.1, which provides little evidence of any correlation.

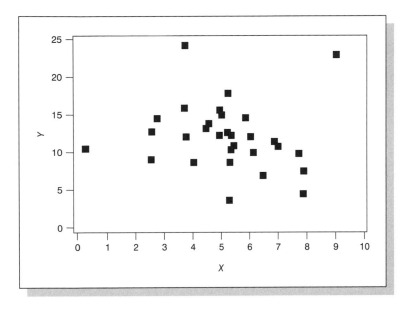

Figure 4.6
Negligible correlation

The things to remember about the sample correlation coefficient, r are that:

- It measures the strength of the connection or association between observed values of two variables.

- It can take any value from −1 to +1 inclusive.

- If it is positive it means there is a direct or upward-sloping relationship.

- If it is negative it means there is an inverse or downward-sloping relationship.

- The further it is from zero the stronger the association.

4.1.2 The coefficient of determination

The square of the correlation coefficient is also used as a way of assessing the connection between variables. Although it is the square of r, the symbol used to represent it is R^2. It is called the *coefficient of determination* because it can help you to measure how much the values of one variable are decided or *determined* by the values of another.

As we saw, the correlation coefficient is based on the standard deviation. Similarly the square of the correlation coefficient is based on the square of the standard deviation, the variance.

Like the correlation coefficient, the coefficient of determination is a ratio, the ratio of the amount of the variance that can be explained by the relationship between the variables to the total variance in the data. Because it is a ratio it cannot exceed one and because it is a square it is always a positive value. For convenience it is often expressed as a percentage.

Example 4.3

Calculate the coefficient of determination, R^2, for the data in Example 4.1.

The correlation coefficient for the data was −0.96. The square of −0.96 is 0.92 (to 2 decimal places) or 92 per cent. This is the value of R^2. It means that 92 per cent of the variation in the prices can be explained by the variation in the distances.

You may find R^2 an easier way to communicate the strength of the relationship between two variables. Its only disadvantage compared to the correlation coefficient is that the figure itself does not convey whether the association is positive or negative. However, there are other ways of showing this, including the scatter diagram.

4.1.3 Simple linear regression analysis

Measuring correlation tells you how strong the linear relationship between two variables might be but it doesn't tell us exactly what that relationship is. If we need to know about the way in which two variables are related we have to use the other part of basic bivariate analysis, *regression analysis*.

The simplest form of this technique, *simple linear regression* (which is often abbreviated to SLR) enables us to find the straight line most appropriate for representing the connection between two sets of observed values. Because the line that we 'fit' to our data can be used to represent the relationship it is rather like an average in two dimensions, it summarizes the link between the variables.

Simple linear regression is called *simple* because it analyses two variables, it is called *linear* because it is about finding a straight line, but why is it called *regression*, which actually means going backwards? The answer is that the techniques was first developed by the genetics pioneer Galton, who wanted a way of representing how the height of children was genetically restrained or 'regressed' by the height of their parents.

In later work you may encounter *multiple* regression, which is used to analyse relationships between more than two variables, and *non-linear* regression, which is used to analyse relationships which do not have a straight line pattern.

You might ask why it is necessary to have a technique to fit a line to a set of data? It would be quite easy to look at a scatter diagram like Figure 4.1, lay a ruler close to the points and draw a line to represent the relationship between the variables. This is known as fitting a line 'by eye' and is a perfectly acceptable way of getting a quick approximation particularly in a case like Figure 4.1 where there are few points which form a clear linear pattern.

The trouble with fitting a line by eye is that it is inconsistent and unreliable. It is inconsistent because the position of the line depends on the judgement of the person drawing the line. Different people will produce different lines for the same data.

For any set of bivariate data there is one line which is the most appropriate, the so-called 'best-fit' line. There is no guarantee that fitting a line by eye will produce the best-fit line, so fitting a line by eye is unreliable.

We need a reliable, consistent way of finding the line which best fits a set of plotted points, which is what simple linear regression analysis is. It is a technique that finds the line of best fit, the line that travels as closely as possible to the plotted points. It identifies the two defining characteristics of that line, its *intercept*, or starting point, and its *slope*, or rate of increase or decrease.

We can use these defining characteristics to compose the equation of the line of best fit, which represents the line using symbols. The equation enables us to plot the line itself.

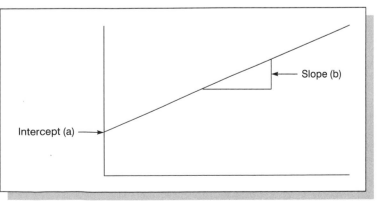

Figure 4.7
The intercept and slope of a line

Simple linear regression is based on the idea of minimizing the differences between a line and the points it is intended to represent. Since all the points matter, it is the sum of these differences that needs to be minimized. In other words the best-fit line is the line that results in a lower sum of differences than any other line would for that set of data.

The task for simple linear regression is a little more complicated because the difference between a point and the line are positive if the point is above the line, and negative if the point is below the line. If we were to add up these differences we would find that the negative and positive differences cancel each other out.

This means the sum of the differences is not a reliable way of judging how well a line fits a set of points. To get around this problem, simple linear regression is based on the squares of the differences because they will always be positive.

Example 4.4

A new ice cream parlour has been open three days. The sales (in £'000) and the lunch time temperatures (in degrees Celsius) for these three days were:

Sales (Y)	4	3	6
Temperature (X)	15	20	25

Which of the two lines best fits the data, the one in Figure 4.8 or the one in Figure 4.9?

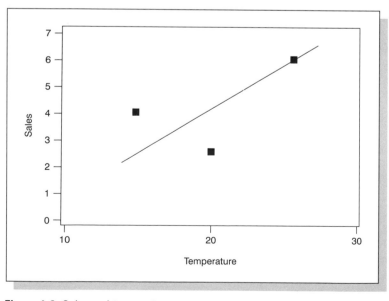

Figure 4.8 Sales and temperature

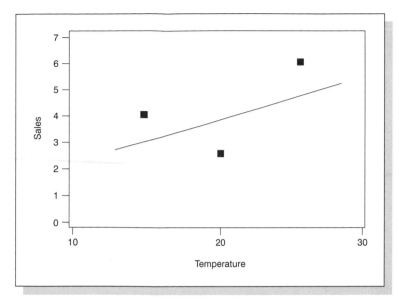

Figure 4.9 Sales and temperature

The deviations between the points and the line in Figure 4.8 are, from left to right, +1.5, –1.5 and 0. The total deviation is:

$$1.5 + (-1.5) + 0 = 0$$

The deviations between the points and the line in Figure 4.9 are, from left to right, +1, –1 and +1. The total deviation is:

$$1 + (-1) + 1 = 1$$

The fact that the total deviation is smaller for Figure 4.8 suggests that its line is the better fit. But if we take the sum of the squared deviations the conclusion is different.

Total squared deviation in Figure 4.8 $= 1.5^2 + (-1.5)^2 + 0^2 = 2.25 + 2.25 + 0 = 4.5$

Total squared deviation in Figure 4.9 $= 1^2 + (-1)^2 + 1^2 = 1 + 1 + 1 = 3$

This apparent contradiction has arisen because the large deviations in Figure 4.8 cancel each other out when we add them together.

The best-fit line that simple linear regression finds for us is the line which takes the path which results in there being the least possible sum of squared differences between the points and the line. For this reason the technique is sometimes referred to as *least squares regression*.

For any given set of data, as you can imagine, there are many lines from which the best-fit line could be chosen. To pick the right one we could plot each of them in turn and measure the differences using a ruler. Fortunately, such a laborious procedure is not necessary. Simple linear regression uses calculus, the area of mathematics that is partly about finding minimum or maximum values, to find the intercept and slope of the line of best-fit directly from the data.

The procedure involves using two expressions to find firstly the slope and then the intercept. Since simple linear regression is almost always used to find the line of best fit from a set of sample data the letters used to represent the intercept and the slope are a and b respectively. The equivalent Greek letters, α and β are used to represent the intercept and slope of the population line of best fit.

According to simple linear regression analysis the slope of the line of best fit:

$$b = \frac{\Sigma xy - (\Sigma x \times \Sigma y)/n}{\Sigma x^2 - (\Sigma x)^2/n}$$

And the intercept:

$$a = (\Sigma y - b\Sigma x)/n$$

These results can then be combined to give the equation of the line of best fit, which is known as the *regression equation*:

$$Y = a + bX$$

The expressions for getting the slope and intercept of the line of best fit look daunting, but this need not worry you. If you have to find a best-fit line you can use a statistical or a spreadsheet package, or even a calculator with a good statistical facility, to do the hard work for you. They are quoted here, and used in Example 4.5 below merely to show you how the procedure works.

Example 4.5

Find the equation of the line of best fit for the data in Example 4.1.

We need to find four summations; the sum of the x values, the sum of the y values, the sum of the x squared values and the sum of the products of each pair of x and y values multiplied together.

Distance (x)	x^2	Price (y)	xy
8	64	18	144
6	36	20	120
5	25	25	125
2	4	27	54
2	4	28	56
1	1	32	32
$\Sigma x = 24$	$\Sigma x^2 = 134$	$\Sigma y = 150$	$\Sigma xy = 531$

$$b = \frac{\Sigma xy - (\Sigma x \times \Sigma y)/n}{\Sigma x^2 - (\Sigma x)^2/n} = \frac{531 - (24 \times 150)/6}{134 - 24^2/6} = \frac{531 - 3600/6}{134 - 576/6}$$

$$= \frac{531 - 600}{134 - 96} = \frac{-69}{38} = -1.82$$

$$a = (\Sigma y - b\Sigma x)/n = (150 - (-1.82)24)/6 = (150 + 43.58)/6 = 193.58/6 = 32.26$$

The equation of the line of best fit is:

$$Y = 32.26 - 1.82X$$

This is a laborious procedure, even with a relatively simple set of data. You can use MINITAB to perform this type of analysis by selecting **Basic Statistics** from the **Stat** menu. Choose **Regression** from the **Basic Statistics** sub-menu and you will see another sub-menu. Pick **Regression** from this sub-menu. Specify the column locations of the **Response**, i.e. the values of Y, and the **Predictor**, i.e. the values of X. Click **OK** and the output that appears has the regression equation, the equation of the line of best fit, at the top.

If you want a scatter diagram with the line of best-fit superimposed on the scatter, follow the **Stat – Regression** sequence in MINITAB, and then choose **Fitted Line Plot** from the **Regression** sub-menu. The diagram will include the regression equation and the value of R^2 for the data.

To produce a regression equation in Excel choose **Data Analysis** from the **Tools** pull-down menu. Select **Regression** from the **Data Analysis** menu and specify the input ranges for the values of X and Y in the command window. The output that appears includes the intercept and slope of the line of best-fit in a column headed **Coefficient** towards the bottom. In this column you will see the intercept in the first row and the slope, labelled **X variable**, in the second row.

Example 4.6

Produce a fitted line plot for the data in Example 4.1 using MINITAB.

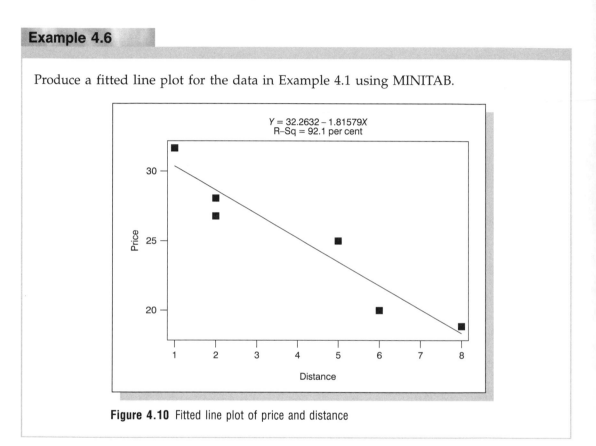

Figure 4.10 Fitted line plot of price and distance

You can see two insertions above the graph in Figure 4.10. The second is the value of the coefficient of determination, R^2, which is written as R-Sq, 92.1 per cent. This is a slightly more precise version of the result we saw in Example 4.3. The first is the regression equation

$$Y = 32.2632 - 1.81597X$$

This is the same equation as we obtained by calculation in Example 4.5, except that here the slope and the intercept are given more precisely. We know that Y is the price and X is the distance, so the equation could be written:

$$\text{Price} = 32.2632 - 1.81597 \text{ Distance}$$

This is a regression 'model' that represents how the two variables are connected based on the sample evidence in Example 4.1. It is the best linear model that can be found for that set of data.

We can use the equation to predict values of Y that should occur with values of X. These are known as *expected* values of Y because they are what the line leads us to *expect* to be associated with the X values. The symbol $\hat{y}$ (y-hat) is used to represent a value of Y that is predicted using the regression equation, so that we can distinguish it from an actual y value.

That is to say the regression equation $Y = a + bX$ can be used to predict an individual y value that is expected to occur with an observed x value:

$$\hat{y} = a + bx$$

Example 4.7

Use the regression equation from Example 4.6 to find the price per guest the couple should expect to pay if they wanted a venue that was a distance of 4 miles from the ceremony.

The regression equation tells us that:

Price = 32.2632 − 1.81597 distance

If we put the figure '4' in where the word 'distance' appears in the equation we can work out what, according to the equation, the price should be.

Price (when distance is 4) = 32.2632 − 1.81597 (4)

= 32.2632 − 7.26388 = 24.99932

That suggests that if the couple want a reception 4 miles from the ceremony they should expect it to cost £25 per guest.

4.2 Summarizing data collected over time

Data collected over time, time series, is very important for the successful performance of organizations in the hospitality and tourism sectors. For instance, such data can reveal trends in consumer expenditure and taste that these organizations need to follow.

Businesses use information based on data collected by other agencies over time to help them understand and evaluate the environment in which they operate. Perhaps the most important and widespread example of this is the use of *index numbers* to monitor general trends in prices and costs. For instance, the Retail Price Index is used as a benchmark figure in the context of wage bargaining, and Share Price Indices are reference points in financial decisions that companies face.

Businesses also produce a variety of data that is collected over time in order to understand and communicate its progress. For instance, every company report contains charts and tables showing data that demonstrate its development over the period of a year, e.g. sales, profits, number of employees.

4.2.1 Index numbers

Most businesses attach a great deal of importance to changes in the costs of things they buy and the prices of things they sell. During periods of high inflation these changes are more dramatic, in periods of low inflation they are modest. Over recent decades, when the level of inflation has fluctuated so much, companies have got used to tracking general price and cost movements carefully. To help them do this they have turned to index numbers.

Index numbers can be used to represent movements of many things over time in a series of single figures. A simple index number is a ratio that expresses the value of something at one point, maybe the current value, in relation to its value at another point, the base period. The ratio is usually expressed as a percentage.

Example 4.8

The wholesale price of fish bought by the proprietor of a fish and chip shop was £6.75 per kilo in 1999. It was £5.40 in 1995. Calculate a simple price index to represent the change in price over the period.

$$\text{Simple price index} = \frac{\text{current price}}{\text{base period price}} = p_c/p_0 = 6.75/5.40 = 1.25$$

Where p_c represents the price in the current year and p_0 represents the price in the base year (i.e. period 0).

You can express the result as a percentage by multiplying it by 100.

$$\text{Simple price index} = p_c/p_0 \times 100 = 1.25 \times 100 = 125$$

This tells us that the price of fish has increased by 25 per cent over this period.

However businesses usually buy and sell more than a single item so this type of index number is of limited use. Of much greater importance are *aggregate* indices that summarize price movements of many items in a single figure.

We can calculate a simple aggregate price index for a combination of goods by taking the sum of the prices for the goods in the current period and dividing it by the sum of the prices of the same goods in the base period. That is:

$$\text{Simple aggregate price index} = \Sigma p_c / \Sigma p_0 \times 100$$

Example 4.9

The fish and chip shop proprietor referred to in Example 4.8 regularly buys fish, potatoes and salt. The prices of these goods in 1999 and 1995 were:

	1995	1999
Fish (per kg)	£5.40	£6.75
Potatoes (per kg)	£0.35	£0.70
Salt (per kg)	£1.40	£1.50

Calculate a simple aggregate price index to compare the prices in 1999 to the prices in 1995.

Simple aggregate price index:

$$\Sigma p_c / \Sigma p_0 \times 100 = \frac{6.75 + 0.70 + 1.50}{5.40 + 0.35 + 1.40} \times 100 = \frac{8.95}{7.15} \times 100 = 125.17$$

This result indicates that prices paid by the proprietor have increased by 25.17 per cent from 1995 to 1999.

The result we obtained in Example 4.9 may well be more useful because it is an overall figure that includes all the commodities. However, it does not differentiate between prices of items that are purchased in greater quantity than other items, which implies that their prices are of much greater significance.

In a simple aggregate price index each price is given equal prominence, you can see that it appears once in the expression. Its numerical 'clout' depends simply on whether it is a large or small price. In Example 4.9 the result, 125.17, is close to the value of the simple price index of fish calculated in Example 4.8, 125. This is because fish happens to have the largest of the prices in the set.

In practice the importance of the price of an item is a reflection of the quantity that is bought as well as the price itself. To measure changes in movements of prices in a more realistic way we need to *weight* each price in proportion to the quantity purchased. We can then calculate a weighted aggregate price index.

There are two ways we can do this. The first is to use the quantity figure from the base year, represented by the symbol q_0, to weight the price of each item. This type of index is known as the Laspeyre price index. To calculate it we need to work out the total cost of the base-period quantities at current prices, divide that by the total cost of the base period quantities at base period prices, and multiply the result by 100:

$$\text{Laspeyre price index} = \Sigma q_0 p_c / \Sigma q_0 p_0 \times 100$$

Example 4.10

The fish and chip shop records show that in 1995 500 kg of fish, 1000 kg of potatoes and 25 kg of salt were purchased. Use these figures and the price figures from Example 4.9 to produce a Laspeyre price index to compare the prices of 1999 to those of 1995.

$$\Sigma q_0 p_c / \Sigma q_0 p_0 \times 100 = \frac{(500 \times 6.75) + (1000 \times 0.70) + (25 \times 1.50)}{(500 \times 5.40) + (1000 \times 0.35) + (25 \times 1.40)} \times 100$$

$$= \frac{4112.5}{3075} \times 100$$

$$= 133.74$$

This result suggests that the prices have increased by 33.74 per cent between 1995 and 1999.

The Laspeyre technique uses quantities that are historical. The advantage of this is that such figures are usually readily available. The disadvantage is that they may not accurately reflect the quantities used in the current period.

The alternative approach, which is more useful when quantities used have changed considerably, is to use quantity figures from the current period. This type of index is known as the Paasche price index. To calculate it you work out the total cost of the current period quantities at current prices, divide that by the total cost of the current period quantities at base period prices, and multiply the result by 100:

$$\text{Paasche price index} = \Sigma q_c p_c / \Sigma q_c p_0 \times 100$$

Example 4.11

The fish and chip shop purchased 500 kg of fish, 600 kg of potatoes and 20 kg of salt in 1999. Use these figures and the price figures from Example 4.9 to produce a Paasche price index to compare the prices of 1999 to those of 1995.

$$\Sigma q_c p_c / \Sigma q_c p_0 \times 100 = \frac{(500 \times 6.75) + (600 \times 0.70) + (20 \times 1.50)}{(500 \times 5.40) + (600 \times 0.35) + (20 \times 1.40)} \times 100$$

$$= \frac{3825}{2938} \times 100 = 130.19$$

This result suggests that the prices have increased by 30.19 per cent between 1995 and 1999.

The figure we obtained in Example 4.11 is lower because the weight given to the price of potatoes, the price that has changed most, is much lower in the Paasche index.

The advantage of using a Paasche price index is that the quantity figures used are more up-to-date and therefore realistic. But it is not always possible to get current period quantity figures, particularly when there is a wide range of items and a large number of organizations or consumers that buy them.

The other disadvantage of using the Paasche price index is that new quantity figures must be available for each period we want to compare with the base period. If our fish and chip shop proprietor wants a Paasche price index for prices in 2000 compared to 1995 you could not provide one until you know the quantities used in 2000. By contrast, to calculate a Laspeyre price index for 2000 you only need to know the prices in 2000.

If you look carefully at Example 4.10 and 4.11 you will see that whichever index is used the same quantity figures weight the prices from the different years. This is an important point, they are *price* indices, and they are used to compare prices across the time period, not quantities.

Organizations tend to use index numbers that have already been compiled rather than construct their own. Probably the most common use of index numbers that you will meet is in the adjustment of financial amounts to take into account changes in price levels.

A sum of money in one period is not necessarily the same as the same amount in another period because its purchasing power changes. This means that if we want to compare an amount from one period with an amount from another period we have to make some adjustment for price changes. The most common way of doing this is to use the Retail Price Index (RPI), an index the Government Statistical Service calculates to monitor price changes, changes in the cost of living.

Example 4.12

The annual salary of the manager of a leisure centre has changed in the following way between 1995 and 1998. Use the RPI figures for those years to see whether the increases in her salary have kept up with the cost of living.*

	1995	1996	1997	1998
Salary (£'000)	15	17	18	20
RPI (1993 = 100)	109	115	121	130

We can 'deflate' the figures for 1996, 1997 and 1998 so that they are expressed in '1995 pounds' by multiplying each of them by the ratio between the RPI for 1995 and the RPI for the year concerned.

Adjusted 1996 salary = 17 × 109/115 = 16.113   i.e. £16,113

Adjusted 1997 salary = 18 × 109/121 = 16.215   i.e. £16,215

Adjusted 1998 salary = 20 × 109/130 = 16.769   i.e. £16,769

These results suggest that her salary has increased more than the cost of living throughout the period.

4.2.2 Basic time series analysis

Organizations collect time series data, which is data made up of observations taken at regular intervals, as a matter of course. Look at the operations of any organization and you will usually find figures such as daily receipts, weekly staff absences, and monthly payroll. If you look at the report it produces to present its performance you will find more time series data such as quarterly turnover and annual profit.

Sometimes each observed value of a time series is only looked at when it is collected. But often organizations need to look at the sequence that is unfolding as more observed values are collected. This can help them review their performance over the period covered by the time series and it can help them predict future values of the time series.

* (Source: 'Retail Price Index', Office for National Statistics, © Crown Copyright 1999)

It is possible to do both of these things using a time series chart, a graph that shows the progression of observations in a time series. You can look for an overall movement, a *trend*, and recurrent fluctuations around the trend.

This is a good way to get a 'feel' for the way the time series is behaving, but to analyse a time series properly we need to use a more systematic approach. One way of doing this is called *decomposition*, which involves breaking down or *decomposing* the series into different parts. This approach is suitable for time series data that has a repeated pattern, which includes many time series that occur in the hospitality and tourism sectors.

The decomposition approach assumes that a time series is made up, or composed, of three types of parts, or *components*. These are:

1 A trend, an underlying longer-term movement in the series.
2 A recurrent component, which may be daily, weekly, monthly, seasonal or cyclical.
3 An error, the amount that isn't part of either the trend or recurrent components.

The type of recurrent component we find in a time series depends on how regularly the data is collected. We would expect to find daily components in data collected each day, weekly components in data collected each week and so on. Seasonal components are usually a feature of data collected quarterly, whereas cyclical components, patterns that recur over many years, crop up in data collected annually.

It is possible that a time series includes more than one recurrent component, for instance weekly figures may exhibit a regular monthly fluctuation as well as a weekly one. However, usually the decomposition of a time series involves looking for the trend and just one recurrent component.

Example 4.13

The numbers of students using a college cafeteria each day for the first three weeks of the college term are:

	Monday	Tuesday	Wednesday	Thursday	Friday
Week 1	187	259	226	308	132
Week 2	213	298	263	349	161
Week 3	236	343	311	359	166

Construct a time series chart and examine it for evidence of a trend and a recurrent daily component.

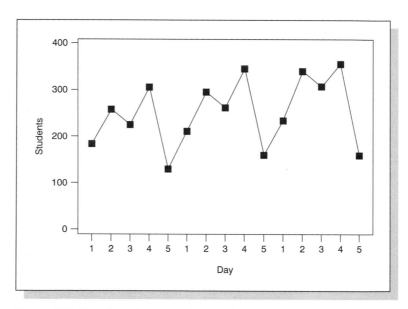

Figure 4.11 Use of a college cafeteria over three weeks

If you look carefully at Figure 4.11 you can see that there is a gradual upward drift in the points that represent the time series. This suggests the trend is that the number of students using the cafeteria is increasing.

You can also see that within the figures for each week, plotted as Days 1 (Mondays) to 5 (Fridays) there is considerable variation. The points for Tuesdays and Thursdays tend to peak whilst the figures for Mondays, Wednesdays and Fridays tend to dip.

The first stage we take in decomposing a time series is to try and separate out the trend. We can do this by calculating a set of *moving averages* for the series. Moving averages are sequential, they are averages calculated from sequences of values in a time series.

A moving average (MA) is the mean of one of each time period in the time series. In Example 4.13 each moving average will be the mean of one Monday figure, one Tuesday figure and so on. Because the moving average is calculated from five observations it is called a *five-point* moving average.

The first moving average in the set will be the mean of the figures for the first week. The second moving average is the mean of the figures from Tuesday to Friday of the first week and the Monday of the second week. The result will still be the mean of five figures, one from each day of the week. We continue doing this, dropping the first value of the sequence out and replacing it with a new figure until we reach the end of the series.

Example 4.14

Calculate moving averages for the data in Example 4.13.

The first MA $= (187 + 259 + 226 + 308 + 132)/5 = 1112/5 = 222.4$

The second MA $= (259 + 226 + 308 + 132 + 213)/5 = 1138/5 = 227.6$

The third MA $= (226 + 308 + 132 + 213 + 298)/5 = 1177/5 = 235.4$

and so on.

The complete set of moving averages is:

222.4 227.6 235.4 242.8 251.0 256.8 261.4 270.4 280.0 282.0 283.0

If you count the number of moving averages in Example 4.14 you will find there are only eleven, four fewer than the number of observations in the time series. This is because each moving average summarizes five observations that come from a series of different points in time.

Like any other average we can think of a moving average as being in the middle of the set of data from which it has been derived. In the case of moving averages we can think of them as belonging to the middle of the period covered by the observations that we used to calculate it. The first moving average therefore belongs to the Wednesday of the first week because that is the middle of the first five days, the days whose observed values were used to calculate it.

If the first moving average belongs to the first Wednesday, we don't have moving averages that belong to the first Monday and Tuesday. Similarly, the last moving average belongs to the last Wednesday and we have no moving averages for the last Thursday and Friday.

The process of positioning the moving averages in line with the middle of the observations they summarize is called *centering*.

Example 4.15

Centre the moving averages in Example 4.14.

		Monday	*Tuesday*	*Wednesday*	*Thursday*	*Friday*
Week 1		187	259	226	308	132
MA				222.4	227.6	235.4
Week 2		213	298	263	349	161
MA		242.8	251.0	256.8	261.4	270.4
Week 3		236	343	311	359	166
MA		280.0	282.0	283.0		

The process of centering is a little more complicated if you have a time series with a periodicity of four, such as quarterly data. To centre the moving averages for quarterly data, for instance, you have to split the difference between two moving averages because the moving averages you calculate are 'out of phase' with the time series observations.

Example 4.16

Calculate and centre the moving averages for the data below. They are the numbers of bookings for Mediterranean holidays taken by a travel agent over two years.

	Winter	Spring	Summer	Autumn
Year 1	597	351	266	185
Year 2	541	286	192	137

Moving averages for these figures will be four-point moving averages.

First MA $= (597 + 351 + 266 + 185)/4 = 1399/4 = 349.75$

Second MA $= (351 + 266 + 185 + 541)/4 = 1343/4 = 335.75$

and so on.

	Winter	Spring		Summer		Autumn	
Year 1	597	351		266		185	
MA			349.75		335.75		319.50
Year 2	541	286		192		137	
MA			301.00		289.00		

The moving averages straddle two quarters because the middle of four periods is between two of them. To centre them, that is to bring them in line with the series itself, we have to split the difference between pairs of them.

The centred four-point MA for the Summer of Year 1 $= (349.75 + 335.75)/2 = 342.75$

The centred four-point MA for the Autumn of Year 1 $= (335.75 + 319.50)/2 = 327.63$

and so on.

	Winter	Spring		Summer		Autumn	
Year 1	597	351		266		185	
MA			349.75		335.75		319.50
Centred MA				342.75		327.63	
Year 2	541	286		192		137	
MA			301.00		289.00		
Centred MA	310.25		295.00				

Centering moving averages is important because the moving averages are the figures that we need to use as estimates of the trend at particular points in time. We want to be able to compare them directly with observations in order to separate out other components of the time series.

The procedure we adopt to separate the components of a time series depends on how we assume they are combined in the observations. The simplest case is to assume that the components are added together, that is each observation, y, is the sum of a set of components:

$$y = \text{Trend component } (T) + \text{Recurrent component } (R)$$
$$+ \text{Error component } (E)$$

This is called the *additive* model of a time series. You may also come across the *multiplicative* model. If you want to analyse a time series which you assume is additive, you have to subtract the components from each other to decompose the time series. If you assume it is multiplicative, you have to divide to decompose it.

We begin the process of decomposing a time series assumed to be additive by subtracting the centred moving averages, the estimated trend values, from the observations they sit alongside. What we are left with are deviations from the trend, a set of figures that contain only the recurrent and error components, that is:

$$y - T = R + E$$

Example 4.17

Subtract the centred moving averages from the observations in Example 4.13.

	Monday	Tuesday	Wednesday	Thursday	Friday
Week 1	187	259	226	308	132
MA (T)			222.4	227.6	235.4
$y - T$			3.6	80.4	−103.4
Week 2	213	298	263	349	161
MA (T)	242.8	251.0	256.8	261.4	270.4
$y - T$	−29.8	47.0	6.2	87.6	−109.4
Week 3	236	343	311	359	166
MA (T)	280.0	282.0	283.0		
$y - T$	−44.0	61.0	28.0		

The next stage is to arrange these $y - T$ results by the days of the week and calculate the mean of the deviations from the trend for each day. These will be our estimates for the recurrent component for each day, the differences we expect between the trend and the observed value on each day of the week.

Example 4.18

Find the estimates for the daily components from the figures in Example 4.17. What do they tell us about the pattern of demand for the cafeteria?

	Monday	Tuesday	Wednesday	Thursday	Friday
$y - T$			3.6	80.4	−103.4
$y - T$	−29.8	47.0	6.2	87.6	−109.4
$y - T$	−44.0	61.0	28.0		

The estimated daily components are:

On Mondays $((−29.8) + (−44.0))/2 = −36.9$
On Tuesdays $(47.0 + 61.0)/2 = 54.0$
On Wednesdays $(3.6 + 6.2 + 28.0)/3 = 12.6$
On Thursdays $(80.4 + 87.6)/2 = 84.0$
On Fridays $((−103.4) + (−109.4)/2 = −106.4$

These figures suggest that the cafeteria regularly attracts more students on Tuesdays and Thursdays, rather less on Mondays, almost the same as the trend on Wednesdays and considerably less students on Fridays.

We can take the analysis a stage further by subtracting the recurrent components from the $y - T$ figures to isolate the error components. That is:

$$E = y - T - R$$

Example 4.19

Find the error components for the data in Example 4.13.

	Monday	Tuesday	Wednesday	Thursday	Friday
Week 1	187	259	226	308	132
$y - T$			3.6	80.4	−103.4
R			12.6	84.0	−106.4
$E = (y - T) - R$			−9.0	−3.6	3.0
Week 2	213	298	263	349	161
$y - T$	−29.8	47.0	6.2	87.6	−109.4
R	−36.9	54.0	12.6	84.0	−106.4
E	7.1	−7.0	−6.4	3.6	−3.0
Week 3	236	343	311	359	166
$y - T$	−44.0	61.0	28.0		
R	−36.9	54.0	12.6		
E	−7.1	7.0	15.4		

The error terms enable us to review the performance over the period. A large negative error component suggests we have under-performed in that period and might lead us to investigate reasons that may explain why. A large positive error component suggests we have performed better than expected and we would look for reasons to explain the success. This type of evaluation should enable us to improve the performance because we can tackle the factors that lead us to under-perform and build on the factors that lead us to perform well.

The error components in Example 4.19 suggest that the number of students using the cafeteria on Wednesdays is rather erratic, but on Wednesday of Week 3 something seems to have attracted disproportionately more students than on previous Wednesdays. Perhaps a special promotion or bad weather affecting sporting commitments may have played a part?

As well as using the results of decomposition to review performance we can use them to construct forecasts for future periods. There are two stages in doing this. The first is to project the trend into the periods we want to predict, and the second is to add the appropriate recurrent components to the trend projections. We can represent the process as:

$$\hat{y} = T + R$$

where $\hat{y}$ is the estimated future value, T and R are the trend and recurrent components respectively. You can see there is no error component. The error components are, by definition, unpredictable.

You could produce trend projections by plotting the centred moving averages and fitting a line to them by eye, then simply continuing the line into the future periods you want to predict. However, a much better way is to use regression analysis to get the equation of the line that best fits the moving averages and use the equation to project the trend. The regression equation in this context is called the *trend line equation*.

Example 4.20

Find the trend line equation for the moving averages in Example 4.15 by simple linear regression analysis. Use the equation to predict the trend values in Week 4 and construct forecasts for Week 4 by adding the daily components from Example 4.18.

We have to use numbers for the regression analysis so we cannot use the names of the days of the week. Instead we number them, starting with 1 for the Monday of Week 1 and so on.

MA	222.4	227.6	235.4	242.8	251.0	256.8	261.4	270.4	280.0	282.0	283.0
Day	3	4	5	6	7	8	9	10	11	12	13

Using simple linear regression analysis the trend line equation is:

Trend = 217.6 + 4.56 day

Week 4 will consist of Days 16 to 20.

Forecast trend on Day 16 = 217.6 + 4.56 (16) = 290.56
Forecast trend on Day 17 = 217.6 + 4.56 (17) = 295.12
Forecast trend on Day 18 = 217.6 + 4.56 (18) = 299.68
Forecast trend on Day 19 = 217.6 + 4.56 (19) = 304.24
Forecast trend on Day 20 = 217.6 + 4.56 (20) = 308.80

Adding the appropriate daily components gives the forecast values for Week 4:

Forecast for Day 16 (Monday)   = 290.56 + (−36.9) = 253.66 round to 254
Forecast for Day 17 (Tuesday)   = 295.12 + 54.0   = 349.12 round to 349
Forecast for Day 18 (Wednesday) = 299.68 + 12.6   = 312.28 round to 312
Forecast for Day 19 (Thursday) = 304.24 + 84.0   = 388.24 round to 388
Forecast for Day 20 (Friday)   = 308.80 + (−106.4) = 202.40 round to 202

Forecasts like the ones we have obtained in Example 4.18 can be used as the basis for setting budgets, for assessing future staffing levels and so forth. In practice computer software would be used to derive them.

In MINITAB there is a **Decomposition** facility that you can enter via the **Time Series** option in the **Stat** menu. It can produce graphics like Figure 4.12 to portray the process.

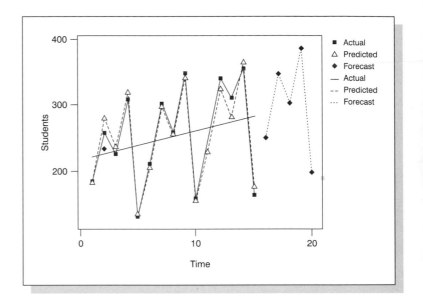

Figure 4.12
College cafeteria usage

In Figure 4.12 the solid line that zigzags depicts the original series, the smooth line running upwards through it is the trend line, and the broken line that follows the original series closely is a plot of the trend plus the daily components. The differences between the latter line and the line representing the original values are the error components. The broken line on the right-hand side is a plot of the predictions the package has made for the days in Week 4.

In Excel the **Moving average** facility in the **Data Analysis** option from the **Tools** menu can provide you with moving averages for a time series. If you tick the **Chart output** box in the **Moving average** command window you can get a plot of the time series alongside its moving averages.

Review questions

4.1 Select the appropriate definition for each term on the left-hand side from the list on the right-hand side:

(a) a regression equation   (i) is another name for the dependent variable, Y

(b) a correlation coefficient   (ii) is an underlying movement in a time series

(c) a moving average   (iii) measures price changes over time

(d) an inverse relationship   (iv) is another name for the independent variable, X

(e) a predictor   (v) is a mean of a sequence of time series values

(f) a response   (vi) measures association between two variables

(g) a trend   (vii) is when Y goes down as X goes up

(h) a weighted price index   (viii) represents the line of best fit

4.2 Consider which of the relationships below are likely to have a positive and which are likely to have a negative correlation coefficient:

(a) The length of stay at a hotel and the total cost of the accommodation
(b) The time customers wait to be served in a restaurant and the number of staff on duty
(c) The average temperature of countries and the number of tourists they attract
(d) The alcohol content of beers and their price
(e) The age of people and the number of times they visit nightclubs
(f) The income of people and the number of holidays they take per year

4.3 Nine males were each asked their age and the number of times they had visited a theme pub during the last month.

Age	18	19	22	24	26	29	35	46	51
Visits	11	7	14	9	5	3	4	0	1

(a) Calculate the correlation coefficient for this set of data and interpret its value
(b) Which of the two variables should logically be the Y variable?
(c) Plot a scatter diagram to portray the data
(d) Find the regression equation for the line of best fit

Hospitality, Leisure & Tourism Series

(e) Use the regression equation to predict how many times a month a 30-year-old male is likely to visit a theme pub

(f) Plot the regression equation and use it to suggest what age group should be targeted by the manager of a theme pub who wants to attract customers who will visit the pub ten times or more a month.

4.4 A contract-catering firm has a fleet of three vans. The main expenses incurred in running this fleet are fuel, servicing and tax and insurance. The figures for these expenses and the amount of each commodity purchased are given in the table below:

Year	1997	1998	1999
Fuel price (per litre)	£0.50	£0.58	£0.66
Fuel usage (litres)	6000	6250	6200
Servicing (per service)	£120	£135	£145
Number of services	6	7	6
Tax and insurance (per vehicle)	£1500	£1700	£2000
Number of vehicles	3	3	3

(a) Calculate Laspeyre price indices for the years 1998 and 1999 using 1997 as the base year

(b) Calculate Paasche price indices for the years 1998 and 1999 using 1997 as the base year

(c) Which type of price index is more appropriate in this case, and why?

4.5 The annual revenue figures, in millions of pounds, for two theme parks from 1994 to 1998 are as follows:

Year	1994	1995	1996	1997	1998
Park A	10.0	10.8	12.1	12.3	12.6
Park B	11.5	12.0	12.5	13.5	14.5
Retail Price Index	104	109	115	121	130

Use the Retail Price Index figures in the bottom row of the table to adjust the figures for the effects of inflation. Use the adjusted figures to compare the performances of the two parks.

4.6 The travel agent in Example 4.15 received the following number of bookings for Mediterranean holidays in Year 3:

Winter	Spring	Summer	Autumn
562	301	253	149

(a) Use these figures and those quoted in Example 4.15 to calculate more four-point moving averages for the time series and centre them

(b) Find estimates of the seasonal components for each quarter

(c) Identify the error components in the series and use them to assess the travel agent's record

(d) Construct predictions for the bookings that the travel agent will receive in the four quarters of Year 4

4.7 Using the analysis of the college cafeteria trade in Example 4.20 provide forecast values for Week 5, that is Days 21 to 25.

CHAPTER 5

Assessing risk

This chapter will help you:

- To understand why probability is important.
- To appreciate how chance and risk can be measured.
- To identify different types of probability.
- To analyse the chances of sequences and combinations.

In this chapter you will find:

- The scale of probability.
- Different approaches to assessing probabilities.
- Analysis of simple and compound probabilities.
- The addition rule of probability.
- The multiplication rule of probability and dependency.
- Venn and tree diagrams.

'The chances are . . .'

This chapter is intended to introduce you to the subject of probability, the branch of mathematics that is about finding out how likely real events or theoretical results are to happen. The subject originated in gambling, in particular the efforts of two seventeenth-century French mathematical pioneers, Fermat and Pascal, to calculate the odds of certain results in dice games.

The science of probability may well have remained a historical curiosity within the field of mathematics that was little-known outside casinos and race-tracks if it were not for the fact that probability has proved to be invaluable in fields as varied as psychology, economics, physical science, market research and medicine. In these and other fields, probability offers us a way of analysing chance and allowing for risk so that it can be taken into account whether we are investigating a problem or trying to make a decision.

Probability makes the difference between facing *uncertainty* and coping with *risk*. Uncertainty is a situation where we know that it is possible that things could turn out in different ways but we simply don't know how probable each result is. Risk, on the other hand, is when we know there are different outcomes but we also have some idea of how likely each one is to occur.

In the hospitality and tourism sectors organizations inevitably have to operate in conditions that are far from certain. Fast-food restaurants cannot be sure how many customers will come through their doors, and how much they will spend from one day to another. Hotels cannot rely on exactly the same staff working for them from one month to another. Companies that build large theme parks or multi-screen cinemas don't know whether their project will be finished on time or if it will make a profit from one year to another.

As well as these examples of what we might call normal commercial risk, there is the added peril of unforeseen risk. A successful holiday destination may be torn apart by war, demand for certain food products may be undermined by contamination, there may be an accident on a theme park ride, etc.

The topics that you will meet in this chapter will help you to understand how organizations can measure and assess the risks they have to deal with. But there is a second reason why probability is a very important part of your studies; because of the role it plays in future statistical work.

Almost all the statistical research that you are likely to come across at college and in you future career, whether it is intended to investigate consumer behaviour, employee attitudes, product quality, or whatever, will have one important thing in common; it will involve the collection and analysis of a sample.

In almost every case the people who commission the research and those who carry it out want to know about an entire population. They may want to know the opinions of all customers, the attitudes of all employees, the characteristics of all products, but it would be far too expensive or time consuming or simply impractical to study every item in a population. The only alternative is to study a sample and use the results to gain some insight into the population.

This can work very well, but only if we have a sample that is random and we take account of the risk associated with sampling.

A sample is called a random sample if every item in the population has the same chance of being in it as every other item in the population. If a sample is not random it is of very little use in helping us to understand a population.

Taking samples involves risk because we can take different random samples from a single population. These samples will be composed of different items from the population and produce different results. Some samples will produce results very similar to those that we would get from the population itself if we had the opportunity to do so. Other samples will produce results that are not typical of the population as a whole.

To use sample results effectively we need to know how likely they are to be close to the population results even though we don't actually know what the population results are. Assessing this involves the use of probability.

5.1 Measuring probability

A *probability*, usually represented by a capital *P*, is a measure of the likelihood of a particular result or outcome. It is a number on a scale that runs from zero to one inclusive, although it can be expressed as a percentage.

If there is a probability of zero that an outcome will occur it means there is literally no chance that it will happen. At the other end of the scale, if there is a probability of one that something will happen, it means that it is absolutely certain to occur. Half way between these extremes, a probability of one half means that a result is equally likely to occur as not to occur. Sometimes such a probability is described as a fifty-fifty chance.

So how do we decide what the probability of something happening is? The answer is that there are three distinct approaches that can be used to attach a probability to a particular outcome. We can describe these as the *judgemental*, *experimental*, and *theoretical* approaches to identifying probabilities.

The judgemental approach means evaluating the chance of something happening on the basis of opinion alone. Usually the something is relatively uncommon, which rules out the use of the experimental approach, and doesn't occur within a context of definable possibilities, which rules out the use of the theoretical approach. The opinion on which the probability is based is usually someone with some expertise in the subject.

You will often find judgemental probabilities in assessments of political stability and economic conditions, perhaps concerning investment prospects or currency fluctuations. You could, of course, use a judgemental approach to assessing the probability of any outcome even when there are more sophisticated means available. For instance, some people assess the chance that a horse wins a race solely on their opinion of the name of the horse when they could investigate the horse's record.

If you did investigate the horse's record you would be using an experimental approach, looking into the results of the previous occasions when the 'experiment', in this case the horse entering a race, was conducted. You could work out the number of times the horse has won a race as a proportion of the total number of races it has entered. This is the *relative frequency* of wins and this can be used to estimate the probability that the horse wins its next race.

A relative frequency based on a limited number of experiments is really an estimate of the probability because it only approximates the 'true' probability, which is the relative frequency based on an infinite number of experiments.

Example 5.1

The horse 'Loshad' has entered sixteen races and won five of them. What is the probability that it will win its next race?

The relative frequency of wins is the number of wins, five, divided by the total number of races, sixteen.

Relative frequency = 5/16 = 0.3125 or 31.25 per cent

We can conclude therefore that on the basis of its record, the probability that the horse wins its next race is:

P (Loshad wins its next race) = 0.3125

In other words a little less than a one-third or a one in three chance.

Of course Example 5.1 is a simplified version of what horse racing analysts actually do. They would probably consider ground conditions, other horses in the race and so on, but essentially they base their assessment of a horse's chances on the experimental approach to setting probabilities.

There are other situations when we want to establish the probability of a certain result of some process and we could use the experimental approach. Perhaps we could consult the results of previous 'experiments', or conduct some ourselves.

The results we found would provide a suitable relative frequency figure for us to use as the probability, but we need not go to the trouble of using the experimental approach if we can deduce the probability using the theoretical approach. You can deduce the probability of a particular outcome if the process that produces it has a constant, limited and identifiable number of possible outcomes, one of which must occur whenever the process is repeated.

There are many examples of this sort of process in gambling, including many where the number of possible outcomes is very large indeed such as bingo and lotteries. However, even in these the number of outcomes is finite, the possible outcomes remain the same whenever the process takes place, and they could all be identified if we had the time and patience to do it.

Probabilities of specific results in bingo and lotteries can be deduced because the same number of balls and type of machine are used each time. In contrast probabilities of horses winning races can't be deduced because different horses enter each race, the length of races varies and so on.

Example 5.2

A 'Wheel of Fortune' machine in an amusement park has thirty-six segments. Ten of the segments would give the player a cash prize. What is the probability that you win a cash prize if you play the game?

To answer this we could build a wheel of the same type, spin it thousands of times and work out what proportion of the results would have given us a cash prize. Alternatively, we could question people who have played the game previously and find out what proportion of them won a cash prize. These are two ways of finding the probability experimentally.

It is far simpler to deduce the probability. Ten outcomes out of a possible thirty-six would give us a cash prize so:

P (cash prize) $= 10/36 = 0.2778$ or 27.78 per cent

This assumes that the wheel is fair, in other words that each outcome is as likely to occur as any other outcome.

Gambling is a rich source of illustrations of the use of probabilities because it is about games of chance. However, it is by no means the only field where you will find probabilities. Whenever you buy insurance you are buying a product whose price has been decided on the basis of the rigorous and extensive use of the experimental approach to finding probabilities.

5.2 Different types of probabilities

So far the probabilities that you have met in this chapter have been what are known as *simple* probabilities. Simple probabilities are probabilities of single outcomes. In Example 5.1 we wanted to know the chance of the horse winning its next race. The probability that the horse wins its next two races is a *compound* probability.

A compound probability is the probability of a compound or combined outcome. In Example 5.2 winning a cash prize is a simple outcome, but winning a cash or a non-cash prize, like a cuddly toy, is a compound outcome.

To illustrate the different types of compound probability we can apply the experimental approach to bivariate data. That is we can estimate compound probabilities by finding appropriate relative frequencies from data that has been tabulated by categories of attributes or classes of values of variables.

Example 5.3

A survey of the orders and methods of payment of 500 customers of a café-bar produced the following results.

Payment	Non-alcoholic beverages	Alcoholic beverages	Meal	Total
Cash	87	189	15	291
Debit card	11	5	62	78
Credit card	4	12	115	131
Total	102	206	192	500

What is the probability that a customer coming into the café-bar will pay by credit card?

What is the probability that a customer coming into the café-bar will order a meal?

These are both simple probabilities because they each relate to only one variable, method of payment in the first case, type of order in the second.

The total column on the right of the table tells us that in all 131 of the 500 customers paid by credit card.

P (Payment by credit card) $= 131/500 = 0.262$ or 26.2 per cent
which is the relative frequency of credit card payment

Similarly, by using the totals row along the bottom of the table:

P (Customer orders a meal) $= 192/500 = 0.384$, or 38.4 per cent
which is the relative frequency of orders that are for meals

If we want to use a table such as in Example 5.3 to find compound probabilities we must use figures from the cells within the table, rather than the column and row totals, to produce relative frequencies.

Example 5.4

What is the probability that a customer coming into the café-bar in Example 5.3 orders non-alcoholic beverages and pays by cash?

The number of customers in the survey who did this was 87 so:

$$P \text{ (non-alcoholic beverages and cash)} = 87/500$$
$$= 0.174 \text{ or } 17.4 \text{ per cent}$$

It is rather laborious to write descriptions of the outcomes in full so they are normally abbreviated; we could use 'NA' to represent an order for non-alcoholic beverage, 'A' for alcoholic beverage and 'M' for meal. Likewise we could use 'Ca' for cash payment, 'Cr' for credit card payment and 'D' for debit card payment. So we can express the probability in Example 5.4 in a more convenient way.

$$P \text{ (non-alcoholic beverages and cash)} = P \text{ (NA and Ca)}$$
$$= 0.174$$

This type of compound probability, which includes the word 'and' measures the chance of the *intersection* of two outcomes. The relative frequency we have used as the probability is based on the number of people who are in two specific categories of the 'order' and 'payment' characteristics. It is the number of people who are at the 'cross-roads' or intersection between the 'non-alcoholic' and the 'cash' categories.

Finding the probability of an intersection of two outcomes is quite straightforward if we are assessing it by applying the experimental approach to bivariate data. In other situations, for instance where we only have simple probabilities to go on, we need to use the *multiplication rule* of probability which we will discuss later in the chapter.

There is second type of compound probability, which measures the probability that one out of two or more alternative outcomes occurs. This type of compound probability includes the word 'or' in the description of the outcomes involved.

Example 5.5

Use the data in Example 5.3 to find the probability that a customer coming into the café-bar orders a meal or pays by debit card.

The probability that one (or, by implication, both) of these outcomes occurs is based on the relative frequency of all the people who are in one or other category. This implies that we should add the number of people who ordered a meal to the number of people who paid by debit card, and divide the result by the total number of people in the survey.

Number of people who ordered a meal = 15 + 62 + 115 = 192

Number of people who paid by debit card - 11 + 5 + 62 = 78

If you look carefully you will see that the number 62 appears in both of these expressions. This means that if we use the sum of the number of people who ordered a meal and the number of people who paid by debit card to get our relative frequency figure we will double count the 62 people who ordered a meal and paid by debit card. This means the probability we get will be too big.

The problem arises because we have added the 62 people who ordered a meal and paid by debit card in twice so to correct this we have to subtract the same number once.

$$P \text{ (M or D)} = \frac{(15 + 62 + 115) + (11 + 5 + 62) - 62}{500} = \frac{192 + 78 - 62}{500}$$

$$= 208/500 = 0.416 \text{ or } 41.6 \text{ per cent}$$

This type of probability measures the chance of a *union* of two outcomes. The relative frequency we have used as the probability is based on the combined number of people who are in two specific categories of the 'order' and 'payment' characteristics. It is the number of people who are in the union or 'merger' between the 'non-alcoholic' and the 'cash' categories.

To get a probability of a union of outcomes from other probabilities, rather than by applying the experimental approach to bivariate data, we use the *addition rule* of probability. You will find this discussed later in the chapter.

The third type of compound probability is the *conditional* probability. Such a probability measures the chance that one outcome occurs given that, or on *condition* that, another outcome has already occurred.

Example 5.6

Use the data in Example 5.3 to find the probability that a customer who has ordered alcoholic beverages pays by cash.

Another way of measuring this is as the probability that a customer pays by cash given that they have ordered alcoholic beverages. It is represented as:

$$P\,(Ca/A)$$

Where the forward slash is shorthand for 'given that'.

We find this probability by taking the number of people who paid cash and ordered alcoholic beverages as a proportion of the total number of people who ordered alcoholic beverages.

$$P\,(Ca/A) = 189/206 = 0.9175 \text{ or } 91.75 \text{ per cent}$$

This is a proportion of a subset of the 500 customers in the sample. The majority of them, the 294 people who did not order alcoholic beverages, are excluded because they didn't meet the condition on which the probability is based, i.e. ordering alcoholic drinks.

It is always possible to identify compound probabilities directly from the sort of bivariate data in Example 5.3 by the experimental approach. But what if we don't have this sort of data? Perhaps we have some probabilities that have been obtained judgementally or theoretically and we want to use them to find compound probabilities. Perhaps we have some probabilities that have been obtained experimentally but the data is not at our disposal.

5.3 The rules of probability

In situations where we do not have recourse to appropriate experimental data we need to have some method of finding compound probabilities. These are the two rules of probability, the addition rule and the multiplication rule.

5.3.1 The addition rule

The addition rule of probability specifies the procedure for finding the probability of a union of outcomes, that is a compound probability that is defined using the word 'or'.

According to the addition rule the compound probability of one or both of two outcomes, which we will call A and B for convenience, is the simple probability that A occurs added to the simple probability that B occurs. From this total we subtract the compound probability of the intersection of A and B, the probability that both A and B occur. That is:

$$P \text{ (A or B)} = P \text{ (A)} + P \text{ (B)} - P \text{ (A and B)}$$

Example 5.7

Use the addition rule to calculate the probability that a customer coming into the café-bar in Example 5.3 orders a meal or pays by debit card.

Applying the addition rule:

$$P \text{ (M or D)} = P \text{ (M)} + P \text{ (D)} - P \text{ (M and D)}$$

The simple probability that a customer orders a meal, P (M) = 192/500

The simple probability that a customer pays by debit card, P (D) = 78/500

The probability that a customer orders a meal and pays by debit card:

$$P \text{ (M and D)} = 62/500$$

So:

$$P \text{ (M or D)} = 192/500 + 78/500 - 62/500$$

$$= \frac{192 + 78 - 62}{500} = 208/500 = 0.416 \text{ or } 41.6 \text{ per cent}$$

If you compare this answer to the answer we obtained in Example 5.5 you will see they are exactly the same. In this case the addition rule is an alternative means of getting to the same result. In some ways it is more convenient because it involves row and column totals of the table in Example 5.3 rather than numbers from different cells within the table.

The addition rule can look more complicated than it actually is because it is called the addition rule yet it includes a subtraction. It may help to represent the situation in the form of a *Venn diagram*; the sort of diagram used in part of mathematics called *set theory*.

In a Venn diagram the complete set of outcomes that could occur, known as the *sample space*, is represented by a rectangle. Within the rectangle circles are used to represent sets of outcomes.

In Figure 5.1 the circle on the left represents the ordering a meal outcome, and the circle on the right represents the payment by debit card outcome. The area covered by both circles represents the probability that a customer orders a meal or pays by debit card. The area of overlap represents the probability that a customer orders a meal and pays by debit card.

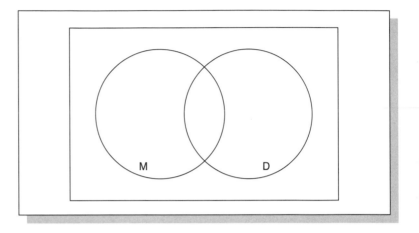

Figure 5.1
A Venn diagram to illustrate Example 5.7

By definition the area of overlap is part of both circles. If you simply add the areas of the two circles together to try and get the area covered by both circles, you will include the area of overlap twice. If you subtract it once from the sum of the areas of the two circles you will only have counted it once.

The addition rule would be simpler if there were no overlap; in other words there is no chance that the two outcomes can occur together. This is when we are dealing with outcomes that are known as *mutually exclusive*. The probability that two mutually exclusive outcomes both occur is zero.

In this case we can alter the addition rule:

$$P \text{ (A or B)} = P \text{ (A)} + P \text{ (B)} - P \text{ (A and B)}$$

to $$P \text{ (A or B)} = P \text{ (A)} + P \text{ (B)}$$

because $P \text{ (A and B)} = 0$

Example 5.8

A group of 178 holidaymakers arrive at a resort in the Aegean on a charter flight. One day during their holiday they are offered a choice of three different excursions: visiting ancient ruins, a boat trip, or visiting a craft museum. Forty-three choose the ancient ruins, 61 the boat trip, and 29 the craft museum.

What is the probability that a holidaymaker from the group has chosen the boat trip or the craft museum?

The choices are mutually exclusive because each holidaymaker can choose only one excursion. We can therefore use the simpler form of the addition rule.

For convenience we can use the letter A for the ancient ruins, B for the boat trip, and C for the craft museum.

$$P \text{ (B or C)} = P \text{ (B)} + P \text{ (C)} = 61/178 + 29/178 = 90/178$$

$$= 0.5056 \text{ or } 50.56 \text{ per cent}$$

If you read Example 5.8 carefully you can see that although the three excursions are mutually exclusive, they do not constitute all of the alternative outcomes. That is to say they are not *collectively exhaustive*. As well as choosing one of the three excursions each holidaymaker has a fourth choice, to decline an excursion. If you subtract the number of holidaymakers taking an excursion from the total number of holidaymakers you will find that 45 of the holidaymakers have not chosen one of the excursions.

A footnote to the addition rule is that if we have a set of mutually exclusive and collectively exhaustive outcomes their probabilities must add up to one. A probability of one means certainty, which reflects the fact that in a situation where there are a set of mutually exclusive and collectively exhaustive outcomes, one and only one of them is certain to occur.

Example 5.9

What is the probability that one of the holidaymakers in the group in Example 5.8 chooses to visit the ancient ruins or to take the boat trip or to go to the craft museum or to do none of these things? For convenience we will use the letter N to denote the latter.

The simple probability that a holiday maker visits the ancient ruins = P (A) = 43/178

The simple probability that a holiday maker takes the boat trip = P (B) = 61/178

The simple probability that a holiday maker visits the craft museum = P (C) = 29/178

The simple probability that a holiday maker doesn't do A, B or C = P (N) = 45/178

$$P \text{ (A or B or C or N)} = \frac{43 + 61 + 29 + 45}{178} = 178/178 = 1$$

This footnote to the addition rule can be used to derive probabilities of one of a set of mutually exclusive and collectively exhaustive outcomes if we know the probabilities of the other outcomes.

Example 5.10

Deduce the probability that a holidaymaker from the group in Example 5.8 chooses none of the excursions using the simple probabilities of the other outcomes.

P (Holiday maker chooses no excursion) = $1 - P$ (A) $- P$ (B) $- P$ (C)

$$= 1 - 43/178 - 61/178 - 29/178$$

$$= 1 - 0.2416 - 0.3427 - 0.1629$$

$$= 1 - 0.7472 = 0.2528 \text{ or } 25.28 \text{ per cent}$$

The result we obtained in Example 5.10, 0.2528, is the same as the figure of 45/178 that we used for P (N) in Example 5.9.

5.3.2 The multiplication rule

The multiplication rule of probability specifies the procedure for finding the probability of an intersection of outcomes, that is a compound probability that is defined using the word 'and'.

According to the multiplication rule the compound probability that two outcomes both occur is the simple probability that the first one occurs multiplied by the *conditional* probability that the second outcome occurs, given that the first outcome has already happened. That is:

$$P \text{ (A and B)} = P \text{ (A)} \times P \text{ (B/A)}$$

The multiplication rule is what bookmakers use to work out odds for 'accumulator' bets, that is bets that a sequence of outcomes, like several specific horses winning races, occurs. To win the bet the first horse must win the first race; the second horse must win the second race and so on. The odds of this sort of thing happening are often something like five hundred to one. The numbers, like five hundred, are large because they are obtained by multiplication.

Example 5.11

Use the multiplication rule to calculate the probability that a customer coming into the café-bar in Example 5.3 orders non-alcoholic drinks and pays by cash.

We will use the abbreviations NA for non-alcoholic beverages and Ca for cash.

$P \text{ (NA and Ca)} = P \text{ (NA)} \times P \text{ (Ca/NA)}$

From the table in Example 5.3:

$P \text{ (NA)} = 102/500$

that is the relative frequency of customers ordering non-alcoholic drinks and

$P \text{ (Ca/NA)} = 87/102$

is the relative frequency of customers ordering non-alcoholic drinks who pay by cash.

So

$P \text{ (NA and Ca)} = 102/500 \times 87/102 = 0.204 \times 0.853 = 0.174$ or 17.4 per cent

If you compare this answer to the answer we obtained in Example 5.4 you will see that they are exactly the same.

The multiplication rule can look more complex than it actually is because it includes a conditional probability. We use a conditional probability for the second outcome because the chances of it occurring could be influenced by the first outcome. This is called *dependency*; in other words one outcome is dependent on the other.

A useful way of telling whether two outcomes are dependent is to compare the conditional probability of one outcome given that the other has happened, with the simple probability that it happens. If the two figures are different the outcomes are dependent.

Example 5.12

Analysis of a survey of 200 first-time visitors to a prominent stately home and gardens showed that 122 of them enjoyed their visit. Of these, 45 said they would definitely visit the establishment again. Overall 59 of the 200 respondents said they would definitely return.

Are enjoyment of the first visit and the intention to return dependent?

The simple probability that a first-time visitor expresses a definite intention to return is 59/200 or 29.5 per cent.

The conditional probability that a first-time visitor expresses a definite intention to return given that they have enjoyed their visit is 45/122 or 36.9 per cent.

You can see that there is a difference between these two figures, which suggests that the expression of a firm intention to return is dependent on the enjoyment of the first visit.

The multiplication rule can be rearranged to provide us with a way of finding a conditional probability. That is if:

$$P \text{ (A and B)} = P \text{ (A)} \times P \text{ (B/A)}$$

then if we divide both sides by P (A) we get:

$$P \text{ (A and B)}/P \text{ (A)} = P \text{ (B/A)}$$

that is:

$$P \text{ (B/A)} = P \text{ (A and B)}/P \text{ (A)}$$

Example 5.13

What is the probability that a customer of the café-bar in Example 5.3 pays by cash given that they have ordered alcoholic beverages?

We will use the abbreviations A for alcoholic beverages and Ca for cash.

$$P (Ca/A) = P (Ca \text{ and } A)/P (A)$$

From the table in Example 5.3:

$$P (Ca \text{ and } A) = 189/500 = 0.378$$

and $P (A) = 206/500 = 0.412$

so $P (Ca/A) = 0.378/0.412 = 0.9175 \text{ or } 91.75 \text{ per cent}$

You might like to compare this to the answer we obtained in Example 5.6.

If there had been no difference between the two probabilities in Example 5.12 there would be no dependency, that is the outcomes would be *independent*.

Because the conditional probabilities of independent outcomes are the same as their simple probabilities, we can simplify the multiplication rule when we are dealing with independent outcomes. We can replace the conditional probability of the second outcome given that the first outcome has occurred with the simple probability that the second outcome occurs. That is instead of:

$$P (A \text{ and } B) = P (A) \times P (B/A)$$

we can use $P (A \text{ and } B) = P (A) \times P (B)$

because $P (B) = P (B/A).$

Example 5.14

What is the probability that a player who plays the Wheel of Fortune in Example 5.2 twice wins cash prizes both times?

Ten of the thirty-six segments give a cash prize, so the probability of a cash prize in any one game is 10/36.

The probability that a player gets a cash prize in their second game given that they have won a cash prize in their first game is also 10/36. The outcomes are independent; in other words the result of the second game is not influenced by the result of the first. (If this is not clear because you feel there is a connection, you might ask yourself how the Wheel of Fortune remembers what it did the first time!)

We will use the letter C to represent a cash prize. The first cash prize the player wins can then be represented as C_1, and the second as C_2.

$$P (C_1 \text{ and } C_2) = P (C) \times P (C) = 10/36 \times 10/36 = 0.77 \text{ or } 7.7 \text{ per cent}$$

5.4 Tree diagrams

If you have to investigate the probabilities of sequences of several outcomes it can be difficult to work out the different combinations of outcomes in your head. It helps if you write down all the different variations, and you may find a Venn diagram a useful way of arranging them in order to work out probabilities of certain types of combinations. But perhaps the best way of sorting out this kind of problem is to use a *tree diagram*.

A tree diagram, which is sometimes called a *probability tree*, represents the different sequences of outcomes in the style of a tree that 'grows' from left to right. Each branch of the tree leads to a particular outcome.

On the right-hand side of the diagram, at the end of each branch, we can insert the combination of outcomes that the sequence of branches represents and, using the multiplication rule, the probability that the sequence of outcomes happens.

Example 5.15

Three married couples, the Akhtars, the Bennetts, and the Carters, begin a pub management course run by a brewery. The pass rate for couples taking this course is 70 per cent. Construct a tree diagram and use it to work out:

- The probability that all three couples pass.

- The probability that two of the couples pass.

- The probability that one of the couples pass.

We will use A to represent the Akhtars, B for the Bennetts and C for the Carters. To indicate a couple failing we will use the appropriate letter followed by a ' mark, so A' represents the outcome that the Akhtars fail, whereas A alone represents the outcome that the Akhtars pass.

The pass rate suggests the probability that a couple passes is 0.7, and given that the 'pass' and 'fail' outcomes are mutually exclusive and collectively exhaustive, the probability they fail is 0.3.

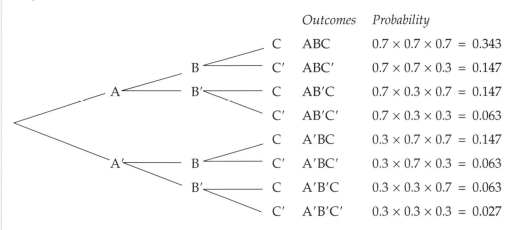

	Outcomes	Probability
C	ABC	$0.7 \times 0.7 \times 0.7 = 0.343$
C'	ABC'	$0.7 \times 0.7 \times 0.3 = 0.147$
C	AB'C	$0.7 \times 0.3 \times 0.7 = 0.147$
C'	AB'C'	$0.7 \times 0.3 \times 0.3 = 0.063$
C	A'BC	$0.3 \times 0.7 \times 0.7 = 0.147$
C'	A'BC'	$0.3 \times 0.7 \times 0.3 = 0.063$
C	A'B'C	$0.3 \times 0.3 \times 0.7 = 0.063$
C'	A'B'C'	$0.3 \times 0.3 \times 0.3 = 0.027$

The probability that all three couples pass, that is P (ABC), is the probability at the top on the right-hand side, 0.343 or 34.3 per cent.

The probability that two couples pass is the probability that one of three sequences occurs, either ABC' or AB'C or A'BC. Since these combinations are mutually exclusive we can apply the simpler form of the addition rule:

P (ABC' or AB'C or A'BC) $= 0.147 + 0.147 + 0.147 = 0.441$ or 44.1 per cent

The probability that one couple passes is the probability of either AB'C' or A'BC' or A'B'C. These combinations are also mutually exclusive so again we can apply the simpler form of the addition rule:

P (AB'C' or A'BC' or A'B'C) $= 0.063 + 0.063 + 0.063 = 0.189$ or 18.9 per cent

A tree diagram should include all possible sequences. One way you can check that it does is to add up the probabilities on the right-hand side. Because these outcomes are mutually exclusive and collectively exhaustive their probabilities should add up to one. We can check that this is the case in Example 5.15.

$$0.343 + 0.147 + 0.147 + 0.147 + 0.063 + 0.063 + 0.063 + 0.027 = 1$$

Review questions

5.1 Select the appropriate definition for each term on the left-hand side from the list on the right-hand side:

(a) compound probability   (i)   basing a probability on opinion

(b) multiplication rule   (ii)   outcomes that cannot occur together

(c) collectively exhaustive   (iii) $P\,(A \text{ and } B) = P\,(A) \times P\,(B/A)$

(d) dependency   (iv)   a probability of a single outcome

(e) judgemental   (v)   basing a probability on deduction

(f) simple probability   (vi)   all possible outcomes

(g) mutually exclusive   (vii) $P\,(A \text{ or } B) = P\,(A) + P\,(B) - P\,(A \text{ and } B)$

(h) experimental   (viii)   when $P\,(B/A)$ is not equal to $P\,(B)$

(i) addition rule   (ix)   a probability of more than one outcome

(j) theoretical   (x)   basing a probability on evidence

5.2 The following survey results show the social class and type of main holiday destination of 250 adult holidaymakers.

Destination	Social class: AB	CD	E
UK	13	25	26
The rest of Europe	29	60	23
Other	55	14	5

Use these figures to estimate:

(a) The probability that a holidaymaker belongs to social class E

(b) The probability that a holidaymaker takes a main holiday in the UK

(c) The probability that a holidaymaker is in social class AB or takes a main holiday outside Europe

(d) The probability that a holidaymaker takes a main holiday in the rest of Europe or is in social class E
(e) The probability that a holidaymaker is in social class CD and takes a main holiday in the UK
(f) The probability that a holidaymaker takes a main holiday in the rest of Europe and is in social class AB
(g) The probability that a holidaymaker in social class E takes a main holiday outside Europe
(h) The probability that a holidaymaker in social class E takes a main holiday in the UK

5.3 Compare the answers to 5.2(b) and 5.2(h). Are social class and main holiday destination dependent?

5.4 The 120 employees at a hotel were asked which would best improve their working life – better promotion prospects, higher pay or more respect from other staff. The results are tabulated below:

Response Job type:	Manual	Clerical	Managerial
Better promotion prospects	12	12	3
Higher pay	53	19	2
More respect	7	6	6

(a) What is the probability that an employee selected more respect?
(b) What is the probability that an employee is a clerical worker or selected better promotion prospects?
(c) What is the probability that a manual employee selected higher pay?
(d) What is the probability that an employee selected more respect and is a manager
(e) What is the probability that a managerial employee selected higher pay?

5.5 A backpacker is about to cross some dangerous equatorial terrain. According to local experts anyone who does this faces a 5 per cent chance of being fatally mauled by a large mammal, a 10 per cent chance of sinking in quicksand and a 12 per cent chance of a poisonous bite. What is the probability that the backpacker survives the journey?

5.6 Tuesday night is cheap beer night at the Jopper pub. Police records show that on 15 out of the last 52 Tuesdays they were summoned to deal with a disturbance at the pub. Construct a tree diagram and use it to find the probability that over the next three Tuesdays there will be:

(a) no trouble
(b) trouble on the first Tuesday only
(c) trouble on one Tuesday only

(d) trouble on the second and third Tuesdays

(e) trouble on two of the Tuesdays

Assume that the events on any one Tuesday are independent of events on any other Tuesday.

5.7 You win a prize in a charity raffle. The prize, donated by a small hotel chain, is a voucher entitling you to a free double room for a weekend at each of the three hotels in the chain, the Xerxes, the York and the Zetland. The room you stay in at each hotel will be picked at random by the hotel manager. The Xerxes has 12 double rooms, 7 of which are en suite. The York has 28 double rooms, 16 of which are en suite. The Zetland has 18 double rooms, 13 of which are en suite.

(a) What is the probability that none of the rooms you get are en suite?

(b) What is the probability that one of the rooms you get is en suite?

(c) What is the probability that two or more of the rooms you get are en suite?

CHAPTER 6

Putting probability to work

This chapter will help you:

- To understand and use probability distributions.
- To analyse discrete random variables.
- To find and interpret summary measures of probability distributions.
- To apply probability in the analysis of business decisions.

In this chapter you will find:

- Basic discrete probability distributions.
- The binomial and Poisson distributions.
- Mean and standard deviation of probability distributions.
- Expectation.
- Decision trees.
- Guidance on using computer software to access probability distributions.

'Weighing up all the possibilities ...'

The early parts of this chapter are intended to show you how we can *model* or represent the chances of different combinations of outcomes using the same sort of approach as we use to arrange data into frequency distributions. The later sections are designed to illustrate how probability can be used in making decisions, especially when there are several stages in the decision process, such as investment in new facilities.

6.1 Simple probability distributions

In Chapter 2 we looked at how we could present data in the form of a frequency distribution. This involved listing categories of values that occurred in the set of data and finding out how many observed values fell into each category, that is the frequency of those categories of values in the set of data. The result enabled us to see how the observations were distributed over the range of the data, hence the term frequency distribution.

A *probability distribution* is very similar to a frequency distribution. Like a frequency distribution a probability distribution has a series of categories, but instead of categories of values it has categories of types of outcomes. The other difference is that each category has a probability instead of a frequency.

In the same way as a frequency distribution tells us how frequently each type of value occurs, a probability distribution tells us how probable each type of outcome is.

In Chapter 2 we saw how a histogram could be used to portray a frequency distribution. We can use a similar type of diagram to portray a probability distribution.

In Chapter 3 we used summary measures including the mean and standard deviation to summarize distributions of data. We can use the mean and standard deviation to summarize distributions of probabilities.

Just as we need the set of data to construct a frequency distribution to present it, we need to identify the set of compound outcomes in order to create a probability distribution. We also need the probabilities of the simple outcomes that make up the combinations of outcomes.

Example 6.1

The entertainment manager at a large traditional holiday camp decides to spice up the quiz night by selecting teams of three contestants by drawing names out of a hat. If there are equal numbers of female and male contestants what are the chances that a team of three includes zero, one, two and three females?

Because there are equal numbers of females and males the probability that a female is selected is 0.5 and the probability that a male is selected is also 0.5.

The probability that a team includes no females is the probability that a sequence of three males is selected.

$$P \text{ (MMM)} = 0.5 \times 0.5 \times 0.5 = 0.125$$

The probability that one female is selected in a team of three is a little more complicated because we have to take into account the fact that the female could be the first or the second or the third person to be selected. So:

$$P \text{ (1 female)} = P \text{ (FMM or MFM or MMF)}$$

Because these three sequences are mutually exclusive, according to the addition rule:

$$P \text{ (1 female)} = P \text{ (FMM)} + P \text{ (MFM)} + P \text{ (MMF)}$$

Since the probability that a female is selected is the same as the probability that a male is selected each of these three ways of getting one female will have the same probability. That is:

$$P \text{ (FMM)} = P \text{ (MFM)} = P \text{ (MMF)} = 0.5 \times 0.5 \times 0.5 = 0.125$$

So:

$$P \text{ (1 female)} = 0.125 + 0.125 + 0.125 = 0.375$$

We get the same answer for the probability that two females are selected.

$$P \text{ (2 females)} = P \text{ (FFM or FMF or MFF)}$$
$$= P \text{ (FFM)} + P \text{ (FMF)} + P \text{ (MFF)}$$
$$= 0.125 + 0.125 + 0.125 = 0.375$$

Finally:

$$P \text{ (3 females)} = 0.5 \times 0.5 \times 0.5 = 0.125$$

We can bring these results together and present them in the form of a probability distribution.

Number of females (x)	P (x)
0	0.125
1	0.375
2	0.375
3	0.125

In Example 6.1 the probability distribution presents the number of females as a variable, X, whose values are represented as x. The variable X is a *discrete random variable*. It is discrete because it can only take a limited set of values. It is random because the values occur as the result of a random process.

The symbol 'P (x)' represents the probability that the variable X takes a particular value, x. For instance, we can represent the probability that the number of females is one, as:

$$P \ (X \ = \ 1) \ = \ 0.375$$

Figure 6.1 shows the probability distribution we compiled in Example 6.1 in graphical form. We can find summary measures to represent this distribution, in the same way as we could use summary measures to represent distributions of data. However, we don't have a set of data to use to get our summary measures. Instead we have to use the probabilities to 'weight' the values of X, just as we would use frequencies to obtain the mean from a frequency distribution.

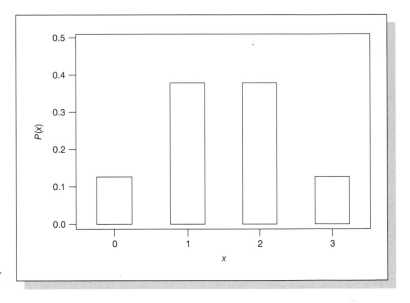

Figure 6.1
The probability distribution of X

You can get the mean of a probability distribution by multiplying each x value by its probability and then adding up the results.

$$\mu \ = \ \Sigma x P(x)$$

Notice that we use the Greek symbol μ here to represent the mean of the distribution. The mean of a probability distribution is a population mean because we are dealing with a distribution that represents the probabilities of all possible values of the variable.

Once we have found the mean we can proceed to find the variance and standard deviation. We can obtain the variance, σ^2, by squaring each x value, multiplying the square of it by its probability and adding the results. From this sum we subtract the square of the mean.

$$\sigma^2 = \Sigma x^2 P(x) - \mu^2$$

You can get the standard deviation, σ, by taking the square root of the variance.

Again you can see that we are using a Greek letter to represent the variance and the standard deviation because they are population measures.

Example 6.2

Calculate the mean and the standard deviation for the probability distribution in Example 6.1.

x	$P(x)$	$xP(x)$	x^2	$x^2P(x)$
0	0.125	0	0	0
1	0.375	0.375	1	0.375
2	0.375	0.750	4	1.500
3	0.125	0.375	9	1.125
		1.500		3.000

The mean, μ is 1.5, the total of the $xP(x)$ column.

The variance, σ^2 is 3, the total of the $x^2P(x)$ column minus the square of the mean.

$$\sigma^2 = 3 - 1.5^2 = 3 - 2.25 = 0.75$$

The standard deviation, $\sigma = \sqrt{\sigma^2} = \sqrt{0.75} = 0.866$.

The mean of a probability distribution is sometimes referred to as the *expected value* of the distribution. Unlike the mean of a set of data, which is based on what the observed values of a variable actually were, the mean of a probability distribution tells us what the values of the variable are likely, or *expected*, to be.

We may need to know the probability that a discrete random variable takes a particular value or a lower value. This is known as a *cumulative* probability because in order to get it we have to add up or *accumulate* other probabilities. You can calculate cumulative probabilities directly from a probability distribution.

Example 6.3

Calculate a set of cumulative probabilities from the probability distribution in Example 6.1.

Suppose we want the probability that X, the number of females, is two or less than two. Another way of saying this is the probability that X is less than or equal to two. We can use the symbol '$\leq$' to represent 'less than or equal to', so we are looking for $P(X \leq 2)$. (It may help you to recognize this symbol if you remember that the small end of the '$<$' part is pointing at the X and the large end at the 2, implying that X is smaller than 2.)

We can find the cumulative probabilities for each value of X by taking the probability that X takes that value and adding the probability that X takes a lesser value. You can see these cumulative probabilities are on the right-hand side of the following table.

Number of females (x)	P(x)	P(X ≤ x)
0	0.125	0.125
1	0.375	0.500
2	0.375	0.875
3	0.125	1.000

The cumulative probability that X is zero or less, $P(X \leq 0)$ is the probability that X is zero, 0.125, plus the probability that X is less than zero. Since it is impossible for X to be less than zero we do not have to add anything to 0.125.

The second cumulative probability, the probability that X is one or less, $P(X \leq 1)$ is the probability that X is one, 0.375, plus the probability that X is less than one, in other words that it is zero, 0.125. Adding these two probabilities together gives us 0.5.

The third cumulative probability is the probability that X is two or less, $P(X \leq 2)$. We obtain this by adding the probability that X is 2, 0.375, to the probability that X is less than 2, in other words that it is one or less. This is the previous cumulative probability, 0.5. If we add this to the 0.375 we get 0.875.

The fourth and final cumulative probability is the probability that X is three or less. Since we know that X can't be more than three (there are only three members in a team), it is certain to be three or less, so the cumulative probability is 1. We would get the same result arithmetically if we add the probability that X is three, 0.125, to the cumulative probability that X is less than 3, in other words that it is 2 or less, 0.875.

The cumulative probabilities like those we worked out in Example 6.3 are perfectly adequate if we want the probability that a variable takes a particular value or a lower one, but what if we need to know the probability that a variable is higher than a particular value?

We can use the same cumulative probabilities if we manipulate them using our knowledge of the addition rule. If for instance we want to know the probability that a variable is more than two, we can find it by taking the probability that it is two or less away from 1.

$$P(X > 2) = 1 - P(X \le 2)$$

We can do this because the two outcomes (X being greater than two and X being less than or equal to two) are mutually exclusive and collectively exhaustive. One and only one of them must occur. There are no other possibilities so it is certain that one of them happens.

In the expression $P(X > 2)$, which represents the probability that X is greater than two, we use the symbol '>' to represent 'greater than'. It may help you to recognize this symbol if you remember that the larger end of it is pointing to the X and the smaller end is pointing to the 2, implying that X is bigger than 2.

Although the situation described in Example 6.1, picking teams of just three people, was quite simple, the approach we used to obtain the probability distribution was rather laborious. Imagine that you had to use the same approach to produce a probability distribution if there were five or six members of a team instead of just three. We had to be careful enough in identifying the three different ways of selecting two females in a team of three. Listing the different ways two females could be selected in a team of five is far more tedious.

Fortunately there are methods of analysing such situations that do not involve strenuous mental gymnastics. These involve using *binomial* distributions.

6.2 Binomial distributions

Binomial distributions are the first of a series of 'model' statistical distributions that you will meet in this chapter and the two that follow it. These distributions have been derived theoretically but are widely used in dealing with practical situations. They are particularly useful because they enable you not only to answer a specific question but also to explore the consequences of altering the situation without actually doing it.

Binomial distributions can solve problems that have what is called a *binomial structure*. These types of problems arise in situations where a series of finite, or limited number of 'experiments', or 'trials' take place repeatedly. Each trial has the same two mutually exclusive and collectively exhaustive outcomes, as the *bi* in the word binomial might suggest. These two outcomes are generally referred to as 'success' and 'failure'.

To analyse a problem using a binomial distribution we have to know the probability of each outcome and it must be the same for

Hospitality, Leisure & Tourism Series

every trial. In other words the results of the trials must be independent of each other.

Words like 'experiment' and 'trial' are used to describe binomial situations because of the origins and widespread use of binomial distributions in science. Although these distributions have become widely used in many other fields, these scientific terms have stuck.

The situation in Example 6.1 has a binomial structure. Selecting a team of three is in effect conducting a series of three trials. In each trial, that is each time a name is selected from the hat, there can be only one of two outcomes, either a female or a male is picked.

In practice we use computer software or printed tables to find binomial distributions. These have been produced using an equation, sometimes called the binomial equation, which you will see below. You won't need to remember it, and you shouldn't need to use it. We will look at it here purely to show that it works.

We can use the symbol X to represent the number of 'successes' in a certain number of trials, n. X can be described as a binomial random variable. The probability of success in any one trial is represented by the letter p.

The probability that there are x successes in n trials is:

$$P(X = x) = \frac{n!}{x!(n-x)!} xp^x(1-p)^{n-x}$$

You will see that an exclamation mark is used several times in the equation. It represents a *factorial*, that is a number multiplied by one less than itself then multiplied by two less itself and so on until we get to one. For instance four factorial, 4! is four times three times two times one, $4 \times 3 \times 2 \times 1$, which comes to 24.

Example 6.4

Use the binomial equation to find the first two probabilities in the probability distribution for Example 6.1.

We can begin by identifying the number that we will insert in the binomial equation.

Selecting a team of three involves conducting three 'trials', so $n = 3$.

The variable X is the number of females selected in a team of three. We need to find the probabilities that X is 0, 1, 2, and 3, so these will be the x values.

If we define 'success' as selecting a female, p, the probability of success in any one trial, is 0.5.

We can now put these numbers into the equation. We will start by working out the probability that no females are selected in a team of three, that is $X = 0$.

$$P(X = 0) = \frac{3!}{0!(3 - 0)!} \times 0.5^0(1 - 0.5)^{3-0}$$

This expression can be simplified considerably. Any number raised to the power zero is one, so $0.5^0 = 1$. Conveniently zero factorial, $0!$, is also one. We can also clear up some of the subtractions.

$$P(X = 0) = \frac{3!}{1(3)!} \times 1(0.5)^3$$

$$= \frac{3 \times 2 \times 1}{3 \times 2 \times 1} \times (0.5 \times 0.5 \times 0.5) = 1 \times 0.125 = 0.125$$

If you look back at Example 6.1 you will find that this is the same as the first figure in the probability distribution. The figure below it, 0.375, is the probability that one female is selected in a team of three, that is $X = 1$. Using the binomial equation:

$$P(X = 1) = \frac{3!}{1!(3 - 1)!} \times 0.5^1(1 - 0.5)^{3-1}$$

$$= \frac{3 \times 2 \times 1}{1(2)!} \times 0.5(0.5)^2$$

$$= \frac{6}{1(2 \times 1)} \times 0.5(0.25) = 3 \times 0.125 = 0.375$$

You may like to try using this approach for $P(X = 2)$ and $P(X = 3)$ as well.

Hospitality, Leisure & Tourism Series

You will find it much easier to use computer software to get these figures. You can do it in MINITAB by selecting the **Probability Distributions** option from the **Calc** menu. Pick the **Binomial** option from the sub-menu. You can choose to obtain probabilities or cumulative probabilities. You will need to specify the **Number of trials** and the **Probability of success**, as well as the column location of the x values.

Alternatively, you can obtain the probabilities one at a time in Excel. Move the cursor to an empty cell then type = **BINOMDIST(x,n,p,FALSE)** in the Formula Bar. The numbers you put in for x, n and p depend on the problem. **FALSE** denotes that we don't want a cumulative probability, **TRUE** denotes that we do. To get the probability that one female is selected in a team of three we would type =**BINOMDIST(1,3,0.5,FALSE)**.

Generating binomial probabilities using software means we don't have to undertake laborious calculations or comb through printed tables to find the figures we are looking for. We can use the software to help us analyse far more complex problems than Example 6.1.

Example 6.5

An international cricket ground is about to stage a major test match. The ground features many corporate hospitality boxes, each of which accommodates eight guests. All of these boxes, like the rest of the ground, have been fully booked for this event for many months.

The Corporate Hospitality Department offers a welcome pack of eight pre-packed meals in each box. These meals contain meat. If 10 per cent of the population are vegetarians, what is the probability that at least one vegetarian occupant of a box will be disappointed with their meal? Assume that all the boxes are fully occupied.

This problem has a binomial structure. The variable X is the number of vegetarians in a box. Each person in a box is a 'trial' that can be a 'success', a vegetarian, or a 'failure', a non-vegetarian. The probability of 'success', in this case the probability that a person in a box is a vegetarian, is 0.1. There are eight people per box, so the number of trials, n, is 8.

The probability distribution, obtained using MINITAB, is:

Binomial with n = 8 and p = 0.100000

x	$P(X = x)$
0.00	0.4305
1.00	0.3826
2.00	0.1488
3.00	0.0331
4.00	0.0046
5.00	0.0004
6.00	0.0000
7.00	0.0000
8.00	0.0000

We need the probability that there is at least one vegetarian in a box, that is the probability that X is greater than or equal to one, $P(X \geq 1)$. We could get it by adding up all the probabilities in the distribution except the first one, the probability that X is zero, $P(X = 0)$. However, it is easier to take $P(X = 0)$ away from one.

$$P(X \geq 1) = 1 - P(X = 0) = 1 - 0.4305 = 0.5695 \text{ or } 56.95 \text{ per cent}$$

We can show the probability distribution in Example 6.5 in graphical form.

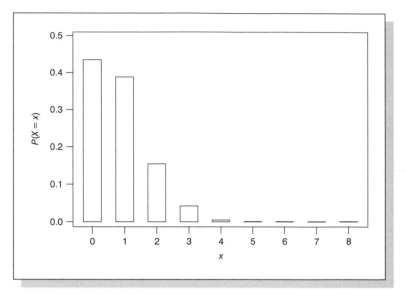

Figure 6.2
The probability distribution in
Example 6.5

In Figure 6.2 the block above 0 represents the probability that $X = 0$. The other blocks combined represent the probability that X is larger than 0.

It is quite easy to find the mean and variance of a binomial distribution. The mean, μ, is simply the number of trials multiplied by the probability of success, that is $\mu = np$. The variance, $\sigma^2 = np(1 - p)$.

Example 6.6

Calculate the mean, variance and standard deviation of the binomial distribution in Example 6.5.

In Example 6.5 the number of trials, n, was 8, and the probability of success, p, was 0.1.

The mean:

$$\mu = np = 8 \times 0.1 = 0.8$$

The variance:

$$\sigma^2 = np(1 - p) = 8 \times 0.1(1 - 0.1) = 0.8 \times 0.9 = 0.72$$

The standard deviation:

$$\sigma = \sqrt{\sigma^2} = \sqrt{0.72} = 0.849$$

Binomial distributions are called *discrete probability distributions* because they describe the behaviour of some discrete random variables, binomial variables. These variables concern the number of times things happen in the course of a finite number of trials.

But what if we need to analyse how many things happen over a period of time? For this sort of situation we can use other types of discrete probability distribution known as Poisson distributions.

6.3 Poisson distributions

Some types of business problem involve the analysis of incidents that are unpredictable. Usually they are things that can happen over a period of time such as the number of telephone calls coming through to a hotel reception desk. However, it could be a number of things over a space such as the number of stains in a carpet. Poisson distributions describe the behaviour of these variables and enable us to find the probability that a specific number of incidents happen over a particular period.

Using a Poisson distribution is quite straightforward. In fact you may find it easier than using a binomial distribution because we need to know fewer things about the situation. To identify which binomial distribution to use we had to specify the number of trials and the probability of success, these are the two defining characteristics, or *parameters*, of a binomial distribution. In contrast Poisson distributions are single parameter distributions, the one parameter being the mean.

If we have the mean of the variable we are investigating we can obtain the probabilities of a Poisson distribution using computer software.

In MINITAB this means selecting **Probability Distributions** from the **Calc** menu, and then picking **Poisson** from the sub-menu. In the command window you can choose to obtain probabilities or cumulative probabilities. You will need to provide the **Mean** as well as the column location of your x values.

You can also obtain the Poisson distribution probabilities in Excel. Move the cursor to an empty cell then type

=POISSON(x,Mean,FALSE)

in the Formula Bar. The numbers you put in for x and the mean depend on the problem. **FALSE** denotes that we don't want a cumulative probability, **TRUE** denotes that we do.

Example 6.7

Two lifeguards are employed to look after the bathers at a private beach. The size of the beach means that they can't deal with more than one incident each per hour. If the mean number of incidents per hour is 1, what is the probability that they will not be able to deal with all the incidents that occur in an hour?

The variable, X in this case, is the number of incidents per hour. The mean of X is 1.

The lifeguards can deal with two incidents an hour, so the probability that there are more incidents than they can handle is the probability that X is more than 2, or to put it another way, the probability that X is greater than or equal to 3, $P(X \geq 3)$.

To obtain this probability we can subtract the probabilities that X is 0, 1 or 2, that is the numbers of incidents the lifeguards can deal with in an hour, from one. We can use the simpler form of the addition rule, because they are mutually exclusive:

$$P(X = 0 \text{ or } 1 \text{ or } 2) = P(X = 0) + P(X = 1) + P(X = 2)$$

These probabilities, obtained using MINITAB, are:

Poisson with $\mu = 1.00000$

x	$P(X = x)$
0.00	0.3679
1.00	0.3679
2.00	0.1839
	0.9197

The probability that there are 0, 1 or 2 incidents is the total of these probabilities, 0.9197 or 91.97 per cent. The probability that there are three or more incidents is therefore 0.0803 or 8.03 per cent.

If we had to produce the Poisson probabilities in Example 6.7 without the aid of computer software we could calculate them using the formula for the distribution. You won't have to remember it, and probably won't need to use it, but it may help your understanding if you know where the figures come from.

The probability that the number of incidents, X, takes a particular value, x, is:

$$P(X = x) = \frac{e^{-\mu} \mu^x}{x!}$$

You can see the letter e, which represents a mathematical constant known as Euler's number. The value of this, to 4 places of decimals is 2.7183, so we can put this in the formula.

$$P(X = x) = \frac{2.7183^{-\mu} \mu^x}{x!}$$

The symbol μ represents the mean of the distribution and x is the value of x whose probability we want to know. In Example 6.7 the mean is 1, so the probability that there are no incidents, that is the probability that X is zero is:

$$P(X = 0) = \frac{2.7183^{-\mu}\mu^0}{0!}$$

To work this out we need to be aware that any quantity (in this case μ) raised to the power zero is one and the value of zero factorial (0!) is one. So:

$$P(X = 0) = \frac{2.7183^{-1}1^0}{1} = 2.7183^{-1} = 1/2.7183 = 0.3679$$

Notice that 2.7183^{-1} becomes $1/2.7183$. Any number raised to a negative power is a reciprocal, for instance 2^{-2} is $1/2^2$, in other words $\frac{1}{4}$.

If you look back at Example 6.7 you will see that the result we have calculated is the same as the first figure in the list of probabilities. The next figures were the probabilities that there were one and two incidents respectively.

$$P(X = 1) = \frac{2.7183^{-\mu}\mu^1}{1!} = \frac{2.7183^{-1} \times 1}{1} = 1/2.7183 = 0.3679$$

$$P(X = 0) = \frac{2.7183^{-\mu}\mu^2}{2!} = \frac{2.7183^{-1} \times 1^2}{2} = 1/2.7183 \times 2 = 0.1839$$

In Example 6.7 we only looked at part of the Poisson distribution that has a mean of one. Figure 6.3 displays the distribution.

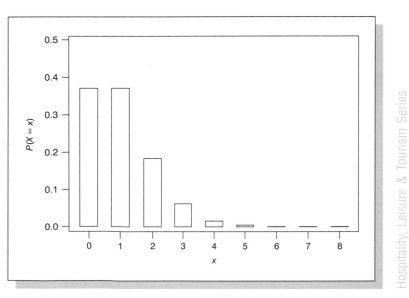

Figure 6.3
The probability distribution in Example 6.7

The task involved in Example 6.7 could be made a little easier by using cumulative probabilities of the Poisson distribution. MINITAB offers us the opportunity to obtain these by clicking **Cumulative probability** in the **Poisson** command window.

Poisson with μ = 1.00000

x	$P(X \leq x)$
0.00	0.3679
1.00	0.7358
2.00	0.9197

You can see that the last figure in the right-hand column is the same as the figure we subtracted from one to get the answer to Example 6.7. It is the cumulative probability that X is less than or equal to 2, $P(X \leq 2)$, which is another way of saying the probability that X is 0 or 1 or 2.

You can use Excel to get $P(X \leq 2)$. Locate the cursor in an empty cell then type **=POISSON(2,1,TRUE)** in the Formula Bar. You will see the probability in the cell where you have located the cursor.

6.4 Expectation

Earlier in the chapter we referred to the mean of a probability distribution as the expected value of the distribution because it can be used as a guide to what we could expect or predict that the values will be like. In fact one of the most important uses of probabilities is to make predictions. The production of predicted, or expected values is called *expectation*.

A probability assesses the chance of a certain outcome in general. To use it to make predictions we have to apply it to something specific. If the probability refers to a process that is repeated, we can predict how many times the outcome will occur if the process happens a specific number of times by multiplying the probability by the number of times the process happens.

Example 6.8

In Example 6.1 the probability that a quiz team of three members chosen at random contained one female was 0.375. If there are enough contestants for 200 teams, how many teams will contain exactly one female?

Selecting these quiz teams is a process that is to be repeated 200 times so we can work out how many teams include one female by multiplying the probability that a team contains one female, 0.375, by the number of times the process is repeated, 200.

Expected number of teams with one female = $0.375 \times 200 = 75$

So we would expect 75 of the teams to contain one female.

The result we obtained in Example 6.8 is a prediction, and like any prediction it won't always be true. We shouldn't therefore interpret the result as meaning that every time 200 quiz teams are selected at random there will be exactly 75 teams that contain one female.

What the result in Example 6.8 does mean is that if 200 quiz teams were selected at random every night, in the long run we would expect that the average number of teams containing one female will be 75.

Expectation also allows us to predict incidences over time. To do this you multiply the probability that a certain number of incidences occur over a period of time by the time you want your prediction to cover.

Example 6.9

In Example 6.7 we found that the probability that the number of incidents on the beach is more than two in any hour was 0.0803. If the beach is open 80 hours per week, in how many hours will there be more than two incidents?

We can obtain the answer by multiplying the probability of more than two incidents per hour by the number of hours the beach is open.

Expected hours with more than two incidents $= 0.0803 \times 80 = 6.424$

Since the two lifeguards can only handle two incidents an hour, we would expect them to have to summon help during 6 or 7 hours in a week.

In some situations the outcomes are associated with specific financial results. In these cases the probabilities can be applied to the monetary consequences of the outcomes to produce a prediction of the amount of money that the process will generate. These types of prediction are often called *expected monetary values* (EMVs).

Example 6.10

An airline incurs extra hospitality costs if its planes are delayed. If the delay is only a few hours the passengers are given a free meal. The airport restaurant makes a fixed charge of £500 for this service irrespective of the number of passengers involved. If there is an overnight delay the passengers are given free accommodation and breakfast at the airport hotel. The cost of this is £6000 whatever the number of passengers concerned.

If the probability that a plane is delayed a few hours is 10 per cent and the probability a plane is delayed overnight is 2 per cent, what is the expected monetary value of the airline's extra hospitality costs?

To answer this we need to take the probability of each of the three possible outcomes (no delay, short delay, and overnight delay) and multiply them by their respective costs (£0, £500, and £6000). The expected monetary value is the sum of these results.

$$EMV = (0.88 \times 0) + (0.1 \times 500) + (0.02 \times 6000) = 0 + 50 + 120 = 170$$

The airline can therefore expect that extra hospitality costs will amount to £170 per flight.

6.5 Decision trees

Expected monetary values play an important part in models that can be used to analyse business situations that involve a number of stages of outcomes and decisions. These models are called *decision trees*.

As their name might suggest, decision trees depict the different sequences of outcomes and decisions in the style of a tree spreading from left to right. Each branch of the tree represents an outcome or a decision. The junctions or points at which branches separate are called *nodes*. If the branches that stem from a node represent outcomes, the node is called a *chance node* and depicted using a small circle. If the branches represent different decisions that could be made at that point, the node is a *decision node* and depicted using a small square.

All the paths in a decision tree should lead to a specific monetary result that may be positive (an income or a profit) or negative (a cost or a loss). The probability that each outcome occurs is written alongside the branch that represents the outcome. We use the probabilities and the monetary results to work out the expected monetary value (EMV) of each possible decision. We write the EMV of a decision alongside the branch that represents it. The final task is to select the decision, or series of decisions if there is more than one stage of decision making, that yields the highest EMV.

Hospitality, Leisure & Tourism Series

Example 6.11

A fast-food company is interested in building a new restaurant on the outskirts of a major town. Because of local opposition to their proposal there is only a 65 per cent chance that they will be granted planning permission. If they do obtain planning permission there is an 80 per cent chance that their main rivals will open a similar facility close enough to seriously affect the prospects of the restaurant.

Financial planners at the company say that the venture would make a profit of £2 million in its first five years of operation if the rival facility is not built, and a loss of £0.4 million over the five years if the rival facility is built.

Assuming that the company takes all investment decisions on the basis of financial prospects over the first five years of any venture, should they proceed with their plan?

We can begin by distinguishing between the decisions the company can take and the outcomes they could face. The decisions are to build the restaurant or not to build the restaurant. The outcomes are whether they get planning permission or not, and whether the rival facility is built or not.

Although granting planning permission and building the rival facility are decisions, they are decisions taken by people outside the company. As far as the company is concerned they are outcomes and they do not have direct control over them.

In the diagram we will use the abbreviations:

- 'B' for building the restaurant and 'No B' for not building it.

- 'PP' for planning permission and 'No PP' for no planning permission.

- 'RF' for a rival facility and 'No RF' for no rival facility.

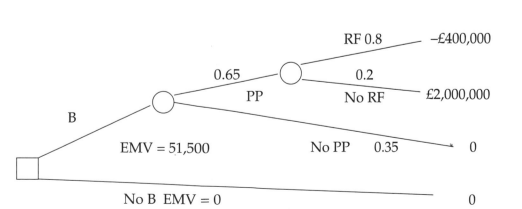

We can start with the EMV of the 'No build' decision. If they decide not to build the monetary result is certain to be zero.

If they decide to build there is a probability of 0.35 that they fail to get planning permission and get a monetary result of zero. The probability that they make a loss of £400,000 is the probability that they get planning permission and that the rival facility is built. The probability that they make a profit of £2,000,000 is the probability that they get planning permission and that the rival facility is not built.

The EMV of building the restaurant is the sum of these probabilities multiplied by their respective monetary results.

$$\text{EMV (build)} = (0.35 \times 0) + (0.65 \times 0.8 \times (-400{,}000)) + (0.65 \times 0.2 \times 2{,}000{,}000)$$

$$= 0 + (-208{,}000) + 260{,}000 = 52{,}000$$

Since the expected monetary value of building the restaurant, £52,000, is greater than the expected monetary value of not building, £0, they should build.

Although decision trees can be a useful approach to weighing up decisions, they do have several shortcomings as techniques for taking decisions.

Their first weakness is that they are only as good as the information that you put into them. If the probabilities and monetary figures are not reliable then the conclusion is also unreliable. This is an important issue when, as in Example 6.11, the figures are speculative assessments of future events over a considerable period of time.

The second shortcoming is that they take no account of the attitude that the people making the decision have towards risk. For instance, if the fast-food company in Example 6.11 has high profits and is cash rich it might be prepared to accept the risk of a loss more readily than if it has low profits and a liquidity problem.

The third drawback is that it is difficult to introduce factors that are non-quantifiable or difficult to quantify into the process. For instance, the location where the company in Example 6.11 wants to build the restaurant may be in an area where recruiting part-time staff for peak periods is easier than in a city-centre location.

Despite these weaknesses decision trees can help to investigate decisions and their consequences, especially when we are interested in the effects of altering some of the figures to see whether the conclusion changes.

Example 6.12

The rival company in Example 6.11 publishes financial results that show an improvement in profits. As a result the fast-food company that wants to build the restaurant now puts the probability that a rival facility will be built at 0.9. Should the company change its mind about building the restaurant?

We need to put the new probability that there is no rival facility (0.1) into the expression for the expected monetary value of the decision to build.

$$\text{EMV (build)} = (0.35 \times 0) + (0.65 \times 0.9 \times (-400{,}000)) + (0.65 \times 0.1 \times 2{,}000{,}000)$$

$$= 0 + (-234{,}000) + 130{,}000 = -104{,}000$$

The expected monetary value of building is negative, −£104,000, so it is now lower than the expected monetary value of not building, £0, so they should not build.

Review questions

6.1 Select the appropriate description for each term on the left-hand side from the list on the right-hand side.

(a) cumulative probability   (i) consist of probabilities of incidents over time

(b) expected value   (ii) the expected monetary value of a decision

(c) binomial distributions   (iii) the probability of one value or a lower one

(d) Poisson distributions   (iv) consist of probabilities of successes in trials

(e) EMV   (v) represent decisions and outcomes

(f) decision trees   (vi) a name for a probability distribution mean

6.2 The head of the Corporate Hospitality Department at the cricket ground in Example 6.5 decides to include one vegetarian meal in the welcome packs for guests in the hospitality boxes. How does this affect the probability that at least one vegetarian occupant of a box will be disappointed with their meal?

6.3 A large party of Russian tourists is due to stay at a hotel. The hotel manager has been told that only 20 per cent of the group speak English. Each table in the hotel restaurant accommodates six guests. If the Russian

Hospitality, Leisure & Tourism Series

guests only sit with each other and there is no seating plan, what is the probability that a table of six of them contains no one who can speak English?

Binomial with $n = 6$ and $p = 0.200000$

x	$P(X = x)$
0	0.2621
1	0.3932
2	0.2458
3	0.0819
4	0.0154
5	0.0015
6	0.0001

6.4 Only one waitress on the staff of the hotel restaurant in Question 6.3 speaks Russian. If the guests will occupy 60 tables and each waiter and waitress can deal with a maximum of 10 tables can all the orders be taken?

6.5 Between the hours of 7 am and 10 am an average of eighteen guests per hour come to a hotel reception desk to settle their accounts. The current front office staffing levels mean that if more than two guests arrive within a five-minute period during these times at least one guest will have to wait. What is the probability that at least one guest will have to wait?

Poisson with $\mu = 1.50000$

x	$P(X = x)$
0	0.2231
1	0.3347
2	0.2510
3	0.1255
4	0.0471
5	0.0141
6	0.0035
7	0.0008
8	0.0001
9	0.0000

6.6 The average number of violent incidents at the Koshmar pub is 2.1 per week. As a result of being injured at work the pub bouncer will be off for a week.

(a) What is the probability that the week passes without any violent incidents?
(b) What is the probability that the week passes with no more than one violent incident?
(c) If the bouncer's doctor says he only needs three days off work, what is the probability that these three days pass without any violent incidents?

(d) What is the probability that these three days pass with more than one violent incident?

Poisson with $\mu = 2.1$		Poisson with $\mu = 0.9$	
x	$P(X = x)$	x	$P(X = x)$
0	0.1225	0	0.4066
1	0.2572	1	0.3659
2	0.2700	2	0.1647
3	0.1890	3	0.0494
4	0.0992	4	0.0111
5	0.0417	5	0.0020
6	0.0146	6	0.0003
7	0.0044	7	0.0000
8	0.0011		
9	0.0003		
10	0.0001		
11	0.0000		

6.7 A small adventure travel company organizes expeditions in remote areas for small groups of tourists. Most of their expeditions are completed successfully but some have to be abandoned due to political unrest in the area, technical failure of vehicles, or serious illness or injury to members of the expedition. In each case the company incurs extra costs. These amount to £4000 if a trip is abandoned as a result of political unrest, £5000 if the cause is technical failure, and £7500 if there is illness or injury. The probability that a trip is abandoned as a result of political unrest is 0.05, the probability that a trip is curtailed because of technical failure is 0.03 and the probability that the trip is abandoned due to illness or injury is 0.02. Assume that these outcomes are mutually exclusive.

(a) What is the expected extra cost per expedition?
(b) The company can buy insurance against these eventualities for £400 per expedition. Should they buy this insurance?

6.8 Eagraville United are the last lower division football club in the quarter-finals of a major cup competition. The other teams are all prominent clubs with large numbers of supporters. The catering manager at Eagraville has to place the order for perishable goods to sell at the game before the draw for the next stage of the competition takes place. She can place a small or a large order. If she places a large order and the game is played at Eagraville she anticipates a profit of £10,000. If she places a small order and the game is played at Eagraville she anticipates a profit of £3000. If a large order is placed and the game is played elsewhere she estimates a loss of £2500. If a small order is placed and the game is played elsewhere she estimates a loss of £1000. There is a 50 per cent chance that Eagraville will get a home game in the draw, but if they do they expect that the larger club will apply for the fixture to be relocated because of the modest size of the Eagraville ground. The probability that such an application will succeed is 0.4.

Use a decision tree to represent the situation and use it to recommend what size of order the catering manager should place.

CHAPTER 7

Simulating populations

Chapter Objectives

This chapter will help you:

- To use continuous probability distributions.
- To analyse continuous random variables.
- To understand how sample results vary.

In this chapter you will find:

- Normal distributions.
- The Standard Normal Distribution.
- Sampling distributions.
- Guidance on using computer software to access Normal distributions.

In the last chapter we looked at how two different types of theoretical probability distributions, the binomial and Poisson distributions can be used to model or simulate the behaviour of discrete random variables. These types of variable can only have a limited or finite number of values, typically only whole numbers like the number of vegetarians in a group of diners or the number of violent incidents in a pub.

Discrete random variables are not however the only type of random variable. You will also come across continuous random variables, variables whose possible values are not confined to a limited range. In the same way as we used discrete probability distributions to help us investigate the behaviour of discrete random variables we use continuous probability distributions to help us investigate the behaviour of continuous random variables. Continuous probability distributions are also used to investigate the behaviour of discrete variables that can have many different values.

The most important continuous probability distributions in statistics are Normal distributions. As the name, which is always written with a capital N, suggests these distributions represent the patterns of many 'typical' or 'normal' variables.

However Normal distributions have a very special place in Statistics because as well as helping us to investigate variables that behave in the way that Normal distributions portray, they can be used to simulate the way in which results from samples vary. This is of great importance when we want to use sample results to make predictions about entire populations.

7.1 Normal distributions

Just as we saw that there are different binomial distributions that describe the patterns of values of binomial variables, and different Poisson distributions that describe the behaviour of Poisson variables, there are many different Normal distributions that display the patterns of values of Normal variables.

Each binomial distribution is defined by n, the number of trials and p, the probability of success in any one trial. Each Poisson distribution is defined by its mean. In the same way, each Normal distribution is identified by two defining characteristics or parameters, its mean and standard deviation.

Normal distributions have three distinguishing features:

1 They are unimodal, that is there is a single peak.
2 They are symmetrical, one side is the mirror image of the other.
3 They are asymptotic, that is they tail off very gradually on each side but the line representing the distribution never quite meets the horizontal axis.

Because Normal distributions are symmetrical distributions with single peaks, the mean, median and mode all coincide at the middle of the distribution. For this reason we only need to use the mean as a measure of location for a Normal distribution. Since the average we use is the mean, the measure of spread that we use for a Normal distribution is the standard deviation.

Normal distributions are sometimes described as bell-shaped. Figure 7.1 illustrates the shape of a Normal distribution.

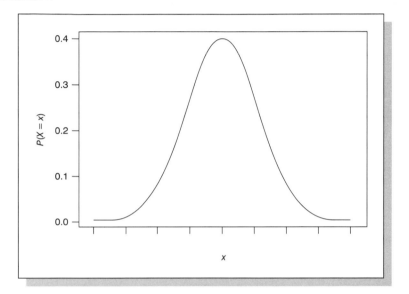

Figure 7.1
A Normal distribution

You can see that the shape of the probability distribution in Figure 7.1 is portrayed by a smooth curve, this is because it represents the probabilities that a continuous variable takes values across the range of the distribution.

If you look back at the diagrams we used to represent discrete probability distributions in Figures 6.1 and 6.2 you will see that they are bar charts that consist of separate blocks. Each distinct block represents the probability that the discrete random variable in question takes one of its distinct values. Because the variable can only take discrete, or distinct, values we can represent its behaviour with a diagram consisting of discrete, or distinct, sections.

If we want to use a diagram like Figure 6.1 or 6.2 to find the probability that the discrete variable it describes takes a specific value, we measure the height of the block against the vertical axis. In contrast using the smooth or continuous curve in Figure 7.1 to find the probability that the continuous variable it describes takes a particular value is not so easy.

Hospitality, Leisure & Tourism Series

To start with we need to specify a range rather than a single variable. For instance, we would have to say what is the probability that the variable x is between 3.500 and 4.499 rather than the probability that x is 4. This probability would be represented in the distribution by that part of the area below the curve between the points 3.500 and 4.499 on the horizontal axis as a proportion of the total area below the curve. Because this sort of thing is very difficult to measure even approximately on a graph, using Normal distributions inevitably involves software or printed tables of probabilities.

In Chapter 6 we saw how we could produce tables of binomial or Poisson probabilities using software as long as we could specify the necessary parameters. We could use the software to produce probabilities for any binomial or Poisson distribution. We can also use the software to produce probabilities for any Normal distribution.

You can do this in MINITAB by selecting the **Probability Distributions** option from the **Calc** menu. Pick the **Normal** option from the sub-menu. In the command window that appears you can choose to obtain probabilities or cumulative probabilities. Because of the nature of continuous variables you will nearly always need cumulative probabilities. You will need to specify the **Mean** and the **Standard deviation** of your Normal distribution, as well as the column location of the x values whose probabilities you want to know.

Alternatively you can obtain the probabilities one at a time in Excel. Move the cursor to an empty cell then type **=NORMDIST(x,mean,standard deviation,TRUE)** in the Formula Bar. The number x is the value whose probability you want to find. The mean and the standard deviation are the parameters of the Normal distribution that x belongs to. **TRUE** denotes that we want a cumulative probability, putting **FALSE** denotes that we don't.

Example 7.1

According to a fast-food chain, the time taken by its customers to consume their purchases in its restaurants is Normally distributed with a mean of 15 minutes and a standard deviation of 3 minutes. What is the probability that a customer selected at random takes less than 10 minutes.

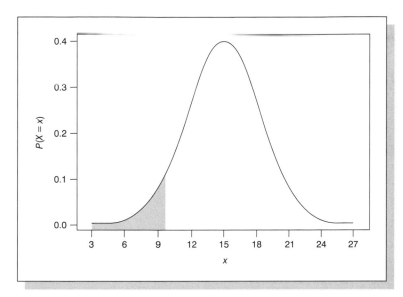

Figure 7.2 The distribution of consumption times of customers in Example 7.1

Figure 7.2 shows the area of the distribution that represents this cumulative probability. We can find it by typing **=NORMDIST(10,15,3,TRUE)** in the Excel Formula Bar. The result is 0.0478 or 4.78 per cent.

The result in Example 7.1 can be interpreted to mean that 4.78 per cent of customers take less than 10 minutes. If we wanted to get a more extensive profile of the probabilities of different times that customers take we could use MINITAB to obtain more details of the distribution.

Hospitality, Leisure & Tourism Series

Example 7.2

Find the probabilities that customers of the fast-food chain in Example 7.1 consume their purchases in less than 6 minutes, less than 9 minutes, less than 12 minutes, less than 15 minutes, less than 18 minutes, less than 21 minutes, and less than 24 minutes.

You can do this by listing these values in a column in the MINITAB worksheet and specify the mean, 15, the standard deviation, 3, and the column location of the values in the command window of the **Normal** option from the **Probability Distributions** sub-menu. You should get the following results.

Normal with mean = 15.0000 and standard deviation = 3.00000

x	$P(X \leq x)$
6.0000	0.0013
9.0000	0.0228
12.0000	0.1587
15.0000	0.5000
18.0000	0.8413
21.0000	0.9772
24.0000	0.9987

You can see from the table in Example 7.2 that the probability that a customer takes less than the mean, 15 minutes, is 0.5, or 50 per cent. This is not too surprising because the mean of a Normal distribution is the figure right in the middle of a symmetrical distribution. We would expect 50 per cent of the values in the distribution to be below it and the other half above it. The probability that any one value is below the mean is therefore exactly the same as the probability that it is above the mean, 0.5.

If the probability that a customer takes less than 15 minutes is 0.5 and the probability that a customer takes more than 15 minutes is 0.5, what is the probability that a customer takes exactly 15 minutes? In theory the probability that a continuous variable has a precise value is infinitely small. The probability that x, the time customers take, is precisely 15, that is 15.000000 . . ., is for all practical purposes zero. If we are more specific about what we mean by '15 minutes', which is probably '15 minutes to the nearest minute', it is clear that we don't mean the probability that x is exactly 15, we mean the probability that x is more than 14.5 and less than 15.5.

An implication of the last point is that there is no tangible difference between the probability that x is less than an amount, and the probability that x is less than or equal to that amount.

The other values in Example 7.2 have been chosen because they are one, two or three standard deviations away from the mean. As a rule of thumb roughly two-thirds of any Normal distribution is between one standard deviation below the mean and one standard deviation above the mean. About 95 per cent of the distribution is within two standard deviation of the mean, and over 99 per cent of the distribution is within three standard deviations of the mean.

Example 7.3

Use the list of probabilities in Example 7.2 to find the proportion of customers that take between 12 and 18 minutes, between 9 and 21 minutes, and between 6 and 24 minutes.

According to the table the probability that X, the time taken by customers, is below 18 minutes is 0.8413 or 84.13 per cent. The probability that X is below 12 minutes is 0.1587, or 15.87 per cent. To find the probability that X is less than 18 minutes and more than 12 minutes we have to subtract the probability that it is less than 12 minutes from the probability that it is less than 18 minutes.

$$P(18 > X > 12) = P(X < 18) - P(X < 12)$$

$$= 0.8413 - 0.1587 = 0.6826 \text{ or } 68.26 \text{ per cent}$$

This is illustrated in Figure 7.3.

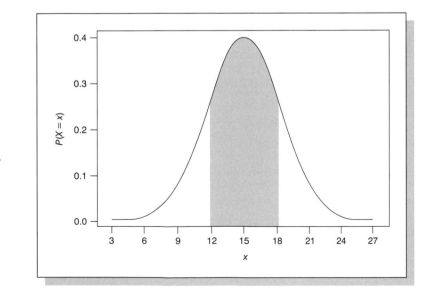

Figure 7.3 Example 7.3 $P(18 > X > 12)$

Hospitality, Leisure & Tourism Series

Similarly, we can get the probability that X is less than 21 minutes and more than 9 minutes by subtracting the probability that X is less than 9 minutes from the probability that it is less than 21 minutes.

$$P(21 > X > 9) = P(X < 21) - P(X < 9)$$
$$= 0.9772 - 0.0228 = 0.9544 \text{ or } 95.44 \text{ per cent}$$

This is illustrated in Figure 7.4.

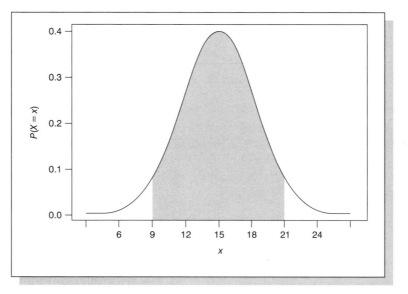

Figure 7.4 Example 7.3 $P(21 > X > 9)$

Finally, the probability that X is less than 24 minutes and more than 6 minutes is the probability that X is less than 24 minutes minus the probability that it is less than 6 minutes.

$$P(24 > X > 6) = P(X < 24) - P(X < 6)$$
$$= 0.9987 - 0.0013 = 0.9974 \text{ or } 99.74 \text{ per cent}$$

This is illustrated in Figure 7.5.

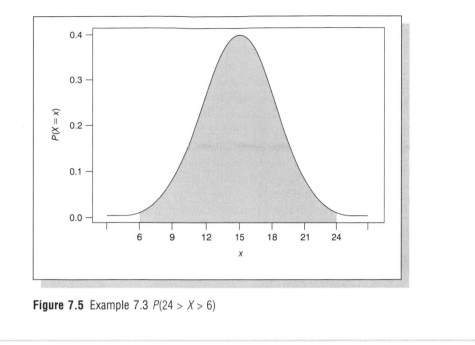

Figure 7.5 Example 7.3 $P(24 > X > 6)$

When we looked at the binomial and Poisson distributions in Chapter 6 we saw how it was possible to calculate probabilities in these distributions using the appropriate formulae. In fact in the days before the sort of software we now have became available, if you needed to use a binomial or a Poisson distribution you had to start by consulting published tables. However, because of the sheer number of different distributions, the one that you wanted may not have appeared in the tables. In such a situation you often had to calculate the probabilities yourself.

Calculating the probabilities that make up discrete distributions is tedious but not impossible, especially if the number of probabilities involved is quite small. The nature of the variables concerned, the fact that they can only take a limited number of values, restricts the number of calculations involved.

In contrast, calculating the probabilities in continuous distributions can be daunting. The variables, being continuous, can have an infinite number of different values and the distribution consists of a smooth curve rather than a collection of detached blocks. This makes the mathematics involved very much more difficult and puts the task beyond the capabilities of many people.

Because it was so difficult to calculate Normal distribution probabilities, published tables were the only viable means of using Normal distributions before computers were available to do the work. However, the number of different Normal distributions is literally infinite, so it was impossible to publish tables for all Normal distributions.

The solution to this problem was the production of tables describing a benchmark Normal distribution known as the *Standard Normal Distribution*. The advantage of this was that you could analyse any Normal distribution by comparing points in it with equivalent points in the Standard Normal Distribution. Once you had these equivalent points you could use published Standard Normal Distribution tables to assist you with your analysis.

Although modern software means that the Standard Normal Distribution is not quite as indispensable as it once was, it is important that you know something about it. Not only is it useful in case you do not have access to appropriate software, but more importantly, there are many aspects of further statistical work you will meet that are easier to understand if you are aware of the Standard Normal Distribution.

7.2 The Standard Normal Distribution

The Standard Normal Distribution describes the behaviour of the variable Z, which is Normally distributed with a mean of zero and a standard deviation of one. Z is sometimes known as the *Standard Normal Variable* and the Standard Normal Distribution is known as the *Z distribution*. The distribution is shown in Figure 7.6.

If you look carefully at Figure 7.6 you will see that the bulk of the distribution is quite close to the mean, and the tails on either side get closer to the horizontal axis as we get further away from the mean, but they never meet the horizontal axis. They are what are called asymptotic.

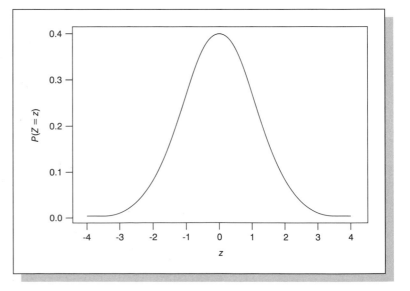

Figure 7.6
The Standard Normal Distribution

Like every other Normal distribution the Standard Normal Distribution is also symmetrical, that is one side is the mirror image of the other. This symmetry meant that tables of the Standard Normal Distribution only needed to list probabilities associated with positive values of Z, that is z values greater than the mean, zero. Probabilities associated with negative z values, those on the left-hand side of the distribution, could be found by using the equivalent positive z values on the right-hand side of the distribution.

Table 7.1 is a set of probabilities of the Standard Normal Distribution, produced using the MINITAB package.

The figures on the left-hand side of the table are values of Z, the Standard Normal Variable. Each figure on the right-hand side is the cumulative probability that the value of Z is less than or equal to the z value to its left.

z	$P(Z \leq z)$
0.00	0.5000
0.10	0.5398
0.20	0.5793
0.30	0.6179
0.40	0.6554
0.50	0.6915
0.60	0.7257
0.70	0.7580
0.80	0.7881
0.90	0.8159
1.00	0.8413
1.10	0.8643
1.20	0.8849
1.30	0.9032
1.40	0.9192
1.50	0.9332
1.60	0.9452
1.70	0.9554
1.80	0.9641
1.90	0.9713
2.00	0.9772
2.10	0.9821
2.20	0.9861
2.30	0.9893
2.40	0.9918
2.50	0.9938
2.60	0.9953
2.70	0.9965
2.80	0.9974
2.90	0.9981
3.00	0.9987

Table 7.1
The Standard Normal Distribution (mean = 0 and standard deviation = 1)

Look back at Figure 7.6 and imagine moving along the horizontal axis starting from the centre of the distribution, where Z is zero. At the point zero, half of the distribution is to your left. If you move to the right along the horizontal axis, the proportion of the distribution to your left gets larger.

In the same way, if you look down Table 7.1 you will see that as the values of Z increase, the cumulative probabilities to their right also increase. This is because the larger z is, the greater the probability that Z will be less than or equal to z. In other words the larger the value of Z the greater the part of the distribution to the left of z.

Example 7.4

Use Table 7.1 to find the following:

(a) The probability that Z is less than or equal to 0.7, $P(Z \leq 0.7)$.

(b) The probability that Z is more than 0.7, $P(Z > 0.7)$.

(c) The probability that Z is more than –1.3, $P(Z > -1.3)$.

(d) The probability that Z is less than or equal to –1.3, $P(Z \leq -1.3)$.

(e) The probability that Z is less than or equal to 2.7 and more than 0.4, $P(0.4 < Z \leq 2.7)$.

(f) The probability that Z is less than or equal to –0.8 and more than –1.9, $P(-1.9 < Z \leq -0.8)$.

(g) The probability that Z is less than or equal to 1.5 and more than –0.6, $P(-0.6 < Z \leq 1.5)$.

Until you are used to dealing with the Standard Normal Distribution you may find it helpful to make a small sketch of the distribution and identify on the sketch the z value(s) of interest and the area that represents the probability you want.

(a) The probability that Z is less than or equal to 0.7, $P(Z \leq 0.7)$.

The figure to the right of 0.7 in Table 7.1 is 0.7580. This is the probability that Z is less than or equal to 0.7. We could also say that 75.80 per cent of z values are no bigger than 0.7. This area is shown in Figure 7.7.

(b) The probability that Z is more than 0.7, $P(Z > 0.7)$.

From (a) we know that 75.80 per cent of z values are no bigger than 0.7. This means that 14.81 per cent of z values are bigger than 0.7, so the answer is $1 - 0.7580$ which is 0.2420. This is shown in Figure 7.8.

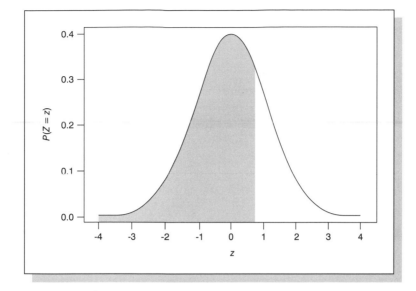

Figure 7.7 Example 7.4(a) $P(Z \le 0.7)$

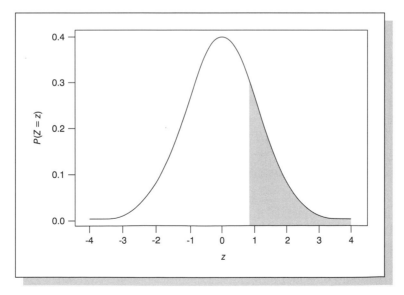

Figure 7.8 Example 7.4(b) $P(Z > 0.7)$

(c) The probability that z is more than –1.3, $P(Z > -1.3)$.

The figure –1.3 does not appear in the list of Z values on the left-hand side of Table 7.1, but the figure 1.3 does. The figure to the right of 1.3, 0.9032, is the probability that z is less than or equal to 1.3, but because the distribution is symmetrical it is the same as the probability that Z is more than –1.3 (by which we mean –1.2, –1.1 and so on). This is shown in Figure 7.9.

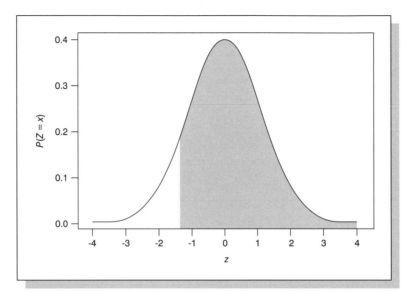

Figure 7.9 Example 7.4(c) $P(Z > -1.3)$

(d) The probability that Z is less than or equal to –1.3, $P(Z \leq -1.3)$.

From (c) we know that the probability that Z is more than –1.3 is 0.9032, so the probability that Z is less than –1.3 (by which we mean –1.4, –1.5 and so on) is 1 – 0.9032 which is 0.0968. This is shown in Figure 7.10.

(e) The probability that Z is less than or equal to 2.7 and more than 0.4, $P(0.4 < Z \leq 2.7)$.

These two figures, 0.4 and 2.7, being positive, do appear in Table 7.1. The figure to the right of 0.4 tells us that the probability that Z is less than or equal to 0.4 is 0.6554. The figure to the right of 2.7 tells us that the probability that Z is less than or equal to 2.7 is 0.9965. We can find the probability that Z is between the two by subtracting the probability that z is less than or equal to 0.4 from the probability that z is less than or equal to 2.7, 0.9965 – 0.6554 which is 0.3411. This is shown in Figure 7.11.

Another way of approaching this is to say that if 99.65 per cent of the area is to the left of 2.7 and 65.54 per cent of the area is to the left of 0.4, then the difference between these two percentages, 34.11 per cent is the area between 0.4 and 2.7.

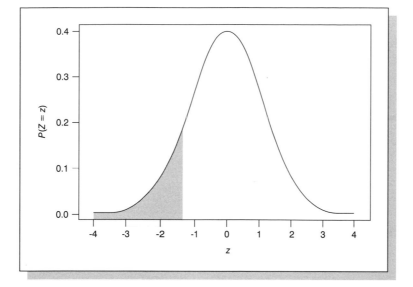

Figure 7.10 Example 7.4(d) $P(Z \leq -1.3)$

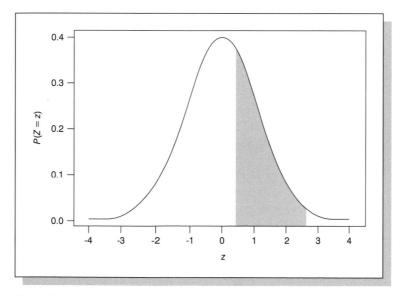

Figure 7.11 Example 7.4(e) $P(0.4 < Z \leq 2.7)$

(f) The probability that Z is less than or equal to –1.9 and more than –0.8, $P(-1.9 < Z \leq -0.8)$.

These are both negative z values so we must start with their mirror images, 0.8 and 1.9, both of which appear in Table 7.1. The probability that Z is less than or equal to 1.9 is 0.9713, which is the same as the probability that Z is more than –1.9. The probability that Z is less than or equal to 0.8, 0.7881, is the same as the probability that Z is more than –0.8. The probability that Z is between –1.9 and –0.8 is 0.9713 – 0.7881 which is 0.1832. This is illustrated in Figure 7.12

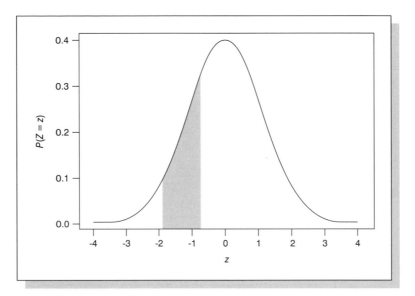

Figure 7.12 Example 7.4(f) $P(-1.9 < Z \leq -0.8)$

(g) The probability that z is less than or equal to 1.5 and more than -0.6, $P(-0.6 < z \le 1.5)$.

The probability that z is less than or equal to 1.5 is 0.9332 according to Table 7.1. From this we need to subtract the probability that z is less than -0.6. The probability that z is less than or equal to 0.6 is 0.7257, which is also the probability that z is more than -0.6. This means that the probability that z is less than -0.6 is $1 - 0.7257$, which is 0.2743. We find the answer by taking this figure away from the probability that z is less than or equal to 1.5, $0.9332 - 0.2743$ which is 0.6589. This is shown in Figure 7.13.

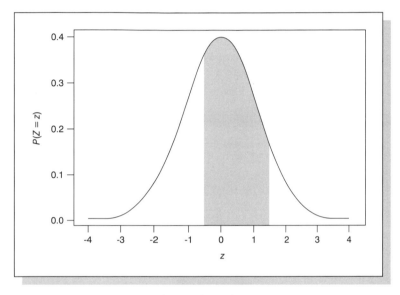

Figure 7.13 Example 7.4(g) $P(-0.6 < Z \le 1.5)$

Sometimes we need to use the Standard Normal Distribution in a rather different way. Instead of starting with a z value and finding a probability, we may have a probability and need to know the z value associated with it.

Example 7.5

Use Table 7.1 to find the value of the specific value of z, which we will call z_α, which means that:

(a) $P(Z \leq z_\alpha) = 0.5793$

(b) $P(Z > z_\alpha) = 0.0446$

(c) $P(Z > z_\alpha) = 0.0026$

(a) If you look down the list of probabilities in the column on the right in Table 7.1, you will see that 0.5793 appears to the right of the z value 0.2, so in this case the value of Z_α is 0.2. This is shown in Figure 7.14.

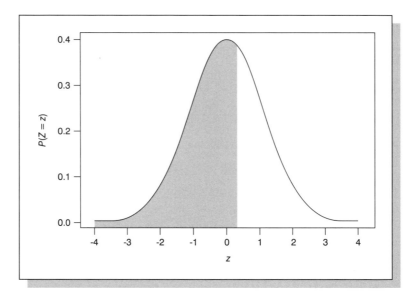

Figure 7.14 Example 7.5(a) 0.5793 = $P(Z \leq 0.2)$

(b) In this case we want the probability that Z is greater than a particular value. The probability that it is less than this value is $1 - 0.0446$ which is 0.9554. This probability appears to the right of 1.7, so here z_α is 1.7. This is shown in Figure 7.15.

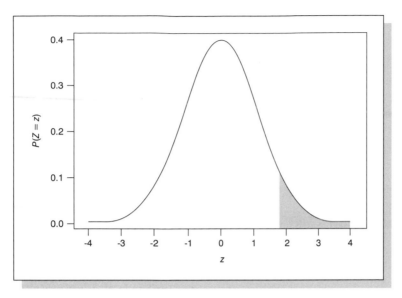

Figure 7.15 Example 7.5(b) $0.0446 = P(Z > 1.7)$

(c) If the probability that Z is greater than z_α is 0.0026, the probability that z is less than or equal to z_α is $1 - 0.0026$ which is 0.9974. This probability appears in Table 7.1 to the right of 2.8, which in this case is the value of z_α. This is illustrated in Figure 7.16.

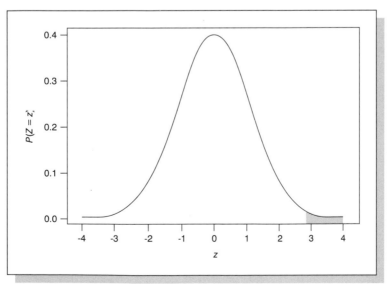

Figure 7.16 Example 7.5(c) $0.0026 = P(Z > 2.8)$

Hospitality, Leisure & Tourism Series

The symbol we used in Example 7.5 to represent the z value we wanted to find, z_α, is a symbol that you will come across in later work. The α in this symbol represents the area of the distribution beyond z_α, in other words the probability that z is beyond z_α.

$$P(Z > z_\alpha) = \alpha$$

In Example 7.5(c), α is 0.0026 and z_α is 2.8, that is $P(Z > 2.8) = 0.0026$, 2.8 is the value of z and 0.0026 or 0.26 per cent is the area of the distribution beyond 2.8. As you can see from Figure 7.16 this small area is in the right-hand tail of the distribution, so we can refer to it as a *tail area*.

Sometimes it is convenient to represent a particular value of Z by the letter z followed by the tail area beyond it in the distribution in the form of a suffix. For instance the z value 2.8 could be written as $z_{0.0026}$ because there is a tail of 0.0026 of the distribution beyond 2.8. We might say that the z value 2.8 'cuts off' a tail area of 0.0026 from the rest of the distribution.

In later work you will find that particular z values are often referred to in this style because it is the area of the tail that leads us to use a particular z value and we may want to emphasize the fact. Values of z that cut off tails of 5 per cent, 2.5 per cent, 1 per cent and $\frac{1}{2}$ per cent crop up in the topics we will look at in the next chapter. The z values that cut off these tail areas, 1.64, 1.96, 2.33 and 2.58 are frequently referred to as $z_{0.05}$, $z_{0.025}$, $z_{0.01}$ and $z_{0.005}$ respectively.

To use the Standard Normal Distribution to analyse other Normal distributions we need to be able to express any value of a Normal distribution that we want to investigate as a value of Z, this is sometimes known as finding its *Z-equivalent* or *Z score*.

The Z-equivalent of a particular value, x, of a Normal variable, X, is the difference between x and the mean of X, μ, divided by the standard deviation of X, σ.

$$Z = \frac{x - \mu}{\sigma}$$

Because we are dividing the difference between the value, x, and the mean of the distribution it belongs to, μ, by the standard deviation of the distribution, σ, to get it, the Z-equivalent of a value is really just the number of standard deviations the value is away from the mean.

Once we have found the Z-equivalent of a value in another Normal distribution we can refer to a Standard Normal Distribution table to assess probabilities associated with it.

Example 7.6

A pub offers a 10 oz Steak Special'. If the steaks they use for these meals have uncooked weights that are Normally distributed with a mean of 9.8 ounces and a standard deviation of 0.5 ounces, what is the probability that a customer will get:

(a) a steak that has an uncooked weight of less than 10 ounces?

(b) a steak that has an uncooked weight of less than 9.5 ounces?

(c) a steak that has an uncooked weight of more than 10.5 ounces?

(a) If X represents the uncooked weights of the steaks, we want to find $P(X < 10)$. This is shown in Figure 7.17.

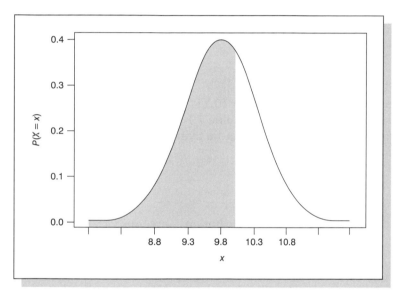

Figure 7.17 Example 7.6(a) $P(X < 10)$

The Z-equivalent of $x = 10$ is:

$$z = \frac{10 - 9.8}{0.5} = 0.4$$

So the probability that X is less than 10 is equivalent to the probability that z is less than 0.4. From Table 7.1:

$$P(Z \leq 0.4) = 0.6554 \text{ or } 65.54 \text{ per cent}$$

Hospitality, Leisure & Tourism Series

(b) The Z-equivalent of 9.5:

$$z = \frac{9.5 - 9.8}{0.5} = -0.6$$

So the probability that X is less than 9.5 is equivalent to the probability that Z is less than −0.6.

$$P(Z < -0.6) = 1 - P(Z > -0.6)$$

From Table 7.1 the probability that Z is less than 0.6, which is the same as the probability that Z is more than −0.6, is 0.7257. The probability that Z is less than −0.6 is therefore 1 − 0.7257 which is 0.2743 or 27.43 per cent.

(c) The Z-equivalent of 10.5:

$$z = \frac{10.5 - 9.8}{0.5} = 1.4$$

The probability that X is more than 10.5 is therefore the same as the probability that Z is more than 1.4. According to Table 7.1 the probability that Z is less than 1.4 is 0.9192, so the probability that Z is more than 1.4 is 1 − 0.9192 which is 0.0808 or 8.08 per cent.

Normal distributions are important statistical distributions because they enable us to investigate the very many continuous variables that occur in business and many other fields, whose values are distributed in a Normal pattern. What makes Normal distributions very important, perhaps even the most important distributions in Statistics, is that they enable us to understand how samples results vary. This is because many *sampling distributions* have a Normal pattern.

7.3 Sampling distributions

Sampling distributions are distributions that show how sample results vary. Such distributions play a crucial role in statistical work because they enable us to use data from a sample to make predictions or judgements about a population. There are considerable advantages in doing this especially when the population is too large to be accessible, or if investigating the population is too expensive or time-consuming.

A sample is a subset of a population, that is, it consists of some observations taken from the population. A random sample is a sample that consists of values taken at random from the population.

You can take many different random samples from the same population, even samples that consist of the same number of observations. Unless the population is very small the number of samples that you could take from it is infinitesimal. A 'parent' population can produce an infinite number of 'offspring' samples.

These samples will have different means, standard deviations and so on. So if we want to use a sample mean to predict the value of the population mean we will be using something that varies, the sample mean, to predict something that is fixed, the population mean.

To do this effectively we have to know how the sample means vary from one sample to another. We have to regard sample means as observations, $\bar{x}$, of a variable, X, and consider how they are distributed. What is more we need to relate the distribution of sample means to the parameters of the population the samples come from so that we can use sample statistics to predict population measures. The distribution of sample means is a sampling distribution.

We will start looking at this by taking the simplest case, in which we assume that the parent population is Normally distributed. If this is the case, what will the sampling distributions of means of samples taken from the population be like?

If you were to take all possible random samples consisting of n observations from a population that is Normal, with a mean μ and a standard deviation σ, and analysed them you would find that the sample means of all these samples will themselves be Normally distributed.

You would find that the mean of the distribution of all these different sample means is exactly the same as the population mean, μ. You would also find that the standard deviation of all these sample means is the population standard deviation divided by the square root of the size of the samples, $\sigma/\sqrt{n}$.

So the sample means of all the samples size n that can be taken from a Normal population with a mean μ and a standard deviation σ are distributed Normally with a mean of μ and a standard deviation of $\sigma/\sqrt{n}$. In other words the sample means are distributed around the same mean as the population itself but with a smaller spread.

We know that the sample means will be less spread out than the population because n will be more than one, so $\sigma/\sqrt{n}$ will be less than σ. For instance, if there are four observations in each sample, $\sigma/\sqrt{n}$ will be $\sigma/2$, that is the sampling distribution of means of samples which have four observations in them will have half the spread of the population distribution.

The larger the size of the samples, the less the spread in the values of their means, for instance if the sample each consist of 100 observations the standard deviation of the sampling distribution will be $\sigma/10$, a tenth of the population distribution.

This is an important but logical point. In taking samples we are 'averaging out' the differences between the values in the population. The larger the samples the more this happens. For this reason it is better to use larger samples to make predictions about a population.

Next time you see an opinion poll look for the number of people the pollsters have canvassed. It will probably be at least one thousand. The results of an opinion poll are a product that the polling organization wants to sell to media companies. In order to do this they have to persuade them that their poll results are likely to be reliable. They won't be able to do this if they only ask a very few people for their opinions!

The standard deviation of a sampling distribution, $\sigma/\sqrt{n}$, is also known as the *standard error* of the sampling distribution because it helps us anticipate the error we will have to deal with if we use a sample mean to predict the value of the population mean.

If we know the mean and standard deviation of the parent population distribution we can find the probabilities of different sample means as we can do for any other Normal distribution, by using software or the Standard Normal Distribution.

Example 7.7

A group of four friends visit the pub in Example 7.6 and each of them orders a Steak Special. What is the probability that the mean uncooked weight of the steaks they order is more than 10 oz?

The uncooked weights of the steaks in the pub in Example 7.6 were Normally distributed with a mean of 9.8 oz and a standard deviation of 0.5 oz.

Imagine we took every possible sample of four steaks from the population of steaks at the disposal of the pub (which we will assume is infinite) and calculated the mean weight of each sample. We would find that the sampling distribution of all these means has a mean of 9.8 and a standard error of $0.5/\sqrt{4}$, which is 0.25.

The probability that one sample of four steaks has a mean of more than 10 is the probability that a Normal variable with a mean of 9.8 and a standard deviation of 0.25 is greater than 10.

The Z-equivalent of the value 10 in the sampling distribution is:

$$z = \frac{\bar{x} - \mu}{\sigma/\sqrt{n}} = \frac{10 - 9.8}{0.5/\sqrt{4}} = \frac{0.2}{0.25} = 0.8$$

From Table 7.1 we find that the probability that z is less than 0.8 is 0.7881, so the probability that z is greater than 0.8 is 0.2119 or 21.19 per cent.

We can conclude that there is a little more than one in five chance that four steaks chosen at random have a mean uncooked weight of more than 10 oz. You might like to compare this with the result in Example 7.6(a), which suggests that the chance a single steak has an uncooked weight of more than 10 oz is 34.46 per cent (the probability of a single steak weighing less than 10 oz was 65.54 per cent).

The procedure we used in Example 7.7 can be applied whether we are dealing with small samples or with very much larger samples. As long as the population the samples come from is Normal we can be sure that the sampling distribution will be distributed Normally with a mean of μ and a standard deviation of $\sigma/\sqrt{n}$.

But what if the population is not Normal? There are many distributions that are not Normal, such as distributions of wealth of individuals or distributions of waiting times.

Fortunately, according to a mathematical finding known as the Central Limit Theorem, as long as n is large (which is usually interpreted to mean more than 30) the sampling distribution of sample means will be Normal in shape and have a mean of μ and a standard deviation of $\sigma/\sqrt{n}$. This is true whatever the shape of the population distribution.

Example 7.8

The times of visitors to a busy Tourist Information Office have to wait to ask for information follow a skewed distribution with a mean of three minutes and a standard deviation of one minute 20 seconds. What is the probability that a random sample of 64 visitors will, on average, have waited more than three and a half minutes?

The sample size, 64, is rather larger than 30 so the sampling distribution of the sample means will have a Normal shape. It will have a mean of 3 minutes, or 180 seconds, and a standard error of $80/\sqrt{64}$.

$$P(\overline{X} > 210 \text{ seconds}) = P\left(Z > \frac{210 - 180}{80/\sqrt{64}}\right)$$

$$= P(Z > 30/10) = P(Z > 3)$$

From Table 7.1 the probability that Z is more than 3 is $1 - 0.9987$ which is 0.0013. So the probability that a random sample of 64 visitors have on average waited more than three and a half minutes is 0.13 per cent, or a little more than a one in a thousand chance.

If the samples taken from a population that is not Normal consist of fewer than 30 observations then the Central Limit Theorem does not apply. The sampling distributions of means of small samples taken from such populations don't have a Normal pattern.

7.4 *t* distributions

The main reason for being interested in sampling distributions is to help us use samples to assess populations because studying the whole population is not possible or practicable. Typically we will be using a sample, which we do know about, to investigate a population, which we don't know about. We will have a sample mean and we will want to use it to assess the likely value of the population mean.

So far we have measured sampling distributions using the mean and the standard deviation of the population, μ and σ. But if we need to find out about the population using a sample, how can we possibly know the values of μ and σ?

The answer is that in practice we don't. In the case of the population mean, μ, this doesn't matter because usually it is the thing we are trying to assess. But without the population standard deviation, σ, we do need an alternative approach to measuring the spread of a sampling distribution.

Because we will have a sample, the obvious answer is to use the sample standard deviation, s, in place of the population standard deviation, σ. So the standard error of the sampling distribution becomes $s/\sqrt{n}$ instead of $\sigma/\sqrt{n}$.

This is fine as long as the sample concerned is large, in practice that n is at least 30. If we are dealing with a large sample we can use $s/\sqrt{n}$ as an approximation of $\sigma/\sqrt{n}$. The means of samples consisting of n observations will be Normally distributed with a mean of μ and a standard error of $s/\sqrt{n}$.

Example 7.9

The mean volume of 'real ale' served as a 'pint' in a particular pub is known to be 0.563 litres. A consumer organization takes a random sample of 100 pints of 'real ale' and finds that the standard deviation of this sample is 0.025 litres. What is the probability that the mean volume of the sample will be more than a pint (0.568 litres)?

The population mean, μ, in this case is 0.563 and the sample standard deviation, s, is 0.015. We want the probability that $\overline{X}$ is more than 0.568, $P(\overline{X} > 0.568)$. The z-equivalent of 0.563 is:

$$z = \frac{\overline{x} - \mu}{s/\sqrt{n}} = \frac{0.568 - 0.563}{0.025/\sqrt{100}} = \frac{0.005}{0.0025} = 2.0$$

So $P(\overline{X} > 0.568) = P(Z > 2.0)$

From Table 7.1 we know that the probability that Z is less than or equal to 2.0 is 0.9772 so the probability that Z is more than 2.0 is 0.0228. So the probability that the sample mean is more than a pint is 0.0228 or 2.28 per cent.

As $s/\sqrt{n}$ is not the real standard error it is usually referred to as the *estimated standard error*, but because the standard deviation of a large sample will be reasonably close to the population standard deviation the estimated standard error will be close to the actual standard error.

If the sample size, n, is less than 30 the estimated standard error is not so close to the actual standard error, and the smaller the sample size, the greater the difference between the two will be. In this situation it is possible to model, or simulate, the sampling distribution using the estimated standard error, as long as the population the sample comes from is Normal, but we have to use a modified Normal distribution in order to do it.

Hospitality, Leisure & Tourism Series

Such modified Normal distributions are known as *t distributions*. The development of these distributions nearly one hundred years ago was a real breakthrough in Statistics because they made it possible to investigate populations using small sample results. Small samples are generally much cheaper and quicker to gather than large sample so *t* distributions transformed the way in which people could use Statistics.

A *t* distribution is a Normal distribution that is more spread out. The greater spread is to compensate for the greater variation in sample standard deviations between small samples than between large samples.

The smaller the sample size, the more compensation is needed, so there are a group of 'standard' *t* distributions. The one that should be used in a particular context depends on the number of degrees of freedom, that is the sample size minus one, $n - 1$.

To work out the probability that the mean of a small sample taken from a Normal population is more, or less, than a certain amount we first need to find its *t*-equivalent, or *t* value. The procedure is very similar to the way we work out a *z*-equivalent.

$$t = \frac{\bar{x} - \mu}{s/\sqrt{n}}$$

Once we have the *t* value equivalent to the sample mean we can use computer software to find the probability associated with it. In MINITAB choose **Probability Distributions** from the **Calc** menu, then **t** from the **Probability Distributions** sub-menu. In the command window you will have to select the **Cumulative probability** options and provide the number of **Degrees of freedom** (the sample size minus one) and the **Input column**, that is the column location of your *t* value(s). The result that you see in the Session window will be the probability that *t* is less than or equal to the value(s) in the **Input column**.

You can also find probabilities of *t* distributions using Excel. The command that you need to type in the Formula Bar is **=TDIST(x,degrees of freedom,tails),** where *x* is the *t* value you are interested in and 'tails' can be either one or two. If you simply want the probability that *t* is bigger than a certain value, specify just one tail. In some circumstances it is useful to know the probability that *t* is more than a certain value or less than its negative equivalent in which case we would specify two tails.

Example 7.10

A customer visiting the pub in Example 7.9 purchases nine pints of real ale. The volumes of the pints served are known to be Normally distributed with a mean of 0.563 litres and the standard deviation of the volumes of the nine pints bought by the customer is 0.03 litres. What is the probability that the mean volume of the nine pints is more than a pint (0.568 litres)?

The population mean, μ, is 0.563 and the sample standard deviation, s, is 0.03. We want the probability that $\overline{X}$ is more than 0.568, $P(\overline{X} > 0.568)$. The t value equivalent to 0.563 is:

$$t = \frac{\overline{x} - \mu}{s/\sqrt{n}} = \frac{0.568 - 0.563}{0.03/\sqrt{9}} = \frac{0.005}{0.01} = 0.5$$

So $P(\overline{X} > 0.568) = P(t > 0.5)$

We can find the probability that t is more than 0.5 by putting =TDIST(0.5,8,1) in the Excel Formula Bar. The figure 8 is the number of degrees of freedom, which is one less than the sample size, 9. The result is 0.3153, so the probability that the mean volume of nine 'pints' is more than a pint is 31.53 per cent.

The t value that led to the result we obtained in Example 7.10 could be written as $t_{0.3153,8}$ because it is the value of t which cuts off a tail area of 31.53 per cent in the t distribution that has 8 degrees of freedom. Similarly $t_{0.05,15}$ represent the t value which cuts off a tail area of 5 per cent in the t distribution that has 15 degrees of freedom.

Review questions

7.1   Select the appropriate description for each term on the left-hand side from the list on the right-hand side:

(a) Normal distributions

(b) the Z distribution

(c) z_α

(d) $z_{0.05}$

(e) a sampling distribution

(i)   the Z value for which $P(Z > z) = 0.05$

(ii)   the estimated standard error

(iii)   a distribution used for small samples

(iv)   symmetrical continuous distributions

(v)   the standard error

(f) $\sigma/\sqrt{n}$

(g) $s/\sqrt{n}$

(h) a t distribution

(vi) the z value for which $P(Z > z) = \alpha$

(vii) the Standard Normal Distribution

(viii) shows how sample results vary

7.2 The journey times of flights to a major European destination from Heathrow are Normally distributed with a mean of three and a half hours and a standard deviation of six minutes.

(a) What proportion of flights will be completed within the advertised journey time of three hours thirty-nine minutes?

(b) What is the probability that a flight takes more than three hours twenty-seven minutes?

(c) What is the probability that a flight takes between three hours twenty-four minutes and three and a half hours?

(d) What is the maximum time taken by the fastest 5 per cent of flights?

(e) What is the minimum time taken by the slowest 25 per cent of flights?

7.3 The cost of renting three-bedroom holiday cottages for a week in a certain part of the UK is Normally distributed with a mean of £320 and a standard deviation of £50.

(a) What is the probability that a cottage chosen at random will cost more than £400?

(b) What is the probability that a cottage chosen at random will cost between £350 and £450?

(c) A family would like to rent a cottage but can only afford £250. What proportion of the cottages fall within their budget?

(d) What proportion of the cottages could the family in Part (c) afford if they were able to increase their budget to £300?

(e) What is the lowest rent of the most expensive 1 per cent of the cottages?

7.4 The ages of unaccompanied business guests of a group of hotels is Normally distributed with a mean of 42 years and a standard deviation of 10 years.

(a) What is the probability that one of these guests selected at random will be older than 38?

(b) What proportion of these guests will be younger than 50?

(c) What proportion of these guests will be between 30 and 45?

(d) What proportion of these guests will be eligible to visit the 'Under 25s' night at a local club?

(e) How old is the youngest member of the oldest 5 per cent of these guests?

(f) How old is the oldest member of the youngest 1 per cent of these guests?

7.5 The size of contributions made by members of coach parties to collections for their driver is Normally distributed with a mean of 75 pence and a standard deviation of 14 pence. If there are 49 seats on a coach:

(a) What is the probability that a full coachload of people will contribute on average more than 80 pence each?

(b) What is the probability that the average contribution of a full coach is between 70 and 77 pence per head?

(c) What is the most generous average contribution of the meanest 5 per cent of coachloads?

(d) What is the meanest average contribution of the most generous 1 per cent of coachloads?

7.6 A large university residence complex consists of small flats that each accommodates four people. Housekeepers are preparing the complex for visitors attending a conference during the summer vacation. These visitors will be staying for five days. As in term time the flats will be either all female or all male.

The housekeepers have been told to supply each flat with two rolls of toilet paper, each of which consists of 240 sheets so there are 120 sheets per guest.

(a) If the usage of toilet paper per day by males is Normally distributed with a mean of 16.5 sheets and a standard deviation of 7.5 sheets, what is the probability that a group of four male guests sharing a flat will run out of toilet paper during their stay?

(b) If the usage of toilet paper per day by females is Normally distributed with a mean of 22.5 sheets and a standard deviation of 10 sheets, what is the probability that a group of four female guests sharing a flat will run out of toilet paper during their stay?

(c) If each flat to be occupied by female guests is given three rolls instead of two what is the probability that the guests will have insufficient?

7.7 A charter airline flies exactly 100 passengers on each of its flights. The amount of money spent by passengers on in-flight purchases is not Normally distributed. The mean amount spent is £8.50 and the standard deviation is £4.00.

(a) What is the probability that the mean in-flight spending of a planeload of passengers is less than £7.50?

(b) What is the probability that the mean in-flight spending of a planeload of passengers is between £8.10 and £9.50?

(c) What is the probability that the mean in-flight spending of a planeload of passengers is more than £8.70?

(d) What mean level of spending will be exceeded by only 5 per cent of planeloads of passengers?

7.8 A featured ride at a theme park involves groups of 16 customers travelling at high speed in a special capsule. The capsule can carry up to 1500 kilograms safely.

(a) If the mean weight of the population is 78.5 kilograms and the standard deviation of one sample of 16 customers is 15.8 kilograms, what is the probability that the capsule will be overloaded?

(b) If the mean weight of customers should be 80.0 if the weight of clothing and baggage that they will take with them on the ride is to be taken into account, what is the probability that the capsule is overloaded? (With 15 degrees of freedom $P(t \le 3.86) = 0.9992$ and $P(t \le 3.48) = 0.9983$.)

Statistical decision making

Chapter Objectives

This chapter will help you:

- To use sample results to make predictions about populations.
- To test assertions about populations.
- To decide how large a sample needs to be.

In this chapter you will find:

- Interval estimates of population means.
- Interval estimates of population proportions.
- Levels of confidence, precision and sample size.
- Hypothesis testing.
- Guidance on using computer software for statistical inference.

Businesses in hospitality and tourism, as well as in other sectors, often use statistical analysis in order to help them study and solve problems. In almost every case the data they use in this analysis will be sample data. Usually it is too expensive, or too time-consuming or simply impossible to obtain population data.

So if there is a problem of customer dissatisfaction they will study data from a sample of customers, not all customers. If there is a problem with product quality they will study a sample of the products not all of them. If a large organization has a problem with staff training they will study the experiences of a sample of their staff rather than all their staff.

Of course they will analyse the sample data in order to draw general conclusions about the population from their analysis. As long as the samples they use are random samples, that is, they consist of observed values chosen at random from the population, it is quite possible to do this.

The use of sample data in drawing conclusions, or making deductions, about populations is known as *statistical inference* from the word *infer* which means to deduce or conclude. It is also referred to as *statistical decision making*, which reflects the fact that this sort of analysis helps organizations and individuals take decisions.

In the last chapter we looked at sampling distributions. These distributions are the theoretical foundations on which statistical inference is built because they connect the behaviour of sample results to the distribution of the population the samples come from. Now we will consider the procedures involved in statistical inference.

There are two types of statistical inference technique that you will encounter in this chapter. The first is *estimation*; the use of sample data to predict population measures like means and proportions. The second is *hypothesis testing*; the use of sample data to verify or refute claims made about population measures.

Collecting sample data can be time-consuming and expensive so in practice organizations don't like to gather more data than they need, but on the other hand they don't want to end up with too little in case they haven't enough for the sort of conclusive results they want. You will find a discussion of this aspect of planning statistical research in this chapter.

8.1 Estimation

Statistical estimation is the use of sample measures such as means or proportions to predict the values of their population counterparts. The easiest way of doing this is to simply take the sample measure and use it as it stands as a prediction of the population equivalent. So we could take the mean of a sample and use it as our estimate of the population mean. This type of prediction is called *point estimation*. It is widely used to get a 'feel' for the population value and in many cases it is a perfectly valid use of the sample result.

The main shortcoming of point estimation is given away by its name; it is a single point, a single shot at estimating one number using another. It is crude way of estimating a population measure because not only is it uncertain whether it will be a good estimate, in other words close to the measure we want it to estimate, but we have no idea of the chance that it is a good estimate.

The best way of using sample information to predict population measures is to use what is known as *interval estimation*, which is the preparation of a range or *interval* as the estimate. The aim is to be able to say how likely it is that the interval we construct is accurate, in other words how *confident* we are that the interval does include within it the population measure. Because the probability that the interval includes the population measure, or the confidence we should have in the interval estimate, is an important issue, interval estimates are often called *confidence intervals*.

Before we look at how interval estimates are constructed and why they work, it will be helpful if we reiterate some key points about sampling distributions. For convenience we will concentrate on sample means for the time being.

- A sampling distribution of sample means shows how all the means of the different sample of a particular size, n, are distributed.

- Sampling distributions that describe the behaviour of means of samples bigger than 30 are always Normal.

- The mean of a sampling distribution is the population mean, μ.

- The standard deviation of a sampling distribution, called the standard error, is the population standard deviation divided by the square root of the sample size, $\sigma \sqrt{n}$.

The sampling distributions that are Normal in shape, the ones that show how sample means of big samples vary, have the same features as other Normal distributions. One of these features is that if we take a point two standard deviations to the left of the mean and another point two standard deviations to the right of the mean, the area between the two points is roughly 95 per cent of the distribution.

To be more precise, if these points were 1.96 standard deviations below and above the mean the area would be exactly 95 per cent of the distribution. In other words 95 per cent of the observations in the distribution are within 1.96 standard deviations from the mean.

This is also true for Normal sampling distributions. Ninety-five per cent of the sample means in a sampling distribution that is Normal will be between 1.96 standard errors below and 1.96 standard errors above the mean. You can see this illustrated in Figure 8.1.

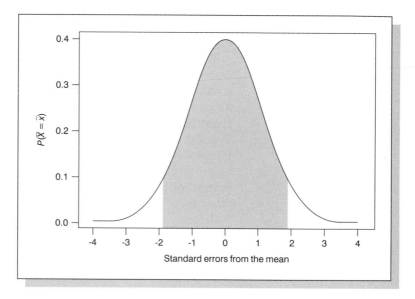

Figure 8.1
Ninety-five per cent of a sampling distribution

The limits of this range, or interval, are:

$$\mu - 1.96 \ \sigma \sqrt{n} \text{ on the left-hand side}$$

and

$$\mu + 1.96 \ \sigma \sqrt{n} \text{ on the right-hand side}$$

The greatest difference between any of the middle 95 per cent of sample means and the population mean, μ, is 1.96 standard errors, 1.96 $\sigma \sqrt{n}$. The probability that any one sample mean is within 1.96 standard errors of the mean:

$$P(\mu - 1.96 \ \sigma \sqrt{n} < \overline{X} < \mu + 1.96 \ \sigma \sqrt{n}) = 0.95$$

The sampling distribution allows us to predict values of sample means like this, using the population mean. But in practice we wouldn't be interested in knowing this because we wouldn't know the value of the population mean. Indeed typically the population mean is the thing we want to find out about using a sample rather than the other way round.

The thing that makes sampling distributions so useful is that we can use them to predict population measures using sample results.

As we have seen, adding and subtracting 1.96 standard errors to and from the population mean creates a range that encompasses 95 per cent of the sample means in the distribution. But what would happen if, instead of adding and subtracting this amount to the population mean, we add and subtract this amount from every sample mean in the distribution?

We would create a range around every sample mean. In 95 per cent of cases, the ranges based on the 95 per cent of sample means that are closest to the population mean (those nearest the middle of the distribution), the range would encompass the population mean itself. In the other 5 per cent of cases, those means furthest away from the population mean and far from the centre of the distribution, the range would not encompass the population mean.

So, suppose we take the mean of a large sample and create a range around it by adding 1.96 standard errors to get an upper figure, and subtracting 1.96 standard errors to get a lower figure. There is a 95 per cent chance that the range between the upper and lower figures will encompass the mean of the population. Such a range is called a 95 per cent confidence interval or a 95 per cent interval estimate because it is an interval, or range, that we are 95 per cent confident, or certain, includes the population mean.

Example 8.1

The levels of discretionary spending, by guests staying at a self-contained holiday village have a mean of £50 per week and a standard deviation of £12.75 per week. A group of researchers, who do not know that the population mean expenditure is £50, finds the discretionary income of a random samples of 100 guests.

The sampling distribution that the mean of their sample belongs to is shown in Figure 8.2. The standard error of this distribution is $12.75/\sqrt{100} = 1.275$.

Ninety-five per cent of the sample means in this distribution will be between 1.96 standard errors below the mean, that is:

$50 - (1.96 \times 1.275) = 47.50$

and 1.96 standard errors above the mean, that is:

$50 + (1.96 \times 1.275) = 52.50$

This is also shown in Figure 8.2.

Hospitality, Leisure & Tourism Series

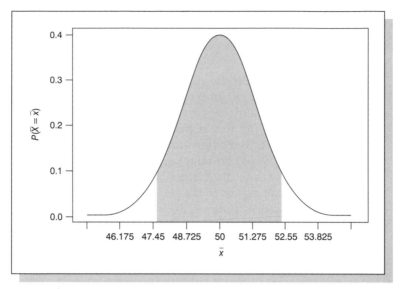

Figure 8.2 Sampling distribution in Example 8.1

Suppose the researchers calculate the mean of their sample and it is £49.25, a figure inside the range 47.50 to 52.50 that encompasses the 95 per cent of sample means within 1.96 standard errors of the population mean. If they add and subtract the same number of standard errors to and from their sample mean:

$$49.25 \pm (1.96 \times 1.275) = 49.25 \pm 2.50 = £46.75 \text{ to } £51.75$$

The interval they create does include the population mean, £50.

Notice the symbol '±' in the expression we have just used. It means we have to carry out two operations: we have to both add *and* subtract the amount that follows it. The addition produces the higher figure, in this case 51.75, and the subtraction produces the lower figure, 46.75.

Imagine they take another random sample of 100 guests and find that the mean expenditure of this second sample is a little higher, but still within the central 95 per cent of the sampling distribution, say £51.87. If they add and subtract 1.96 standard errors to and from this second mean:

$$51.87 \pm (1.96 \times 1.275) = 51.87 \pm 2.50 = £49.37 \text{ to } £54.37$$

This interval also includes the population mean.

If the researchers in Example 8.1 took many samples and created an interval based on each one by adding and subtracting 1.96

standard errors they would find that only occasionally would the interval not include the population mean.

Example 8.2

The researchers in Example 8.1 take a random sample that yields a mean of £47.13. Calculate a 95 per cent confidence interval using this sample mean.

$$47.13 \pm (1.96 \times 1.275) = 47.13 \pm 2.50 = £44.63 \text{ to } £49.63$$

This interval does not include the population mean of £50.

How often should the researchers in Example 8.1 produce an interval that does not include the population mean? The answer is every time they have a sample mean that is amongst the lowest $2\frac{1}{2}$ per cent or the highest $2\frac{1}{2}$ per cent of sample means. If their sample mean is amongst the lowest $2\frac{1}{2}$ per cent the interval they produce will be too low, as in Example 8.2. If the sample mean is amongst the highest $2\frac{1}{2}$ per cent the interval will be too high.

As long as the sample mean is amongst the 95 per cent of the distribution between the lowest $2\frac{1}{2}$ per cent and the highest $2\frac{1}{2}$ per cent, the interval they produce will include the population mean, in other words it will be an accurate estimate of the population mean.

Of course usually when we carry out this sort of research we don't know what the population mean is, so we don't know which sample means are amongst the 95 per cent that will give us accurate estimates and which are amongst the 5 per cent that will give us inaccurate estimates. The important point is that if we have a sample mean and we create an interval in this way, there is a 95 per cent chance that the interval will be accurate. That is why the interval is called a 95 per cent interval estimate or a 95 per cent confidence interval.

We can express the procedure for finding an interval estimate for a population measure as taking a sample result and adding and subtracting an *error*. This error reflects the uncertainties involved in using sample information to predict population measures.

Population measure estimate = sample result ± error

The error is made up of two components, the standard error and the number of standard errors. The number of standard errors depends on how confident we want to be in our estimation.

Suppose you want to estimate the population mean. If you know the population standard deviation, σ, and you want to be $(100 - \alpha)$ per cent confident that your interval is accurate, then:

$$\text{Estimate of } \mu = \bar{x} \pm (z_{\alpha/2} \times \sigma/\sqrt{n})$$

The letter 'z' appears because we are dealing with sampling distributions that are Normal, so we can use the Standard Normal Distribution, the Z distribution, to simulate them. You have to choose which z value to use on the basis of how sure you want or need to be that your estimate is accurate.

If you want to be 95 per cent confident in your estimate, that is $(100 - \alpha)$ per cent = 95 per cent, then α is 5 per cent and $\alpha/2$ is $2\frac{1}{2}$ per cent or 0.025. To produce your estimate you would use $z_{0.025}$, 1.96, the z value that cuts off a $2\frac{1}{2}$ per cent tail in the Standard Normal Distribution. This means that a point 1.96 standard deviations (or standard errors in the case of sampling distributions) away from the mean of any Normal distribution will cut off a tail area of $2\frac{1}{2}$ per cent of the distribution. So:

$$95 \text{ per cent interval estimate of } \mu = \bar{x} \pm (1.96 \times \sigma/\sqrt{n})$$

which is the procedure we used in Example 8.1.

The most commonly used level of confidence in interval estimation is probably 95 per cent, but what if you wanted to construct an interval based on a higher level of confidence, say 99 per cent? A 99 per cent level of confidence means we want 99 per cent of the sample means in the sampling distribution to provide accurate estimates.

To obtain a 99 per cent confidence interval the only adjustment we make is the z value that we use. If $(100 - \alpha)$ per cent = 99 per cent, then α is 1 per cent and $\alpha/2$ is $\frac{1}{2}$ per cent or 0.005. To produce your estimate you would use $z_{0.005}$, 2.58, the z value that cuts off a $\frac{1}{2}$ per cent tail in the Standard Normal Distribution.

$$99 \text{ per cent interval estimate of } \mu = \bar{x} \pm (2.58 \times \sigma/\sqrt{n})$$

The most commonly used confidence levels and the z values you need to use to construct them are given in Table 8.1.

Level of confidence $(100 - \alpha)$ per cent	α/z	$z_{\alpha/2}$
90 per cent	0.05	1.64
95 per cent	0.025	1.96
99 per cent	0.005	2.58

Table 8.1
Selected levels of confidence and associated z values

Example 8.3

Use the sample result in Example 8.2, £47.13, to produce a 99 per cent interval estimate for the population mean.

$$47.13 \pm (2.58 \times 1.275) = 47.13 \pm 3.29 = £43.84 \text{ to } £50.42$$

Notice that this interval in Example 8.3 does include the population mean, £50, unlike the 95 per cent interval estimate based on the same sample mean, £47.13. This is because the sample mean is not amongst the 95 per cent closest to the population mean, but it is amongst the 99 per cent closest to the population mean.

Changing the level of confidence to 99 per cent has meant the interval is accurate, but it is also wider. The 95 per cent interval estimate was £44.63 to £49.63, a width of £5.00. The 99 per cent interval estimate is £43.84 to £50.43, a width of £6.59.

All other things being equal if we want to be more confident that our interval is accurate we have to accept that the interval will be wider, in other words less precise. If we want to be more confident and retain the same degree of precision, the only thing we can do is to take a larger sample.

Example 8.4

If the researchers in Example 8.1 want to construct 99 per cent confidence intervals that are £5 wide, what sample size should they use?

If the estimates are to be £5 wide that means they will be produced by adding and subtracting £2.50 to and from the sample mean. In other words the error will be 2.5. If the level of confidence is to be 99 per cent then the error will be 2.58 standard errors. That is:

$$(z_{\alpha/2} \times \sigma/\sqrt{n}) = 2.50$$

and if $(100 - \alpha)$ per cent = 99 per cent, $z_{\alpha/2} = 2.58$, so:

$$(2.58 \times \sigma/\sqrt{n}) = 2.50$$

We know $\sigma = 12.75$, so $\quad (2.58 \times 12.75/\sqrt{n}) = 2.50$

The only thing we don't know is n, the sample size. Because we know all the other numbers that make up the expression we can work n out.

If
$$(2.58 \times 12.75/\sqrt{n}) = 2.50$$

Then
$$\frac{32.895}{\sqrt{n}} = 2.50$$

If we swap 2.50 and $\sqrt{n}$ $\quad \dfrac{32.895}{2.50} = \sqrt{n} = 13.158$

If the square root of n is 13.158, n itself is 173.13. In practice we would round it up to 174 to be on the safe side.

So if the researchers want 99 per cent interval estimates that are £5 wide they would have to take a sample of 174 guests.

Example 8.1 is artificial because we assumed that we knew the population mean, μ. This helped to explain how and why interval estimation works. In practice we wouldn't know the population mean, and neither would we know the population standard deviation, σ.

8.1.1 Estimating without σ

Practical interval estimation is based on sample results alone, but it is very similar to the procedure we explored in Example 8.1. The main difference is that we have to use a sample standard deviation, s, to produce an estimate for the standard error of the sampling distribution the sample belongs to. Otherwise, as long as the sample concerned is quite large, which we can define as consisting of more than 30 observations, we can follow exactly the same procedure as before.

That is instead of $\qquad$ estimate of $\mu = \bar{x} \pm (z_{\alpha/2} \times \sigma/\sqrt{n})$

we use $\qquad$ estimate of $\mu = \bar{x} \pm (z_{\alpha/2} \times s/\sqrt{n})$

Example 8.5

The mean weight of the cabin baggage checked in by a random sample of 40 passengers at an international airport departure terminal was 3.47 kg. The sample standard deviation was 0.82 kg. Construct a 90 per cent confidence interval for the mean weight of cabin baggage checked in by passengers at the terminal.

90 per cent interval estimate of $\mu = \bar{x} \pm (1.64 \times s/\sqrt{n})$

$$= 3.47 \pm (1.64 \times 0.82/\sqrt{40})$$

$$= 3.47 \pm (1.64 \times 0.82/6.32)$$

$$= 3.47 \pm 0.21 = 3.26 \text{ to } 3.68$$

Notice that in Example 8.5 we are not told whether the population that the sample comes from is Normal or not. This doesn't matter because we have a relatively large sample. In fact given that airlines tend to restrict cabin baggage to 5 kg per passenger the distribution in this case would probably be skewed.

8.1.2 Estimating with small samples

If we want to produce an interval estimate based on a smaller sample, one with less than 30 observations in it we have to be much more careful. First, the population that it comes from must be Normal. Second, because the sample standard deviation of a small sample is not a reliable enough estimate of the population standard deviation to enable us to use the Z distribution, we must use the appropriate t distribution to find how many standard errors are to be added and subtracted.

That is instead of   estimate of $\mu = \bar{x} \pm (z_{\alpha/2} \times \sigma/\sqrt{n})$

we use   estimate of $\mu = \bar{x} \pm (t_{\alpha/2, n-1} \times s/\sqrt{n})$

The number of degrees of freedom, $n-1$ determines the t distribution you use. You will find a selection of t values for commonly used levels of confidence in Table 8.2.

You may recall from the last chapter that t distributions are modifications of the Z distribution. If you compare the figures in the bottom row of Table 8.2 with their equivalents from the Z

Sample size	Degrees of freedom	$t_{0.05,n-1}$	$t_{0.025,n-1}$	$t_{0.005,n-1}$
5	4	2.13	2.78	4.60
10	9	1.83	2.26	3.25
15	14	1.76	2.14	2.98
20	19	1.73	2.09	2.86
25	24	1.71	2.06	2.80
30	29	1.70	2.04	2.76

Table 8.2
Selected levels of confidence and associated t values

distribution in Table 8.1, that is 1.64, 1.96 and 2.58, you can see that they are reasonably close. The figures in the bottom row of Table 8.2 relate to samples of 30. If however you compare the z values with the t values in the top row of Table 8.2, the ones that relate to samples of only 5, you can see that the differences are greater.

Example 8.6

A random sample of 15 employees of a chain of fast-food restaurants are each sent to take a competency test. The mean of the scores achieved by these employees was 56.3 per cent and the standard deviation 7.1 per cent. Results of this test have been found to be Normally distributed in the past. Construct a 95 per cent confidence interval for the mean test score of all the employees of the fast-food chain.

$$\text{estimate of } \mu = \bar{x} \pm (t_{\alpha/2,n-1} \times s/\sqrt{n}).$$

$$95 \text{ per cent estimate of } \mu = \bar{x} \pm (t_{0.025,n-1} \times s/\sqrt{n})$$

$$= 56.3 \pm (t_{0.025,14} \times 7.1/\sqrt{15})$$

$$= 56.3 \pm (2.14 \times 7.1/\sqrt{15})$$

$$= 56.3 \pm 3.92 = 52.38 \text{ per cent to } 60.22 \text{ per cent}$$

8.1.3 Estimating using computer software

You can produce confidence intervals using Excel or MINITAB. In Excel you can find the error, that is the amount that needs to be added and subtracted to create the interval around the sample measure, by typing

=CONFIDENCE(alpha,standard deviation,size)

in the Formula Bar. Alpha is 100 per cent minus the level of confidence expressed as a proportion, standard deviation is the population standard deviation, and size is the sample size. As long as your sample size is at least 30 you can type the sample standard deviation in as the population standard deviation. To produce the error for Example 8.5 we would have to type **=CONFI-DENCE(0.10,0.82,40)**. This will produce the error to six places of decimals, in this case 0.213261. We would then apply this error to the sample mean as a separate numerical operation.

The **CONFIDENCE** command in Excel should only be used if you have a large sample. If you have a small sample you can't use it unless you know the population standard deviation, which is unlikely. However, you could obtain the appropriate t value and sample measures using the other statistical tools available in the package, then assemble the interval yourself.

To construct interval estimates using MINITAB you really need to have the sample data rather than just the sample mean and standard deviation. Put these into a worksheet column then select **Basic Statistics** from the **Stat** menu. Choose **1-Sample Z** from the **Basic Statistics** sub-menu. In the command window that appears you should specify the column location of the sample data, click the **Confidence Interval** button and specify the level of confidence you require. You will also have to provide **Sigma**, the population standard deviation. If your sample consists of at least 30 observations you can type in the sample standard deviation instead.

If you have a small sample follow the same procedure but choose **1-Sample t** from the **Basic Statistics** sub-menu. The command window is almost identical to the one for **1-Sample Z**, except that you do not have to specify **Sigma**, instead the package will calculate the sample standard deviation in the course of providing your interval estimate. Because you do not need to specify a standard deviation you may find **1-Sample t** easier whatever the size of your sample, indeed strictly speaking it is more correct to use a t distribution unless your sample consists of an infinite number of observations!

If you have access to both Excel and MINITAB you may find it convenient to use Excel when you want to produce an interval using results from a large sample, rather than the sample data and MINITAB when you want to produce an interval using small sample data.

8.1.4 Estimating population proportions

Although we have concentrated on how to estimate population means, these are not the only population measures that can be estimated. You will probably also come across estimates of population proportions, indeed almost certainly you already have done.

If you have ever seen an opinion poll, perhaps about voting intentions or a specific issue, you have seen an estimate of a population proportion. To produce the opinion poll result that you read in a newspaper some organization has interviewed a sample of people and used the sample results to predict the voting intentions of the entire population.

In many ways estimating a population proportion is very similar to the estimation we have already studied. We need a sample, we calculate a sample result around which our estimate will be constructed, and we add and subtract an error based on the standard error of the relevant sampling distribution and how confident we want to be that our estimate is accurate.

We have to adjust our approach because of the different nature of the data. When we estimate proportions we are usually dealing with qualitative variables. The values of these variables are characteristics, for instance people voting for Party A or Party B. If there are only two possible characteristics (or we decide to use only two categories in our analysis) the variable will have a binomial distribution.

As we shall see, this is convenient as it means we only have to deal with one sample result (the sample proportion), but it also means that we cannot produce reliable estimates from small samples, those consisting of less than 30 observations. This is because the population distribution must be Normal if we are to use t distributions in estimation.

The sampling distribution of sample proportions is Normal in shape if the samples involved are large, that is more than 30. If the samples are smaller than that, the sampling distribution of sample proportions will not be Normal.

If we have a large sample, we can construct an interval estimate for the population proportion, p, by taking the sample proportion, $\hat{p}$ ('p-hat'), and adding and subtracting an error. The error is the z value appropriate for the level of confidence we want to use multiplied by the estimate standard error of the sampling distribution of sample proportions. The estimated standard error is based on the sample proportion:

$$\text{Estimated standard error} = \sqrt{\hat{p}(1 - \hat{p})/n}$$

$$\text{So an interval estimate of } p = \hat{p} \pm z_{\alpha/2} \times \sqrt{\hat{p}(1 - \hat{p})/n}$$

Example 8.7

A study of a sample of 110 hotels reveals that 31 have facilities suitable for guests with limited mobility. Construct a 95 per cent interval estimate of the proportion of all hotels that have such facilities.

$$\hat{p} = 31/110 = 0.28$$

$$(100 - \alpha) \text{ per cent} = 95 \text{ per cent, so } z_{\alpha/2} = 1.96$$

interval estimate of p

$$= 0.28 \pm 1.96 \times \sqrt{0.28(1 - 0.28)/110}$$

$$= 0.28 \pm 1.96 \times \sqrt{(0.28 \times 0.72)/110}$$

$$= 0.28 \pm 1.96 \times 0.043 = 0.28 \pm 0.084 = 0.196 \text{ to } 0.364$$

These results suggest that we can be 95 per cent confident that the proportion of hotels with suitable facilities for guests with limited mobility will be between 19.6 per cent and 36.4 per cent.

You can produce estimates of population proportions using MINITAB by selecting **Basic Statistics** from the **Stat** menu. Pick the **1 Proportion** option from the **Basic Statistics** sub-menu. In the command window you can choose to submit **Summarized data**. If you do this you will need to provide the number of trials and the number of successes. In Example 8.7 these numbers were 110 and 31 respectively.

8.2 Hypothesis testing

Usually when we make predictions or estimates about population measures we have no idea of the actual value of the measure we are trying to estimate. Indeed the purpose of estimation using sample results is to tell us what the actual value is likely to be.

Sometimes we use sample results to deal with a different situation. This is where the population measure is claimed to be a particular value and we want to see whether the claim is correct. Such a claim is known as a *hypothesis*, and the use of sample results to investigate whether it is true is called *hypothesis testing*. To begin with we will concentrate on testing hypotheses about population means.

The procedure used in hypothesis testing begins with a formal statement of the claim being made for the population measure. This is known as the *null hypothesis* because it is the starting point in the investigation, and is represented by the symbol H_0 ('aitch-nought').

We could find that a null hypothesis turns out to be wrong, in which case we should reject it in favour of an *alternative hypothesis*, represented by the symbol H_1 ('aitch-one'). The alternative hypothesis is the collection of explanations that contradict the claim made in the null hypothesis.

A null hypothesis may specify a single value for the population measure, in which case we would expect the alternative hypothesis to consist of other values both below and above it. Because of this 'dual' nature of the alternative hypothesis, the procedure to investigate such a null hypothesis is known as a *two-sided test*.

In other cases the null hypothesis might specify a minimum or a maximum value, in which case the alternative hypothesis consists of values below, or values above respectively. The procedure we use in these cases is called a *one-sided test*.

The type of null hypothesis that should be used depends on the context of the investigation and the perspective of the investigator.

Example 8.8

A bus company promotes a 'one-hour' tour of a city. Suggest suitable null and alternative hypotheses for an investigation by:

(a) A tourist who wants to know how long the journey will take.
(b) A travel journalist who wants to see whether tourists are being cheated.

In the first case we might assume that the tourist is as concerned about the tour taking too much time as too little time. So appropriate hypotheses would be that the population mean of the times of the tours is either equal to one hour or not.

H_0: μ = 60 minutes H_1: $\mu \neq 60$ minutes

The symbol '$\neq$' represents 'not equal to'.

In the second case we can assume that the investigation is more focused. The journalist is more concerned that the trips might not take the full hour rather than taking longer than an hour, so appropriate hypotheses would be that the population mean tour time is either one hour or more, or it is less than an hour.

H_0: $\mu \geq 60$ minutes H_1: $\mu < 60$ minutes

Once we have established the form of the hypotheses we can begin to test them using the sample evidence at our disposal. We have to decide whether the sample evidence is compatible with the null hypothesis, in which case we cannot reject it. If the sample evidence contradicts the null hypothesis we reject it in favour of the alternative hypothesis.

To guide us in making this decision we need a *decision rule* that we can apply to our sample evidence. The decision rule is based on the assumption that the null hypothesis is true.

If the population mean really does take the value that the null hypothesis specifies, then if we know the value of the population standard deviation, σ, and the size of our sample, n, we can identify the sampling distribution that our sample belongs to ... if the null hypothesis is true.

Example 8.9

The standard deviation of the bus tours in Example 8.8 is known to be 6 minutes. If the duration of a random sample of 50 tours is to be recorded in order to investigate the operation, what can we deduce about the sampling distribution the mean of the sample will belong to?

The null hypotheses in both sections of Example 8.8 specified a population mean, μ, of 60 minutes. The mean of the sampling distribution, the distribution of means of samples consisting of 50 observations, is therefore 60. If the population standard deviation, σ, is 6, then the standard error of the sampling distribution, $\sigma/\sqrt{n}$, is $6/\sqrt{50}$, 0.85 minutes.

We can conclude that the sample mean of our sample will belong to a sampling distribution with a mean of 60 and a standard error of 0.85, if H_0 is true.

The next stage is to compare our sample mean to the sampling distribution it is supposed to come from, if H_0 is true. If it seems to belong to the sampling distribution, in other words it is not too far away from the centre of the distribution, then we can regard the null hypothesis as plausible. If, on the other hand, the sample mean is located on one of the extremes of the sampling distribution we might regard the null hypothesis as suspect.

We can make this comparison by working out the z-equivalent of the sample mean and using it to find out the probability that a sample mean like the one we have comes from the sampling distribution that is based on the null hypothesis being true. Because we are using a z-equivalent, this type of hypothesis test is sometimes called a z test.

Example 8.10

The mean of the random sample in Example 8.9 is 61.87 minutes. What is the z-equivalent of this sample mean, assuming it belongs to a sampling distribution with a mean of 60 and a standard error of 0.85? Use the z-equivalent to find the probability that a sample mean of this magnitude comes from such a sampling distribution.

$$z = (\bar{x} - \mu)/\sigma/\sqrt{n} = \frac{61.87 - 60}{0.85} = 2.2$$

Using Table 7.1 or appropriate software:

$$P(Z \leq 2.2) \quad = 0.986$$

$$\text{So } P(Z > 2.2) \quad = 1 - 0.986 = 0.014$$

This means $P(\bar{X} > 61.87) = 0.014$ or 1.4 per cent

This is shown in Figure 8.3.

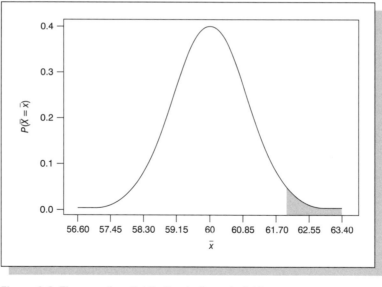

Figure 8.3 The sampling distribution in Example 8.10

Once we know how likely it is that our sample mean belongs to the sampling distribution implied by the null hypothesis, we can make a judgement about the null hypothesis. We have to distinguish between 'acceptable' sample results, those which are compatible with the null hypothesis, and 'unacceptable' sample results, those which conflict with the null hypothesis.

If the probability that a sample mean comes from the sampling distribution that H_0 implies is quite high then it would be 'acceptable'. If it were quite low it would be 'unacceptable'. In Example 8.10 the probability that the sample mean comes from the sampling distributions that H_0 suggests is only 1.4 per cent, a low figure, so we may consider it to be 'unacceptable'.

But what exactly are 'quite high' and 'quite low' probabilities? When you get used to hypothesis testing you may well develop an intuitive 'feel' for what the appropriate dividing line is, but until then you will need to apply a decision rule.

In many practical applications this type of testing is a way of establishing that goods and services meet standards agreed between a supplier and a customer, or between a head office and local management. In these circumstances it is important that a decision rule that defines acceptable sample test results is agreed between the parties involved.

A decision rule should define how low the likelihood of a sample mean has to be before we consider it 'unacceptable'. 'Unacceptable' sample results are often described as *significant*, in the sense that they are significantly different to what the null hypothesis says they should be like. The decision rule specifies what is called the *level of significance*.

If we say that we will use a 5 per cent level of significance in our testing we are saying that if there is less than a 5 per cent chance that a sample mean belongs to the sampling distribution based on H_0 then we will consider it 'unacceptable'. This is a little misleading because it is really the null hypothesis that we would have found to be unacceptable in the light of the sample evidence. So if our sample result is 'unacceptable' we should reject the null hypothesis.

A 5 per cent level of significance means that if the chance that the sort of sample mean our investigation produces does come from the sampling distribution H_0 implies is less than one in twenty, then it is such an unlikely result we believe that the sample evidence disproves the null hypothesis. Another way of putting it is to say that if our sample mean is amongst the 5 per cent least likely to come from the sampling distribution that it should belong to if H_0 were true, then we will reject H_0.

The implication of rejecting H_0 is that the sample mean we have actually belongs to a different sampling distribution, because it is very unlikely to belong to the one that H_0 implies. Very unlikely, but not impossible. The sort of sample mean that our decision rule says is significant, or 'unacceptable', could, just possibly, belong to the sampling distribution H_0 implies. In that case the decision to reject H_0 would be wrong. The level of significance that we specify in a decision rule is also therefore the risk we are prepared to take that we wrongly reject H_0.

When we apply our decision rule we need to take into account the type of null hypothesis we are dealing with. If it suggests that the population mean equals a particular figure we should conduct a two-sided test in order to assess it. That is, if the sample mean we produce is *either* too high *or* too low, then we should reject H_0.

In two-sided tests there are two types of 'unacceptable', or significant, sample result. Because of this if we use a 5 per cent level of significance, the 5 per cent least likely sample means that would lead us to reject the null hypothesis will consist of the lowest $2\frac{1}{2}$ per cent of sample means and the highest $2\frac{1}{2}$ per cent of sample means. If therefore the probability that the sample mean we have belongs to the sampling distribution were less than $2\frac{1}{2}$ per cent, or 0.025, we would reject H_0. We would say that we reject it *at the 5 per cent level*.

Sometimes these lowest and highest extremes of the sampling distribution are called the *rejection regions*, since we reject the null hypothesis if our sample mean is located in one of those parts of the distribution. Another way of applying the decision rule is to use the z values that cut off the tails on the Standard Normal Distribution equivalent to the rejection regions as benchmarks which we compare to the z-equivalent of the sample mean. In this context the z-equivalent of the sample mean is sometimes called the *test statistic*.

In a two-sided, or *two-tail*, test using a 5 per cent level of significance the rejection regions of the furthest $2\frac{1}{2}$ per cent on the left and right sides of the sampling distribution are equivalent to the area of the Standard Normal Distribution beyond the z values -1.96 and $+1.96$ respectively. If the z-equivalent of our sample mean, the test statistic, is either less than -1.96 or greater than $+1.96$, we should reject H_0. This is illustrated in Figure 8.4.

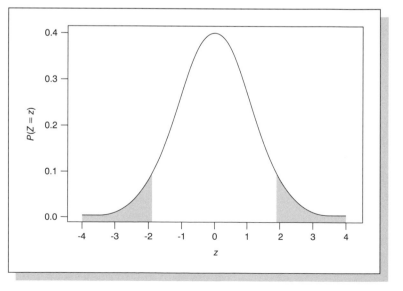

Figure 8.4
Rejection regions for a two-tail test at a 5 per cent level of significance

Example 8.11

Test the hypothesis that the population mean duration of the bus tours in Example 8.8 is 60 minutes, H_0: μ = 60. Use the sample mean given in Example 8.10 and apply a 5 per cent level of significance.

From Example 8.10 we know that the probability that the sample mean, 61.87, belongs to a sampling distribution with a mean of 60 and a standard error of 0.85 is 0.014 or 1.4 per cent. Since this is less than $2\frac{1}{2}$ per cent we can reject the null hypothesis at the 5 per cent level.

Alternatively, we can compare the test statistic, the z-equivalent of the sample mean, 2.2, to the z values that cut off $2\frac{1}{2}$ per cent tails of the Standard Normal Distribution, −1.96 and +1.96. Because it is larger than +1.96, we reject the null hypothesis, our sample evidence suggests that the tours take longer than 60 minutes.

On the other hand, if the null hypothesis suggests that the population mean is less than or equal to a particular figure we conduct a one-sided, or *one-tail*, test. If we do this using a 5 per cent level of significance we reject the null hypothesis if our sample mean is amongst the highest 5 per cent of samples in the sampling distribution that H_0 implies.

Since the null hypothesis includes the possibility that the population mean is lower than a particular value, a very low sample mean is compatible with the null hypothesis. It is only if the sample mean is very high that we would reject H_0.

The decision rule in this case means that if the probability that the sample mean comes from the sampling distribution implied by H_0 is less than 5 per cent or 0.05 and the sample mean is higher than the population mean specified in H_0, then we reject H_0. Alternatively, we could say that if the test statistic, the z-equivalent of our sample mean is higher than 1.64, the z value that cuts off a tail of 5 per cent on the right-hand side of the Standard Normal Distribution, we will reject H_0. This is illustrated in Figure 8.5.

If the null hypothesis states that the population mean is greater than or equal to a particular value, we would also conduct a one-tail test. But this time we would reject the null hypothesis if our sample mean is amongst the lowest 5 per cent of samples in the sampling distribution that H_0 implies.

If the null hypothesis includes the possibility that the population mean is higher than a particular value, a very high sample mean is compatible with the null hypothesis. It is only if the sample mean is very low that we would reject H_0.

Hospitality, Leisure & Tourism Series

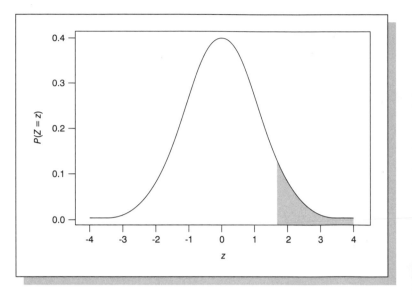

Figure 8.5
Rejection region for a one-tail
test of a 'less than' hypothesis

The decision rule is that if the probability that the sample mean comes from the sampling distribution implied by H_0 is less than 5 per cent or 0.05 and the sample mean is lower than the population mean specified in H_0, then we reject H_0. Alternatively, we could say that if the test statistic were less than -1.64, the z value that cuts off a tail of 5 per cent on the left-hand side of the Standard Normal Distribution, we would reject H_0. This is illustrated in Figure 8.6.

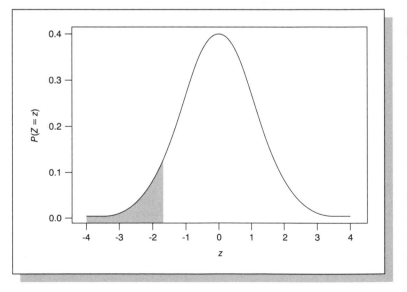

Figure 8.6
Rejection region for a 5 per
cent test of a 'greater than'
hypothesis

Example 8.12

Use the sample mean in Example 8.10 to test the hypothesis that the tours in Example 8.8 take at least 60 minutes, $H_0: \mu \geq 60$, at the 5 per cent level of significance.

The sample mean is 61.87 and in Example 8.10 we found that the probability that it comes from a sampling distribution with a mean of 60 and a standard error of 0.85 was 0.014 or 1.4 per cent. However, because the null hypothesis includes the possibility that the population mean is larger than 60 we cannot reject it.

If we compare the test statistic, 2.2, with the z value that cuts off the 5 per cent tail on the left-hand side of the Standard Normal Distribution, −1.64, we can see that 2.2 cannot be in the rejection region because it is not less than −1.64.

8.2.1 Hypothesis testing without σ

In the hypothesis testing we have looked at so far we have assumed that we know the population standard deviation, σ. This could be the case, particularly if you are trying to find out whether a change had an effect by comparing sample data collected after the change with a previous situation that was well established and known. Perhaps a brewery wants to know if the refurbishment of a pub has a significant effect on trade. In such a case the brewery records are likely to be comprehensive and they could be used to calculate the population standard deviation of the turnover per week. You could then use this figure to calculate the standard error of the sampling distribution that would provide the context for the test.

However in the majority of cases we are unlikely to know the population standard deviation. In these situation the sample size is the first key factor. If our sample evidence comes from a sample that consists of 30 or more observations the sample standard deviation will be sufficiently close to the population standard deviation to allow us to use a z test, that is to base our decision rule on the Standard Normal Distribution. We simply use the sample standard deviation in place of the population distribution when we calculate the standard error, that is instead of $\sigma/\sqrt{n}$ we would use $s/\sqrt{n}$.

Example 8.13

A fast-food chain claims that the burgers in its 'quarter-pounders' have a mean uncooked weight of 4.5 oz. As part of an internal quality control audit a random sample of 40 burgers were weighed. The mean uncooked weight of this sample was 4.39 oz with a standard deviation of 0.29 oz. Do these results support the claim that the mean weight is 4.5 oz? Use a 1 per cent level of significance.

We can assume that the audit is about consistency, in this case to ensure that the burgers are neither too big nor too small, so we should use a two-tail test.

$$H_0: \quad \mu = 4.5 \qquad H_1: \quad \mu \neq 4.5$$

If $\mu = 4.5$, the mean of a sample size of 40 will belong to a sampling distribution that has a mean of 4.5 and a standard error of $0.29/\sqrt{40}$. The test statistic is:

$$z = \frac{4.39 - 4.5}{0.29/\sqrt{40}} = \frac{-0.11}{0.046} = -2.4$$

The probability that a z value is less than -2.4 is 0.0082 or 0.82 per cent.

If we apply a 1 per cent level of significance, this probability must be less than 0.005 or 0.5 per cent in order to reject H_0. In this case we cannot reject H_0.

The z values that cut off tails of $\frac{1}{2}$ per cent are -2.58 and $+2.58$. H_0 cannot be rejected because the test statistic is within rather than outside these values.

8.2.2 Hypothesis testing with small samples

Suppose we want to test a hypothesis using the mean of a sample that consists of less than 30 observations and we don't know the population standard deviation. We can do this but we have to be reasonably sure that the population that the sample comes from is Normal.

The sample standard deviation from a small sample will not be close enough to the population standard deviation to allow us to simply substitute s for σ as we could do with larger samples. This means we have to use t distributions for benchmarks to use in comparing sample results to sampling distributions that null hypotheses imply. Because a t distribution is used you will find that hypothesis tests based on small samples are often called t tests.

Example 8.14

The mean weekly sales of an 'alco-pop' drink at a city centre pub frequented by clubbers is 74.9 units. The manager puts on a special promotion to boost sales of the product. During the five weeks following the promotion the mean sales were 82.4 units per week with a standard deviation of 7.3 units. Test the hypothesis that the promotion has improved sales using a 5 per cent level of significance.

We are only interested in proving that sales have improved, so we need to conduct a one-tail test. The null hypothesis assumes that the sales have not improved, the alternative hypothesis assumes that they have.

$$H_0: \quad \mu \leq 74.9 \qquad H_1: \quad \mu > 74.9$$

The test statistic is $t = \dfrac{(\bar{x} - \mu)}{s/\sqrt{n}} = \dfrac{82.4 - 74.9}{7.3/\sqrt{5}} = \dfrac{7.5}{3.26} = 2.3$

According to Table 8.2 $t_{0.05,4}$ is 2.13, which means that the top 5 per cent of values in a t distribution with 4 degrees of freedom will be greater than 2.13. Our test statistic is larger so we can conclude that there has been a significant increase in sales.

8.2.3 Hypothesis testing using computer software

If you want to use MINITAB to test hypotheses you need to use the same commands as you use to produce estimates, either **1-Sample Z** or **1-Sample t** from the **Basic Statistics** sub-menu in **Stat**. Both of these commands assume that you have stored your sample data in a column in the worksheet.

In the command window for **1-Sample Z** you should specify the column location of your data, then click the **Test mean** button and type into the box next to it the value of the population mean you want to test, i.e. the population mean featured in the null hypothesis. Below this you will see **Alternative**, which invites you to select the type of alternative hypothesis you want to use. The default is **not equal** but if you click the pull-down menu you could select **less than** or **greater than** instead. You will also have to type the value of the population standard deviation in the box next to **Sigma**. If you click the **Graphs** button the package will offer you a selection of diagrams that will portray your data and superimpose on the diagram the population mean being tested.

The command window for **1-Sample t** is very similar to the **1-Sample Z**; the only difference is that you don't have to specify the population standard deviation.

You can test a hypothesis in Excel by typing **=ZTEST (array,x,sigma)** in the **Formula Bar**. The array is the sample data, which must be bracketed, x is the population mean that you want to test, and sigma is the population standard deviation. The result you get, described as a *P*-value, is the probability that the sample mean belongs to the sampling distribution based on the population mean you are testing. *P*-value is an abbreviation of 'population value'.

If you do not provide the population standard deviation the package will use the sample standard deviation instead. This is sound enough if the sample size is at least 30, but the results you get with smaller samples should be treated as rough approximations. There is a separate **TTEST** facility within Excel but it performs more complex tests, such as comparisons between sample means, than the relatively straightforward *t* tests we have considered.

8.2.4 Testing population proportions

In many respects the procedure we use to test hypotheses about population proportions is similar to the way we test other types of hypothesis. We begin with a null hypothesis that specifies a population proportion to be tested, which we represent by the symbol p_0. If the null hypothesis is one of the 'equal to' type we conduct a two-tail test. If it is 'less than' or 'greater than', we conduct a one-tail test.

We calculate the test statistic from the sample proportion, represented by the symbol $\hat{p}$, which comes from the sample data that we want to use to test the hypothesis. We assume that the sample proportion belongs to a sampling distribution that has a mean of p_0 and a standard error of:

$$\sqrt{p_0(1 - p_0)/n}$$

Notice that we use the proportion from the null hypothesis to calculate the standard error, not the sample proportion.

The test statistic is:

$$z = \frac{\hat{p} - p_0}{\sqrt{p_0(1 - p_0)/n}}$$

Because sample proportions are only distributed Normally if they come from large samples, we use the Standard Normal Distribution as the benchmark for the test; in other words it will be a *z* test.

As we have done before we use a decision rule that specifies a level of significance in order to assess the validity of the null hypothesis.

Example 8.15

In her annual report the general manager of a large hotel observes that commercial bookings constituted 32 per cent of the bookings received over the previous year. Out of 146 bookings received for the current year, 40 are commercial bookings. Test the hypothesis that the proportion of commercial bookings in the current year is at least as high as the proportion received last year using a 5 per cent level of significance.

We are interested in proving that the proportion is no lower than it was, so we will use a one-tail test. The hypotheses are:

$H_0: p_0 \geq 0.32$ $H_1: p_0 < 0.32$

The sample proportion, $\hat{p} = 40/146 = 0.274$

The test statistic, $z = \dfrac{\hat{p} - p_0}{\sqrt{p_0(1 - p_0)/n}} = \dfrac{0.274 - 0.32}{\sqrt{0.32(1 - 0.32)/146}}$

$$= -0.046/0.039 = -1.2$$

The probability that Z is -1.2 or less is 0.115, or 11.5 per cent. Since this is more than 5 per cent we cannot reject the null hypothesis.

Another way of assessing the test statistic is to compare it to the z value that cuts off a tail of 5 per cent on the left-hand side of the distribution, -1.64. Because the test statistic is not less than this, the sample result is not significant. We can conclude that, although the sample proportion is lower than the proportion last year, it is not significantly lower.

You can test a hypothesis about a population proportion using MINITAB if you select **1 Proportion** from the **Basic Statistics** selection in the **Stat** menu. You will have to specify whether you have Samples in columns or **Summarized data**. You will also have to click the **Options** button and specify in the **Options** window the **Confidence level** you want to use (100 per cent minus the level of significance), the **Test proportion** featured in the null hypothesis, and the style of the **Alternative** hypothesis. By default MINITAB tests proportions using the appropriate binomial distribution, so to use the Standard Normal Distribution you have to tick the box next to **Use test and interval based on normal distribution**.

Review questions

8.1 Select the appropriate definition from the list on the right-hand side for the terms listed on the left-hand side:

(a) point estimate   (i) the likelihood that an estimate is accurate

(b) z interval   (ii) a result that refutes a null hypothesis

(c) error   (iii) another name for an interval estimate

(d) confidence   (iv) an interval estimate based on a small sample

(e) t interval   (v) a single figure estimate

(f) confidence interval   (vi) an interval estimate based on a large sample

(g) null hypothesis   (vii) the amount added and subtracted to create an interval estimate

(h) significant   (viii) a claim, to be tested, about a population measure.

8.2 The duration of the stay of each of a random sample of 45 people visiting a museum was recorded. The mean length of their visits was 1.85 hours with a standard deviation of 0.64 hours.

(a) Construct a 95 per cent interval estimate for the mean duration of time visitors spend in the museum.
(b) Construct a 99 per cent interval estimate for the mean duration of time visitors spend in the museum.

8.3 A holidaymaker wants to know how much guest-house accommodation will cost in a large seaside resort. A random sample of ten guest houses offer the following rates per night for a double room with breakfast and evening meal:

£35 £26 £29 £22 £27 £28 £32 £38 £30 £32

Construct (a) a 90 per cent interval estimate and (b) a 95 per cent interval estimate for the mean price of this type of accommodation.

8.4 A random sample of 80 restaurant silver-service staff was asked to record their income from tips during one working week. The sample mean was £62.38 with a standard deviation of £18.03.

(a) Construct a 90 per cent interval estimate for the mean income from tips these workers receive.
(b) What sample size would be needed to construct a 95 per cent interval estimate that is no more than £5 wide?

8.5 A survey of 143 licensed premises chosen at random showed that 37 of them had a female manager or assistant manager. Construct a 95 per cent interval estimate for the proportion of licensed premises that have female management staff.

8.6 A ramblers' guide describes a country walk as taking 'the average walker' $2\frac{3}{4}$ hours. A random sample of 40 walkers recorded the time they took to complete the walk. The sample mean was 2.83 hours and the sample standard deviation was 0.31 hours. Test the hypothesis that the mean duration of the walk is 2.75 hours using a 5 per cent level of significance.

8.7 Visitors to a country pub spend an average of £3.28 on alcoholic beverages during Sunday lunchtimes. When the landlord introduces free savoury 'nibbles' at the bar one Sunday lunchtime, the 68 customers spend on average £3.62 on alcoholic beverages, with a standard deviation of £0.47. Test the hypothesis that the availability of the savoury snacks has had no effect on the sales of alcoholic beverages. Use a 1 per cent level of significance.

8.8 The cheese sandwiches supplied by a contract caterer to a large workplace canteen are supposed to contain a mean of 80 g of cheese. A random sample of 25 of these cheese sandwiches was found to contain a mean of 78.5 g of cheese with a standard deviation of 4.8 g. Test the hypothesis that the caterer's sandwiches really do contain 80 g of cheese at the 5 per cent level of significance.

8.9 'Mystery guests' visiting a chain of fast-food restaurants give each restaurant they visit a score out of a hundred. The mean score awarded to restaurants on the UK mainland was 74. When 'Mystery guest' visits were conducted in the 10 restaurants in offshore UK locations, these restaurants were given a mean score of 68.3 with a standard deviation of 6.1. Does this evidence suggest that the performance of these restaurants is significantly worse than those on the UK mainland? Test a suitable hypothesis using a 5 per cent level of significance.

8.10 The mayor of a large island resort claims that no more than 5 per cent of holidaymakers coming to the resort suffer from stomach upsets. Out of a random sample of 110 holidaymakers, 21 reported that they had suffered a stomach upset during their stay. Does this evidence refute the mayor's claim? Use a 1 per cent level of significance to test an appropriate hypothesis.

CHAPTER 9

Statistical decision making using bivariate data

This chapter will help you:

- To analyse the connection between variables.
- To test bivariate models.
- To use bivariate models to make sophisticated predictions.

In this chapter you will find:

- Contingency tests for qualitative data.
- Tests of the correlation coefficient.
- Tests of components of bivariate models.
- Predictions with confidence intervals.
- Guidance on using computer software for statistical inference using bivariate data.

'Looking for the ties that bind . . .'

The purpose of this chapter is to introduce you to methods of statistical inference, or statistical decision making that enable us to draw conclusions about connections between variables in populations based on sample data. The sample data we will be using is described as *bivariate* data because it consists of observed values of two variables. This sort of data is usually collected in order to establish whether there is a connection between the two variables, and if so, what sort of connection it is.

Many organizations use this type of analysis to study consumer behaviour, patterns of costs and revenues, and other aspects of their operations. Sometimes the results of such analysis have far-reaching consequences. For example, if you look at a tobacco product you will see a health warning prominently displayed. It is there because some years ago researchers used these types of statistical methods to establish that there was a connection between tobacco consumption and certain medical conditions.

We shall consider two types of statistical decision-making techniques. The first, tests of association or *contingency*, are designed to investigate connections between qualitative variables, or characteristics. The second are tests that enable us to investigate connections between quantitative variables. The latter usually take the form of bivariate models, and we shall also be looking at how we can use such models to produce confidence intervals for predictions.

9.1 Contingency tests

These tests are used primarily with qualitative data, which is data that consists of different categories of attributes or characteristics. They can help us determine whether one characteristic is associated with, or *contingent* upon, another characteristic. They can be used with quantitative data as long as it discrete data which can take only a very few values or it is arranged in relatively few categories.

If you conduct a questionnaire survey, or have to analyse the results of questionnaire research, you may well want to find out from the data how different characteristics are related to each other. For instance, you may want to look into the possible connection between the gender of respondents and the importance they attach to personal security in hotels. You would need to conduct a contingency test in order to ascertain whether a connection you might find in your sample results is strong enough to enable you to conclude that there is a connection in the population at large. In other words to see if the sample results are *significant*.

Contingency tests are conducted in the same way as the hypothesis tests we looked at in the last chapter. We begin with

Hospitality, Leisure & Tourism Series

a null hypothesis, H_0, which in contingency analysis says that there is no association between the characteristics, whereas the alternative hypothesis, H_1, says that there is an association between them.

The next stage is to analyse the sample results that we want to use to decide which hypothesis is the more plausible. We can start by putting the data into a *contingency table*.

Example 9.1

In a sample survey of consumer preferences in restaurants, 100 respondents were asked if they supported a ban on smoking in restaurants. Of the 40 smokers in the sample, 15 said they supported a ban. Of the 60 non-smokers in the sample, 35 said they supported a ban. Is there a significant connection between whether or not people smoke and their attitude to a smoking ban?

The first stage is to specify suitable hypotheses.

H_0:   There is no association H_1:   There is association

We begin the analysis of the sample results by arranging them in a contingency table.

	Smokers	*Non-smokers*	*Total*
Support ban	15	35	50
Oppose ban	25	25	50
Total	40	60	100

To test the hypotheses the sample results must be combined to produce a measure of contingency, a *test statistic* that we can compare to a benchmark distribution. The test statistic that we use is known as *chi-square* and is represented using the Greek letter chi with a superscript 2, χ^2.

The value of chi-square is calculated by comparing the sample results, which are referred to as the *observed* frequencies and are represented by the letter O, to the results that we would expect if the null hypothesis were true. These values, which we have to work out, are known as the *expected* frequencies and are represented by the letter E.

Example 9.2

Find the results that we would expect to see in the contingency table in Example 9.1 if there is no association between attitude to a smoking ban and whether people smoke.

We can deduce the figures we would expect to see. We know from the totals that the respondents are split equally between the 50 who want a smoking ban in restaurants and the 50 who do not. If there is no association between the attitude that people have towards a ban and whether they smoke or not we would anticipate that both groups, the smokers and the non-smokers, will be evenly split on the issue. In other words if smoking makes no difference to whether people support a ban we would expect the same proportion of smokers as non-smokers to support a ban, and the same proportion of smokers as non-smokers to oppose a ban.

The contingency table would look like this.

	Smokers	Non-smokers	Total
Support ban	20	30	50
Oppose ban	20	30	50
Total	40	60	100

If you look at the table you will see that each group, smokers and non-smokers, has been divided equally between supporters of a ban and opposers of a ban. These figures are the expected figures we need to use in calculating the test statistic. Notice that, although the figures within the table are different, the row and column totals are unchanged.

If you would prefer a rather more formal way of finding expected frequencies you can multiply the row total by the column total and divide the product by the overall total. So to find how many smokers in Example 9.2 we would expect to support a ban, assuming there is no association, we would multiply the total number of smokers by the total number supporting a ban and divide the result by 100, the total number of respondents in the sample. That is:

$$\text{Expected frequency} = \frac{\text{Row total} \times \text{Column total}}{\text{Overall total}}$$

$$= \frac{50 \times 40}{100} = 20$$

Once we have the expected frequencies we can compare them to the observed frequencies, the actual sample results, by putting them together in a single table.

Example 9.3

Produce a contingency table that shows the observed frequencies from Example 9.1 alongside the expected frequencies from Example 9.2. Compare the two sets of frequencies.

In the table below the expected frequencies are shown in brackets:

	Smokers	Non-smokers	Total
Support ban	15 (20)	35 (30)	50
Oppose ban	25 (20)	25 (30)	50
Total	40	60	100

Fewer smokers than we would expect if there were no association support a ban and more non-smokers than we would expect if there were no association support a ban.

The conclusions from Example 9.3 suggest that there is some association in the sample results but is the association strong enough to be significant, in other words does the evidence point to association in the entire population? To find out we need to calculate the test statistic, χ^2.

To do this we subtract each expected frequency from its corresponding observed frequency, then square the result. We will be adding these differences between observed and expected frequencies, so we have to square them otherwise the positive and negative differences will cancel each other out and the test statistic will be of no use. We then divide each squared difference by its expected frequency. This is to *standardize* the test statistic, in other words to enable us to compare it to a standard χ^2 distribution. Finally, we add together the standardized squared differences, we should have one for each section or cell of the contingency table. The total we get is the value of the test statistic, χ^2, for the sample results.

The procedure can be represented using the following formula.

$$\chi^2 = \Sigma(O - E)^2/E$$

Example 9.4

Find the value of χ^2 for the sample data in Example 9.1.

We can work from the contingency table produced in Example 9.3:

	Smokers	Non-smokers
Support ban	15 (20)	35 (30)
Oppose ban	25 (20)	25 (30)

We will start with smokers who support a ban. The observed frequency, O, is 15 and the expected frequency, E, is 20, so:

$$(O - E)^2/E = (15 - 20)^2/20 = 25/20 = 1.25$$

Next we will take the non-smokers who support a ban:

$$(O - E)^2/E = (35 - 30)^2/30 = 25/30 = 0.83$$

Next the smokers who oppose a ban:

$$(O - E)^2/E = (25 - 20)^2/20 = 1.25$$

Last the non-smokers who oppose a ban:

$$(O - E)^2/E = (25 - 30)^2/30 = 0.83$$

The test statistic, χ^2, is the sum of these four results, that is:

$$\chi^2 = 1.25 + 0.83 + 1.25 + 0.83 = 4.16$$

Does the test statistic in Example 9.4 suggest that there is association between whether people smoke or not and their attitude to a smoking ban in restaurants amongst the whole population? We can only establish this by comparing the test statistic to a suitable benchmark distribution.

The type of distribution we will use to assess the test statistic is the *chi-square* distribution, and the procedure is often referred to as a chi-square test. This distribution describes the behaviour of the measure of contingency that we have used, whereas the Standard Normal and t distributions do not. The shape of a typical chi-square distribution is shown in Figure 9.1.

There are in fact many chi-square distributions. The one we use depends on the number of degrees of freedom (DF) we have in

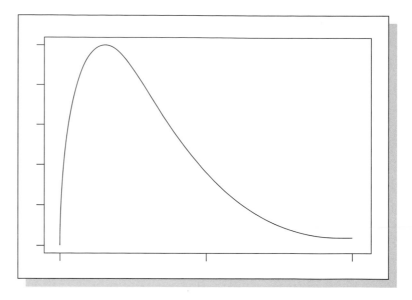

Figure 9.1
A chi-square distribution

our sample results. We can work this out by taking the number of rows in the contingency table, subtracting one, and then multiplying by the number of columns in our contingency table minus one. If we use r to represent the number of rows and c to represent the number of columns:

$$\text{Degrees of freedom} = (r - 1) \times (c - 1)$$

The contingency table in Example 9.4 has two rows and two columns, so the benchmark chi-square distribution is the one that has one degree of freedom. This describes the pattern of chi-square values we would get if we took all the samples we possibly could from a population that had no association between two characteristics, each of which had only two categories, and calculated a chi-square value from each set of sample results.

We need to use the appropriate chi-square distribution to find how likely the test statistic is to arise if there is no association between the characteristics in the population. Using a decision rule that specifies a level of significance we will then be able to arrive at our conclusion.

Although it is possible to find published tables describing chi-square distributions, it is easier to access the one you need using appropriate computer software. The figures in Table 9.1 have been produced using MINITAB.

The first row in Table 9.1 tells us that the probability that χ^2 is larger than 2.71 is 0.10 or 10 per cent. If we wanted to test the null hypothesis of no association at a 10 per cent level of significance, then the test statistic from our sample results would need to be larger than 2.71 in order to reject the null hypothesis.

$P(X^2 \geq \chi^2)$	χ^2
0.10	2.71
0.05	3.84
0.01	6.63

Table 9.1
Chi-square with 1 DF

Table 9.1 also shows that the probability that χ^2 is larger than 3.84 is 0.05 or 5 per cent. If the test statistic is more than this we can reject the null hypothesis at the 5 per cent level of significance. In order to reject the null hypothesis at the 1 per cent level the test statistic would have to be larger than 6.63.

Notice that the larger our test statistic is, the stronger the evidence of association will be. Rejecting the null hypothesis at 1 per cent is far more conclusive than rejecting it at 10 per cent. This is not surprising because the test statistic, χ^2, is based on differences between the actual, or observed, frequencies and those we would expect if there were no association. If there were association then we would anticipate large differences between observed and expected frequencies. If there were no association we would expect small differences.

The test statistic in Example 9.4 was 4.16, which is large enough (larger than 3.84) to enable us to reject the null hypothesis at the 5 per cent level of significance. The sample results suggest that there is association between whether people smoke and their attitude to a smoking ban in restaurants.

An alternative approach is to use computer software to find exactly how likely it is that a χ^2 value of the size of the test statistic or larger occurs, if there is no association in the population. You can do this in MINITAB by selecting **Probability Distributions** from the **Calc** menu and picking the **Chi-Square** option from the sub-menu. In the command window you will need to select **Cumulative probability**, specify the **Degrees of freedom** and specify the test statistic as the **Input constant**. If you try this using the test statistic from Example 9.4, 4.16, you will find that the probability that χ^2 is below 4.16 is 0.9586, so the probability that it is more than 4.16 is 0.0414 or 4.14 per cent. Since this is less than 5 per cent we can reject the null hypothesis at the 5 per cent level of significance and rule out the possibility of no association.

To produce the same figure using Excel, position the cursor in an empty cell and type **=CHIDIST(4.16,1)** in the Formula Bar. The result appears in the cell when you press the **Enter** key.

If you have raw data and you want to use MINITAB to produce a contingency table and test for association, select the **Tables** option from the **Stat** menu, then pick the **Cross Tabulation** option from the sub-menu. You will have to specify the column locations of your data.

Hospitality, Leisure & Tourism Series

If your data is already tabulated you can use MINITAB to test it for association by storing the table in the worksheet and picking the **Chi-Square Test** option from the **Tables** sub-menu. You can perform the same task in Excel by storing the observed frequencies, the 'actual range', in one set of spreadsheet cells, and the expected frequencies, the 'expected range' in another. Type **=CHITEST(actual range,expected range)** in the Formula bar, using the cursor or typing in the cell locations of the **actual range** and the **expected range**.

The set of data we have used to illustrate chi-square tests for association is quite a simple one. In practice we are likely to have more rows and/or columns. Even in the example, we might have had another type of response, perhaps support for non-smoking areas in restaurants, to cope with. Although the table is more elaborate the procedure you have to follow is essentially the same. However there are some important points to remember.

The first is that more rows and columns mean more degrees of freedom, so you must use the correct χ^2 distribution. The second concerns the amount of data. Like other types of statistical testing, all other things being equal, the more data we have the firmer our conclusions will be. We should have enough data to ensure that none of the expected frequencies is less than 5, otherwise our results may be undependable. If any expected frequencies are less than 1, the results of the test will be highly suspect.

If one or more expected frequencies are too low there are two possible solutions. The first is to obtain more data. The second is to merge categories so that there are fewer rows and columns. If you are managing the project yourself you can avoid the problem by planning the research carefully, an issue we will consider in the next chapter.

Example 9.5

In a survey commissioned by a TV travel program, 135 people were asked what their favourite foreign holiday destination was. Some of the results are summarized in the contingency table below:

	Greece	Spain	Thailand	Turkey	USA	Total
Females	4	16	12	10	28	70
Males	3	14	18	10	20	65
Total	7	30	30	20	48	135

Use these sample results to test for association between gender and destination preference using a 5 per cent level of significance.

When we calculate the expected frequencies for Greece we find that for both genders these figures are less than 5.

Expected number of females preferring Greece = $(70 \times 7)/135 = 3.63$
Expected number of males preferring Greece = $(65 \times 7)/135 = 3.37$

These low expected frequencies would weaken the test. We can overcome this by merging the results for the Mediterranean countries.

	Mediterranean	Thailand	USA	Total
Females	30	12	28	70
Males	27	18	20	65
Total	57	30	48	135

The expected values are now:

Expected number of females preferring the Mediterranean = $(70 \times 57)/135 = 29.56$
Expected number of males preferring the Mediterranean = $(65 \times 57)/135 = 27.44$
Expected number of females preferring Thailand = $(70 \times 30)/135 = 15.56$
Expected number of males preferring Thailand = $(65 \times 30)/135 = 14.44$
Expected number of females preferring USA = $(70 \times 48)/135 = 24.88$
Expected number of males preferring USA = $(65 \times 48)/135 = 23.12$

These can now be included in the contingency table.

	Mediterranean	Thailand	USA	Total
Females	30 (29.56)	12 (15.56)	28 (24.88)	70
Males	27 (27.44)	18 (14.44)	20 (23.12)	65
Total	57	30	48	135

The test statistic:

$$\chi^2 = [(30 - 29.56)^2/29.56] + [(12 - 15.56)^2/15.56] + [(28 - 24.88)^2/24.88]$$
$$+ [(27 - 27.44)^2/27.44] + [(18 - 14.44)^2/14.44] + [(20 - 23.12)^2/23.12]$$

$$= 0.0066 + 0.8145 + 0.3913 + 0.0071 + 0.8777 + 0.4210 = 2.5182$$

To find the probability that a χ^2 value of 2.5182 or more occurs if there is no association we use the χ^2 distribution that has two degrees of freedom, since:

$$\text{Degrees of freedom} = (\text{Rows} - 1) \times (\text{Columns} - 1) = (2 - 1) \times (3 - 1) = 2$$

The probability is 0.284 or 28.4 per cent, which means that we cannot reject the null hypothesis of no association at the 5 per cent level of significance. The sample evidence does not suggest that gender and holiday destination preferences are significantly associated.

9.2 Testing and estimating using quantitative bivariate data

The analysis of quantitative bivariate that we looked at in Chapter 4 consisted of two related techniques, correlation and regression. Correlation analysis, which is about the calculation and evaluation of the correlation coefficient, enables us to tell whether there is a connection between the observed values of two variables. Regression analysis, which is about fitting lines of best fit, enables us to find the equation of the line that is most appropriate for the data, the so-called regression or bivariate model.

In this section we will consider how the results from applying correlation and regression to sample data can be used to test hypotheses and make estimates for the populations the sets of sample data belong to.

9.2.1 Testing correlation coefficients

The correlation coefficient, represented by the letter r, measures the extent of the linear association between two variables, X and Y. You can find the correlation coefficient of a set of bivariate data using computer software, or the formula:

$$r = \text{Cov}_{XY}/(s_x \times s_y)$$

where

$$\text{Cov}_{XY} = \Sigma(x - \bar{x})(y - \bar{y})/(n - 1)$$

and s_x and s_y are the standard deviations of the x and y values respectively.

If we select a random sample from populations of X and Y that are *both* Normal in shape, the correlation coefficient calculated from the sample data will be a legitimate estimate of the population coefficient, represented by the Greek r, the letter rho, ρ. In fact the main reason for calculating the sample correlation coefficient is to find out if there is any linear association between the X and Y populations.

The value of the sample correlation coefficient alone is some help in assessing correlation between the populations, but a more thorough approach is to test the null hypothesis that the population correlation coefficient is zero:

$$H_0: \rho = 0$$

The alternative hypothesis we use depends on what we would like to prove. If we are interested in demonstrating that there is significant correlation in the population, then we should use:

$$H_1: \quad \rho \neq 0$$

If we would like to show that there is significant positive correlation in the population:

$$H_1: \quad \rho > 0$$

If we want to indicate that there is significant negative correlation in the population:

$$H_1: \quad \rho < 0$$

If we adopt the first of these versions of the alternative hypothesis, $H_1: \rho \neq 0$, we will need to use a two-tail test, if we use one of the other forms we will conduct a one-tail test.

Once we have established the nature of our alternative hypothesis we need to calculate the test statistic from our sample data. The test statistic:

$$t = \frac{r\sqrt{n-2}}{\sqrt{1-r^2}}$$

where r is the sample correlation coefficient and n is the number of pairs of observations in the sample.

As long as the populations of X and Y are Normal the test statistic will belong to a t distribution with $n - 2$ degrees of freedom and a mean of zero, *if* there is no linear association between the populations of X and Y.

Example 9.6

The proprietor of a take-away business believes that the temperature outside and the number of cans of soft drinks sold are connected. She noted the maximum daytime temperature (in degrees Celsius) and the soft drinks sales on 10 working days chosen at random:

Temperature (°C)	Cans sold
14	19
11	29
17	47
8	12
20	45
13	41
24	67
3	10
16	28
5	21

The correlation coefficient for this sample is 0.871. Test the hypothesis that there is no correlation between temperature and sales at the 5 per cent level of significance. The test statistic:

$$t = \frac{r\sqrt{n-2}}{\sqrt{1-r^2}} = \frac{0.871 \times \sqrt{10-2}}{\sqrt{1-0.871^2}}$$

$$= \frac{0.871 \times \sqrt{8}}{\sqrt{0.24}} = \frac{0.871 \times 2.83}{0.49} = 5.02$$

We need to compare this test statistic to the t distribution that has $n-2$, which in this case is 8 degrees of freedom. The values of t that cut off $2\frac{1}{2}$ per cent tails at either end of this t distribution are -2.306 and 2.306. Since the test statistic is clearly larger than 2.306 we can reject the null hypothesis at the 5 per cent level of significance. The sample evidence strongly suggests that there is correlation between temperature and sales.

We can reach the same conclusion by finding the probability that t with 8 degrees of freedom is 5.02 or larger, which is 0.001 or 0.1 per cent.

MINITAB enables you to test hypotheses about population correlation coefficients without having to calculate a test statistic by providing something called a *P-value* alongside the sample correlation coefficient. You can look at this if you put the data from Example 9.6 in two columns of the worksheet and select

Basic Statistics from the Stat menu. Pick Correlation from the Basic Statistics sub-menu and specify the column locations of your data in the command window, checking that there is a cross in the box next to Display p-values. You should see the following:

Correlation of Temperature and Sales = 0.871

P-value = 0.001

The P-value, or *population value*, is the probability that the null hypothesis of no population correlation is true. If it is below the level of significance in our decision rule, as it is in this case, we can reject the null hypothesis and conclude that there is significant population correlation.

The P-value that MINITAB gives us is based on the assumption that the alternative hypothesis is H_1: $\rho \neq 0$ and therefore the test is a two-tail test. The P-value in this case is therefore the probability that r is 0.871 or more, or *-0.871 or less*. If we want to use another form of alternative hypothesis, one that requires a one tail-test, we would have to divide the P-value by two.

9.2.2 Testing bivariate models

The second technique used to analyse quantitative bivariate data is simple linear regression analysis, the method we used in Chapter 4 to find the equation of the line of best fit between two variables, X and Y. Such a line has two distinguishing features, its intercept and its slope. In the standard formula we used for the line the intercept was represented by the letter a and the slope by the letter b:

$$Y = a + bX$$

The line that this equation describes is the best way of representing the connection between the dependent variable, Y, and the independent variable, X. In practice it is almost always the result of a sample investigation that is intended to shed light on the connection between the populations of X and Y. That is why we have used ordinary rather than Greek letters in the equation.

The results of such a sample investigation can provide an understanding of the relationship between the populations. The intercept and slope of the line of best fit for the sample are point or single-figure estimates for the intercept and slope of the line of best fit for the populations, which are represented by the Greek equivalents of a and b, α and β:

$$Y = \alpha + \beta X$$

The intercept and slope from the analysis of the sample can be used to test hypotheses about the equivalent figures for the populations. Typically we use null hypotheses which suggest that the population values are zero:

$$H_0: \quad \alpha = 0 \quad \text{for the intercept}$$

and

$$H_0: \quad \beta = 0 \quad \text{for the slope}$$

If the population intercept is zero, the population line of best fit will be represented by the equation $Y = 0 + \beta X$, and the line will begin at the origin of the graph, that is where both X and Y are zero. You can see this type of line in Figure 9.2.

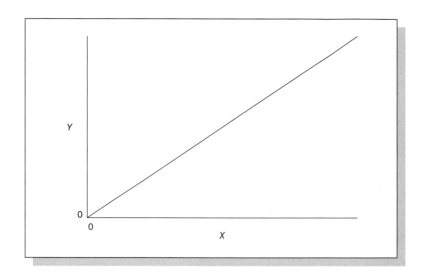

Figure 9.2
$Y = 0 + \beta X$

If we wanted to see whether the population intercept is likely to be zero, we would test the null hypothesis $H_0: \alpha = 0$ against the alternative hypothesis:

$$H_1: \quad \alpha \neq 0$$

When you use regression analysis you will find that investigating the value of the intercept is rarely important. Occasionally it is of interest, for instance, if we are looking at the connection between an organization's levels of operational activity and its total costs at different periods of time, the intercept of the line of best fit represents the organization's fixed costs.

Typically we are much more interested in evaluating the slope of the line of best fit. The slope is pivotal; it tells us how the dependent variable responds to changes in the independent variable. For this reason the slope you will find is also known as the *coefficient* of the independent variable.

If the population slope turns out to be zero, it would tell us that the dependent variable does not respond to the independent variable. The implication of this is that our independent variable is of no use in explaining how our dependent variable behaves and there would be no point in using it to make predictions of our dependent variable.

If the slope of the line of best fit is zero, the equation of the line would be $Y = \alpha + 0X$, and the line would be perfectly horizontal. You can see this illustrated in Figure 9.3.

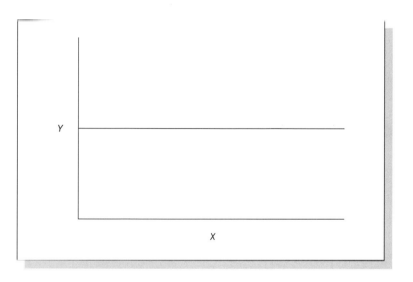

Figure 9.3
$Y = \alpha + 0X$

The line in Figure 9.3 shows that whatever the value of X, whether it is a small one to the left of the horizontal axis or a large one to the right of the horizontal axis, the value of Y remains the same. The size of the x value has no impact on Y whatsoever, and the regression model is useless.

We usually want to use regression analysis to find useful rather than useless models, that is regression models that do help us to understand and anticipate the behaviour of dependent variables. Therefore, in order to demonstrate that a model is valid, it is important that we test the null hypothesis that the slope is zero. Hopefully, the sample evidence will enable us to reject the null hypothesis in favour of the alternative, that the slope is not zero, and we can proceed to use our model.

The test statistic we shall use to test the hypothesis is:

$$t = \frac{b - 0}{s_b}$$

where b is the sample slope, 0 is the value of the population slope suggested by the null hypothesis, and s_b is the estimated standard error of the sampling distributions of sample slopes.

Hospitality, Leisure & Tourism Series

We calculate the estimated standard error, s_b, by dividing s^2, the square of the standard deviation of the sample residuals, that is the parts of the y values that the line of best fit does not explain, by the sum of the squared deviations between the x values and their mean, $\overline{x}$, then taking the square root. That is:

$$s_b = \sqrt{s^2/\Sigma(x - \overline{x})^2}$$

Once we have the test statistic we can assess it by comparing it to the t distribution that has $n - 2$ degrees of freedom, two fewer than the number of pairs of x and y values in our sample data.

Example 9.7

The equation of the line of best fit for the sample data in Example 9.6 is:

Sales = 0.74 + 2.38 Temperature

Test the hypothesis that the population slope is zero using a 5 per cent level of significance. The null hypothesis is:

H_0: $\beta = 0$

The alternative hypothesis is:

H_1: $\beta \neq 0$

To find the test statistic we first need to calculate the standard deviation of the residuals. We can identify the residuals by taking each x value, putting it into the equation of the line of best fit and then working out what Y 'should' be, according to the model. The difference between the y value that the equation says should be associated with the x value and the y value that is actually associated with the x value is called the residual.

To illustrate this, we will look at the first pair of values in our sample data, a day when the temperature was 14°C and 19 cans of soft drink were sold. If we insert the temperature into the equation of the line of best fit we can use the equation to estimate the number of cans that 'should' have been sold on that day:

Sales = 0.74 + (2.38 × 14) = 34.06

The residual is the difference between the actual sales level, 19, and this estimate, that is:

Residual = 19 − 34.06 = 15.04

The standard deviation of the residuals is based on the squared residuals. The residuals and their squares are given in the table below.

Temperature	Sales	Residuals	Squared residuals
14	19	−15.04	226.23
11	29	2.10	4.39
17	47	5.82	33.91
8	12	−7.77	60.35
20	45	−3.31	10.98
13	41	9.34	87.20
24	67	9.17	84.12
3	10	2.13	4.52
16	28	−10.80	116.61
5	21	8.37	70.02
			698.33

We find the standard deviation of the residuals by taking the square root of the sum of the squared residuals divided by n, the number of residuals, minus two. (We have to subtract two because we have 'lost' two degrees of freedom in using the intercept and slope to calculate the residuals.)

$$s = \sqrt{698.33/n - 2} = \sqrt{698.33/8} = 9.343$$

To get the estimated standard error we divide this by the sum of squared differences between the temperature figures and their mean.

Temperature (x)	$\bar{x}$	$x - \bar{x}$	$(x - \bar{x})^2$
14	13.1	0.9	0.81
11	13.1	−2.1	4.41
17	13.1	3.9	15.21
8	13.1	−5.1	26.01
20	13.1	6.9	47.61
13	13.1	−0.1	0.01
24	13.1	10.9	118.81
3	13.1	−10.1	102.01
16	13.1	2.9	8.41
5	13.1	−8.1	65.61
			388.90

The estimated standard error:

$$s_b = \sqrt{s^2/\Sigma(x - \bar{x})^2} = \sqrt{9.343^2/388.90} = 0.4738$$

The test statistic:

$$t = (b - 0)/s_b = 2.38/0.4738 = 5.02$$

The probability that a sample slope as large as this arises if there is a zero slope in the population regression model is 0.001 or 0.1 per cent. This is considerably lower than the 5 per cent level of significance so we can conclusively reject the null hypothesis, the sample evidence suggests that the population slope is not zero.

The implication of the sort of result we arrived at in Example 9.7 is that the model, represented by the equation, is sufficiently sound to enable the temperature variable to be used to predict sales.

If you compare the test statistic for the sample slope in Example 9.7 with the test statistic for the sample correlation coefficient in Example 9.6, you will see that they are both 5.02. This is no coincidence; the two tests are equivalent. The slope represents the form of the association between the variables whereas the correlation coefficient measures its strength. We use the same data in the same sort of way to test the rigour of each of them.

The calculations we had to employ in Example 9.7 are quite laborious, but they should enable you to see how the data is used to produce the conclusion. However, you should seldom, if ever, have to work through this sort of calculation yourself. Regression analysis is a statistical techniques that is very widely used which means that just about every spreadsheet and statistical package will be able to do this sort of work for you.

MINITAB will produce a regression analysis that includes p-values for both the sample intercept and slope. You can obtain it by selecting **Regression** from the **Stat** menu and **Regression** from the **Regression** sub-menu. Try putting the data from Example 9.6 into two columns in the worksheet then specify in the command window the location of the sales figures in the **Response** box and the location of the temperature figures in the **Predictor** box. You should see in the session window an analysis that includes:

The regression equation is

Sales = 0.74 + 2.38 Temperature

Predictor	Coef	StDev	T	P
Constant	0.738	6.874	0.11	0.917
Temperature	2.3788	0.4738	5.02	0.001

S = 9.343

You may recognize some of these figures from Example 9.7. At the top there is the equation of the line of best fit derived from the sample data.

In the next block of output the column headed 'Predictor' contains the two components of the model that we would like to use to predict the sales on the basis of the temperature, the 'Constant' (the intercept) and the temperature variable. The 'Coef', or coefficient column, lists the numerical values of the sample intercept and the sample slope. Under the next heading, 'StDev', standard deviation, we have the estimated standard errors of first the sample intercepts then the sample slopes. The

'T' column contains the test statistics based on first the sample intercept then the sample slope. Finally, the 'P' column contains the '*p*-values' for the sample intercept and the sample slope.

The value labelled S at the bottom is the standard deviation of the residuals. You should recognize this figure as well as the figures in the 'Temperature' row of output.

We can use the figures listed in the 'P' column to assess the hypotheses that the population intercept and slope are zero. The first 'P' value is the probability that we obtain a sample intercept of 0.738 if the population intercept is zero, often described as the probability that the null hypothesis (a population intercept of zero) is true. The 'P' value 0.917 indicates that there is a strong possibility that the population intercept is zero.

The second 'P' value, 0.001 is of more interest. This is the probability that the sample slope is 2.3788 or more if the population slope is zero, or we could say that it is the probability that the null hypothesis (a population slope of zero) is true. Since the figure is well below the level of significance, 5 per cent or 0.05 we would emphatically reject the null hypothesis.

You can use Excel to produce the same analysis, although it will appear in a different sequence, by selecting **Data Analysis** from the **Tools** menu. Pick the **Regression** option from the sub-menu and then provide the cell locations of the values of X and Y. The output will include Table 9.2.

Table 9.2

	Coefficients	Standard error	*t* Stat	*P*-value
Intercept	0.738236	6.873624	0.107401	0.917115
X variable	2.378761	0.473761	5.021009	0.001026

The figures here are the same as the ones we have derived by calculation and using MINITAB. It is the second row that contains the information that we need to assess the null hypothesis that the slope, the coefficient on the X variable, is zero.

9.2.3 Constructing interval predictions

When we use a regression model to make a prediction, as we had to do in Example 9.7 to obtain the residuals, we have a single figure that is the value of Y that the model suggests should be associated with the value of X that we specify.

Example 9.8

Use the regression model in Example 9.7 to predict the level of sales that will be achieved on a day when the temperature is 22° Celsius.

If temperature = 22, according to the regression equation:

Sales = 0.74 + 2.38 (22) = 53.1

Since the number of cans sold is a discrete variable, in practice we would round this to 53 cans.

The problem with all single-figure predictions is that we simply have no idea of how likely they are to be accurate. It is far better to have an interval that we know, with a certain amount of confidence, will be accurate.

Before we look at how we can produce such intervals, we need to clarify exactly what we want to find. The figure we produced in Example 9.8 we described as a *prediction* of sales on a day when the temperature is 22°C. In fact it can also be used as an *estimate* of the mean level of sales that occur on days when the temperature is 22°C. Because it is a single figure it is a point estimate of the sales levels on such days.

We can construct an interval estimate, or confidence interval of the mean level of sales on days when the temperature is at a particular level by taking the point estimate and adding and subtracting an error. The error is the product of the standard error of the sampling distribution of the point estimates and a figure from the appropriate t distribution. The t distribution we use should have $n - 2$ degrees of freedom, n being the number of pairs of data in our sample, and the t value we select from it is based on the level of confidence we want to have that our interval estimate will be accurate.

We can express this procedure using the formula:

$$\text{Confidence interval} = \hat{y} \pm t_{\alpha/2, n-2} \times s \sqrt{\frac{1}{n} + \frac{(x_0 - \bar{x})^2}{\Sigma(x - \bar{x})^2}}$$

where $\hat{y}$ is the point estimate of the mean of the y values associated with x_0 and s is the standard deviation of the sample residuals.

Example 9.9

Construct a 95 per cent confidence interval for the mean sales of soft drinks that the proprietor of the take-away in Example 9.6 can expect on days when the temperature is 22° Celsius.

From Example 9.8 we know that the point estimate for the mean, $\hat{y}$, is 53.1 cans. We will use the original, unrounded figure because the mean, unlike sales on a particular day, does not have to be discrete. We also know from Example 9.8 that s, the standard deviation of the sample residuals, is 9.343, $\bar{x}$ is 13.1, and $\Sigma(x - \bar{x})^2$ is 388.90.

The t value we need is 2.306, the value that cuts off a tail of $2\frac{1}{2}$ per cent in the t distribution that has 10–2, 8, degrees of freedom. The value of x_0, the temperature on the days whose mean sales figure we want to estimate, is 22.

$$\text{Confidence interval} = \hat{y} \pm t_{\alpha/2, n-2} \times s\sqrt{\frac{1}{n} + \frac{(x_0 - \bar{x})^2}{\Sigma(x - \bar{x})^2}}$$

$$= 53.1 \pm 2.306 \times 9.343 \sqrt{(1/10 + (22 - 13.1)^2/388.90)}$$

$$= 53.1 \pm 2.306 \times 9.343 \sqrt{0.304}$$

$$= 53.1 \pm 2.306 \times 5.15$$

$$= 53.1 \pm 11.87 = 41.23 \text{ to } 64.97$$

The confidence interval we produced in Example 9.9 is a reliable guide to what the mean sales are on days when the temperature is 22°C. This is because, although this level of temperature is not amongst the temperature values in our sample data, it is within the range of the temperatures in our sample data, which is from a minimum of 3°C to a maximum of 24°C.

If we produce a confidence interval for the mean of the y values associated with an x value outside the range of x values in the sample it will be both wide and unreliable.

Example 9.10

Construct a 95 per cent confidence interval for the mean sales of cans of soft drinks in the take-away establishment in Example 9.6 on days when the temperature is 35°C.

The point estimate for the mean, $\hat{y} = 0.74 + 2.38\,(35) = 84.04$

$$\text{Confidence interval} = \hat{y} \pm t_{\alpha/2, n-2} \times s \sqrt{\frac{1}{n} + \frac{(x_0 - \bar{x})^2}{\Sigma(x - \bar{x})^2}}$$

$$= 84.04 \pm 2.306 \times 9.343 \sqrt{(1/10 + (35 - 13.1)^2/388.90)}$$

$$= 84.04 \pm 2.306 \times 9.343 \sqrt{1.33}$$

$$= 84.04 \pm 2.306 \times 10.79$$

$$= 84.04 \pm 24.88 = 59.16 \text{ to } 108.92$$

The confidence interval we produced in Example 9.10 is of no real use to us because the temperature on which it is based, 35°C, is beyond the range of temperatures in our sample. Confidence intervals produced from regression lines will be wider when they are based on x values further away from the mean of the x values.

If we want to produce a prediction of an individual value rather than an estimate of a mean of a set of values, with a given level of confidence, we can do so by producing what is called a *prediction interval*. This is to distinguish this type of forecast from a confidence interval, which is a term reserved for estimates of population measures.

The procedure we use to produce prediction intervals is very similar to the one we have used to produce confidence intervals for means of values of dependent variables. It is represented by the formula:

$$\text{Prediction interval} = \hat{y} \pm t_{\alpha/2, n-2} \times s \sqrt{1 + \frac{1}{n} + \frac{(x_0 - \bar{x})^2}{\Sigma(x - \bar{x})^2}}$$

If you look carefully you can see that the difference between this and the formula for a confidence interval is that we have added one to the expression on the right of the square root sign. The effect of this will be to widen the interval considerably. This is to reflect the fact that individual values vary more than statistical measures like means, which are based on sets of values.

Example 9.11

Construct a 95 per cent prediction interval for the sales of cans of soft drinks in the take-away establishment in Example 9.6 on a day when the temperature is 22°C.

$$\text{Prediction interval} = \hat{y} \pm t_{\alpha/2, n-2} \times s \sqrt{1 + \frac{1}{n} + \frac{(x_0 - \bar{x})^2}{\Sigma(x - \bar{x})^2}}$$

$$= 53.1 \pm 2.306 \times 9.343 \sqrt{1 + (1/10 + (22 - 13.1)^2/388.90)}$$

$$= 53.1 \pm 2.306 \times 9.343 \sqrt{1.304}$$

$$= 53.1 \pm 2.306 \times 10.67$$

$$= 53.1 \pm 24.60 = 28.50 \text{ to } 77.70$$

If you compare the prediction interval in Example 9.11 to the confidence interval in Example 9.9 you will see that the prediction interval is much wider, although the level of confidence involved, 95 per cent, is the same.

Just like confidence intervals produced using regression models, prediction intervals are more dependable if they are based on x values nearer the mean of the x values. Prediction intervals based on x values that are well outside the range that we have in our sample are of very little use.

Producing interval estimates from regression models is rather laborious when we have to use a formula and carry out the calculations ourselves. MINITAB will produce both confidence intervals and prediction intervals for you. Select **Regression** from the **Stat** menu then **Regression** from the sub-menu. Specify the column locations of the **Response** and **Predictor** variables, that is Y and X respectively, in the command window then click the **Options** button. In the **Options** window there is a box labelled **Prediction intervals for new observations**. Type the x value that you want the package to use to produce the intervals in the box, then **OK**. If you want intervals based on several different x values, put them in a column in the worksheet and type the column location in the **Prediction intervals for new observations** box. The confidence and prediction intervals, labelled 'CI' and 'PI' respectively, will appear at the end of the regression analysis.

The usefulness of the estimates that you produce from a regression model depends to a large extent on the size of the sample that you have. The larger the sample on which your regression model is based, the more precise and confident your predictions and estimates will be.

As we have seen, the width of the intervals increases the further the x value is away from the mean of the x values, and estimates and predictions based on x values outside the range of x values in our sample are suspect. So, if you know that you want to construct intervals based on specific values of x, try to ensure that these values are within the range of x values in your sample.

Review questions

9.1 Select the appropriate definition from the list on the right-hand side for the terms and symbols listed on the left-hand side.

(a) ρ		(i)	the intercept of the population regression line
(b) contingency test		(ii)	an interval estimate of a population measure
(c) χ^2		(iii)	the probability that a null hypothesis is true
(d) α		(iv)	the slope of the population regression line
(e) β		(v)	the population correlation coefficient
(f) p-value		(vi)	an interval estimate of an individual value
(g) confidence interval		(vii)	a test of association between characteristics
(h) prediction interval		(viii)	a test statistic used in tests of association

9.2 A sample of adults was asked whether they agreed or disagreed with the statement 'zoos are a legitimate leisure attraction'. The respondents were also asked if they had children. The results are summarized in the table below.

	Agree	Disagree
Respondents with children	32	18
Respondents without children	25	28

Test the hypothesis that there is no association between attitude towards zoos and whether or not people have children. Use a 5 per cent level of significance. (The value of χ^2 with one degree of freedom that cuts off a 0.05, or 5 per cent, tail is 3.841.)

9.3 A sample of tourists on package holidays were asked if they would buy a holiday through the internet. They were also asked if they had previously bought a holiday using the internet. The results were as follows:

	Would use internet	Would not use internet
Previously used internet	15	6
Not previously used internet	31	52

Test the null hypothesis that there is no association between previous use of the internet to book a holiday and inclination to use it in the future. Use a 1 per cent level of significance. (The value of χ^2 with one degree of freedom that cuts off a 0.01, or 1 per cent, tail is 6.635.)

9.4 A random sample of male beer drinkers were asked if they preferred to drink bitter or lager. They were also asked to give their age. The results were processed and the following table produced:

	Prefer lager	Prefer bitter
Under 30	27	12
30–45	18	23
Over 45	7	15

Test the null hypothesis that there is no association between preference and age using a 5 per cent level of significance. (The value of χ^2 with two degrees of freedom that cuts off a 0.05, or 5 per cent, tail is 5.991.)

9.5 A random sample of 124 customers using fast-food restaurants were each asked which one of four aspects of these restaurants they rated as most important: cleanliness, speed of service, quality of the food, and value for money. The results were then tabulated against the gender of the respondent.

	Cleanliness	Speed	Quality	Value
Females	26	10	7	19
Males	8	17	14	23

Test the hypothesis that there is no association between gender and the opinions of the respondents in the survey. Use a 0.05 or 5 per cent level of significance. (The value of χ^2 with three degrees of freedom that cuts off a 0.05, or 5 per cent, tail is 7.815.)

9.6 A company that owns a chain of licensed premises commissioned a report that would explore the relationship between the beverage and non-beverage sales in its public houses. Researchers studied the sales records of a random sample of 21 establishments and found a correlation coefficient of 0.46. Test the hypothesis that there is no correlation between the two categories of sales using a 0.05, or 5 per cent, level of significance ($t_{0.025,19} = 2.09$).

9.7 A freelance promoter stages 'retro' discos on an occasional basis at a large city-centre venue. Teams of casual employees handing out 'discount' ticket cards at college and music venues advertise these events. The number of cards handed out before each of the ten events staged so far, and the audience they attracted, are given below.

Number of cards	3750	4100	4500	4750	4800	5250	4600	4800	4320
Audience	925	1000	1150	1200	1100	1680	1480	1370	860

(a) Calculate the correlation coefficient, r, and use it to test whether there is a significant correlation between the number of cards handed out and the audience at the event. Use a 5 per cent level of significance ($t_{0.025,7} = 2.365$).

(b) Find the regression equation and test the hypothesis, at the 5 per cent level of significance, that the population slope is zero.

9.8 A new hotel is being built 15 miles from the location of a prominent annual sporting event. A study of the number of inquiries received by a random sample of 9 established hotels in the area showed that the number of inquiries and the distances, in miles, between the hotels and the event were:

Inquiries	35	61	74	92	113	159	188	217	328
Distance	28	20	17	12	16	8	2	3	1

(a) Find the regression equation and test the hypothesis, at the 5 per cent level of significance, that the population slope is zero ($t_{0.025,7} = 2.365$).

(b) Produce a 95 per cent confidence interval for the mean number of inquiries that hotels 15 miles from the event could expect.

(c) Produce a 95 per cent prediction interval for the number of inquiries that a hotel 15 miles from the event could expect.

9.9 In the process of preparing the company accounts, a contract caterer finds records of the number of guests and the final profit the company made at 8 functions that the company undertook during the previous year.

Number of guests	100	120	140	250	420	470	580	650
Profit (£)		275	192	380	372	518	611	546	973

There is no reason why these figures cannot be treated as if they were from a random sample.

(a) Find the regression equation and test the hypothesis that the population slope is zero at the 5 per cent level of significance ($t_{0.025,6} = 2.447$).

(b) Produce a 95 per cent confidence interval for the mean profit from functions that accommodate 300 guests.

(c) Produce a 95 per cent prediction interval for the profit the company could expect from a function for 300 guests.

9.10 A college canteen has a selection of pre-packed sandwiches on sale. The prices of each of the 10 types of sandwich on sale and the number sold on a single day selected at random were:

Price (£) 1.10 1.20 1.25 1.30 1.45 1.50 1.65 1.80 1.95 2.00
Sales   27   23   20   24   17   14   7   12   3   6

(a) Find the best-fit regression model and test the null hypothesis that the slope of the population line of best fit is zero using a 1 per cent level of significance $(t_{0.005,8} = 3.355)$.

(b) Obtain confidence intervals for the mean sales of sandwiches that cost (i) £1.75 and (ii) 2.50. Which of these estimates is likely to be the more reliable, and why?

CHAPTER 10

Managing statistical research

This chapter will help you:

- To plan statistical work for a project.
- To consider different means of obtaining data.
- To undertake sample surveys.
- To present your results effectively.

In this chapter you will find:

- Suggestions on managing time for statistical research.
- Advice on using secondary data.
- Approaches to sample selection.
- Guidance on questionnaire design.

'Going solo . . .'

When you reach the final stage of your course, or possibly earlier, you will probably be told that one of the course requirements is that you produce a final year project or dissertation. This typically means that you have to identify a project idea, write a project proposal, undertake research to investigate your project idea, and then produce a substantial written document that delivers your findings.

You may see this as a daunting task, particularly when you are trying to think of ideas for a project, but if you approach it positively and manage the task well you can get a great deal out of it. A good final year project could improve the grade of the qualification that you receive. It could also be a useful document to show potential employers as an example of your work.

Your project is probably the first, if not the only time during your course when your tutors offer you the opportunity to study what you like. The parts of your course that you have done so far have probably consisted of studying things that somebody else has decided you should do. Your project is different; it is 'your baby'.

It is very hard to produce a good project if you are not committed to it, so it is worth putting time and effort into thinking up three or four possible ideas at a very early stage. But how can you generate project ideas? It may help if you ask yourself a series of questions:

- Which parts of the course have I enjoyed most?

- Were there any particularly interesting aspects of my experience of work?

- What interests do I have outside my studies?

- What are my academic strengths?

- Do I have any special contacts and resources at my disposal?

Make a list of your responses to these questions. Look at the responses in relation to one another, perhaps there are some interesting combinations? You may have enjoyed marketing as a subject, you may have worked in a catering facility at a football ground on a part-time basis, and you may have a strong interest in football. If all this is true then perhaps a project that looks into how football clubs market food and beverages at their grounds is possible.

If you have thought about your responses and no project ideas come to mind, try talking through your responses with somebody else, perhaps a friend or a tutor. It doesn't matter too much if that person is not involved with your course, simply explaining your thinking to somebody else may prompt some excellent project ideas.

Once you have established at least one viable project idea you will probably have to shape your outline ideas into a formal

Hospitality, Leisure & Tourism Series

proposal and carry out some sort of literature survey. A good proposal will identify specific propositions and hypotheses that your project is intended to investigate. A good literature survey will find what published material is available on the subject you have chosen. This is important because it will influence the nature and scope of the research you will have to undertake.

At this stage you need to consider the data that you will need for your investigation. Perhaps the data is available from published or electronic sources, if not, you will have to consider how you can obtain it yourself. In fact you will probably find that some of the data you need is already available but other data will need to be collected.

Data that is already available, perhaps in a publication in a library or on the internet, is there because somebody else collected and analysed it. As far as you are concerned it is *secondary* data, in other words 'second hand'. Whoever has produced it did so to fulfil their own requirements rather than yours, so be careful.

As we shall see later on in this chapter when you collect data yourself, that is when you gather *primary* or first-hand data, you will have to decide what to ask, who to ask, and so on. These are issues that require careful thought.

Whether the data you analyse in your work is primary or secondary, you will have to consider how to present the analysis in your final document. This is something we will consider in the last section of the chapter.

10.1 Secondary data

If you use secondary data it is the person or agency that collected the data that has decided how the data was collected. You have had no say in the matter. You also have had no say in the way in which the data is presented to you. It may be that the secondary data that you have found is exactly what you require for your investigation, and it could be already presented in a form that will suit your purposes. But you need to look into both of these issues carefully.

There are a number of questions you should consider about the collection of secondary data. First, exactly when was it collected? Published results are by definition historic, they relate to the past. This is inevitable because publication takes time. The data may be fairly recent if it is in a journal or on a web site, but may be much older if it is in a book.

If you are researching a field that has changed relatively little since the publication of the secondary data that you have found then data published some time ago may still be useful.

However, if your field of research is rapidly changing then ageing secondary data is likely to be of limited value to you. If you decide to use it you will have to caution your readers about its validity as a reflection of the current situation and explain how what has happened since the data was collected has reduced its usefulness.

If you want to use the data as the basis of a comparison between then and now, the age of the data is what makes it useful. You will of course need to make sure that if you collect data as part of your investigation of the current situation, you generate data that can be compared to the secondary data. This means you will have to ask or measure the same sort of things about the same sort of sample.

A second issue that you need to look at is how the secondary data was collected. Unless the results are about a small population, it is sample data. So, how large was the sample? How were the people or items in the sample selected? Was it a random or at least a representative sample of the population it came from?

If the population consisted of things, how were the items in the sample measured or counted? If the population consisted of people, how were they asked for the data they provided?

You will probably have to study the source in which you found the secondary data very carefully to find the answers to these questions. Look for a section called 'Methodology', which should explain the methods used to gather the data. Look through any footnotes or notes at the end of the sources for information about how the data was collected, any difficulties the researchers had, and any warnings they give about the validity of their results.

You may be fortunate in finding secondary data that is sufficiently up to date and collected properly. If this is the case the next thing you have to think about is the way in which the secondary data is presented in the secondary source.

The author or authors who prepared the secondary source may have included their original data in their publication, perhaps in an appendix, so check the source carefully. If the original data is included you will be able to consider various ways in which you can present their data in your report. You can decide which form of presentation will be most appropriate for your discussion of the data.

However, it is more likely that the researchers who collected the original data have not included it in their published results. This is almost inevitable if the study they undertook was a large one. The data will probably be presented in the form of statistical measures and diagrams. You may find that although the forms of presentation that have been used in the secondary source may not be the ones that you would have chosen, they are ones that will be appropriate for your discussion.

If the form of presentation used in the published source will not be appropriate for your report the first thing to consider is alternative ways of presenting the data that can be based on the form in which it is published. If the secondary source contains a grouped frequency distribution, you can produce a histogram or an approximation of the mean from it. If they have used a contingency table, you can produce a bar chart, and so on.

But you may not be able to present the data in the form you would like using the forms that appear in the secondary source. This may be a problem if you are trying to compare two or more studies from different points in time or different locations.

If you really would like to present the data in forms that cannot be based on the data as it is published, then it is worth writing to the authors of the study directly to ask whether you can get access to the original data. This may seem a little rude, but remember that the secondary source you have found has been produced by people who have probably spent a great deal of time and effort in carrying out their research and are quite justifiably proud of it. They would probably welcome any inquiry about their work, particularly if it were from somebody like you, somebody who is undertaking their own research and may well introduce their work to a new audience. At the very worst, they could only turn down your request or ignore it.

It is also worth approaching authors of secondary sources if you have questions about their research, or if they know of any follow-up work that has been done on it. However, you must give them time to respond to your request. Perhaps they have changed jobs, or are simply too busy to reply to you right away. Try to contact them at least a month or two before the latest time that you would need to have their response in order to make use of it.

When you prepare your project report for submission you must make sure that you acknowledge the source of all secondary data that you use, even if the form in which it is presented in your report is your own work. There is nothing at all wrong with quoting data or text from other publications in your report, as long as you cite the reference, in other words indicate clearly where it came from.

10.2 Primary data

As we have seen the main difficulty in using secondary data in a project is that it may not fit your requirements. It may not be the data that you would like to have to support the arguments and discussion that you want to develop in your work. You can get around this by collecting primary data. The advantage of doing this is that the data will be up to date and it should be exactly what you want for your project. The disadvantage is that collecting primary data requires careful thought, detailed planning, and plenty of time.

You will have to decide if you are going to collect primary data as early as possible. You should try to identify your data requirements at the same stage as you produce the literature survey. Successful primary data collection is very difficult to do in a short period of time.

After you have identified your data requirements you will need to address two questions: first, whom can you get the data from and, second, how will you be able to get it?

If you require data that you yourself can collect by undertaking a series of experiments in a particular place, perhaps a laboratory or a kitchen, or making a series of direct observations then the first of these questions is answered. You will next need to consider the second question. This means you will have to identify the method of investigation or the means of observation, define the population, decide how large the sample you will study needs to be, and how you will select it.

However, a lot of research into the hospitality and tourism sectors involves getting data from individuals and/or organizations. If this is true in your case then define the types of people or organizations carefully. If the number of people or organizations that fit your definition is quite small then you can carry out a survey of the whole population. This situation is rare, so you will probably have to take a sample from the population.

10.2.1 Selecting your sample

The approach you take to selecting a sample depends on whether you can list all the things, people or organizations that make up the population you want to investigate. Such a list is sometimes called a *sampling frame*. If you can produce a sampling frame, which you should be able to do if you are looking for instance at five-star hotels in the UK, then there are a number of ways in which you can select your sample.

If you want to select a random sample, number each item listed on your sampling frame. One way of picking random samples is called the *lottery* method. Put one numbered ticket for each entry on the list into some sort of receptacle, traditionally a hat, and blindly pick the same number of tickets from the hat as the number of items that you want in your sample. You could write numbers on pieces of paper but it is much easier to buy a set of raffle tickets.

An alternative way of getting a random sample is to use random numbers. These are not, as the name may suggest, numbers that just come into your head (which will not be random), but sequences of numbers generated at random using computer software. You can get such a sequence from Excel by selecting the **Data Analysis** option from the **Tools** menu. Choose the **Random Number Generation** option from the list in the command window.

The way you use the random numbers depends on how many entries there are in your sampling frame. If there are less than ten,

Hospitality, Leisure & Tourism Series

take a sequence of random numbers and use them one at a time to pick your sample. If there are up to a hundred in your sampling frame, use the random numbers two at a time. If you have up to a thousand, use them three at a time and so on.

Example 10.1

A sampling frame identifies 68 restaurants that offer Slavonic cuisine. We want to study a random sample of 10 of these restaurants. The following sequence of random numbers has been produced to help us select a sample:

15030 61249 018029 15719 31751

The sampling frame consists of less than 100 entries so we take the random numbers two at a time:

15   03   06   12   49   01   80   29   15   71   93   17   51

The first pair is 15, so the first restaurant in our sample will be the one that appears 15th in the sampling frame. The second pair is 03, so we pick the 3rd restaurant on the list. As we continue we find that the seventh pair of numbers is 80, which means that the seventh restaurant we should select is the one that appears 80th on the list. As we only have 68 restaurants on the list we ignore the 80 and use the next pair, 29 to select our 7th restaurant. This means the next pair, 15 should be used to select the eighth restaurant. But we have already picked the 15th restaurant, so again we take the next pair of numbers instead.

MINITAB offers a more direct approach to making a random selection. List the number of each of the entries on your sampling frame in a worksheet column. If you have a lengthy sampling frame it will be easier to use the **Make Patterned Data** option on the **Calc** menu, then choose **Simple Set of Numbers** from the sub-menu and you can ask it to generate the list of numbers for you. Once the list is in a column, choose **Random Data** from the **Calc** menu, then **Sample From Columns** from the sub-menu. In the command window you will have to specify the size of the sample, the column where you have located the numbers, and the column where you would like the package to store the random selection it makes.

In general, random sampling is the best way of selecting your sample because it means you will be able to use statistical decision-making techniques to generalize from your results. However, you may need to modify the approach in order to make sure that a balanced sample is produced. This is important when the population is composed of clearly divided categories and you want to ensure that each category is represented in your sample. Such categories are called *strata* and the method we use to take a sample from such a population is called *stratified sampling*.

To use stratified sampling you need to identify how many elements in the population belong to each category. You have to work out the proportion of the population that you want to have in your sample and apply this proportion to the number of elements in each category to find out how many need to be selected from each category. You can then use random sampling to make the selection from each category.

Example 10.2

An organization has 500 employees. Of these, 200 are based at Aberdeen, 180 at Barnet and 120 at Canterbury. We want to select a sample of 100 of the organization's employees.

The sample will consist of 20 per cent of the organization's employees so we will select a random sample of 20 per cent of the employees at each site. To make up our sample we will select a random sample of 20 per cent of the employees at Aberdeen, 20 per cent from Barnet and 20 per cent from Canterbury. The 40 we choose from Aberdeen, with the 36 from Barnet and the 24 from Canterbury will give us the sample of 100.

Using stratified sampling is particularly useful if you want to perform contingency analysis on your data. It should enable you to avoid having too few data in some categories and not being able to get valid test results.

The methods of sampling that we have looked at so far assume that it is possible to compile a list of elements in the population, a sampling frame. But what if this is not possible? Perhaps the population is very large or it is not possible to identify all of the elements in it.

If you can't produce a sampling frame you could use *cluster sampling* to select a sample. This is a good approach to take if the population is finite. For instance you may want to study a sample of gardens that are open to the public in the UK. There are many of these, but not so many that we could describe the number of them as infinite. Constructing a sampling frame may be difficult if they are not all listed in a readily available source.

To apply cluster sampling to produce a sample in such circumstances would mean dividing the UK into areas and selecting a small random sample of areas. Sub-divide these areas into smaller areas and select a small random sample of each of them. Keep going until you have a suitable number of small areas. You then study every element in each of the small areas you have selected.

Hospitality, Leisure & Tourism Series

Using cluster sampling is easier if you use existing ways in which the areas are divided to make your selections. The ways in which the UK is divided up on maps and between different telephone directories and postcodes provide useful frameworks for cluster sampling.

You should be wary of using cluster sampling if your method of data collection entails visiting each person or organization or location in your sample. The expense of making visits to a selection of far-flung areas may be prohibitive. However, you can reduce the prospect of this somewhat by excluding areas that you could not feasibly visit.

If you need to select a sample from a very large population, such as the general public, then the construction of a sampling frame is just not feasible. For instance suppose you want to interview a sample of 100 people in the UK to find out about their experiences of fast-food restaurants. You could find the last official census of the UK population, use it as a sampling frame and select from it a random sample of 100 people, but this would be a huge task.

It would be much more feasible to take a clipboard and ask 100 people that you approach on the street. However, if you do this you should try to ensure that the sample you select is balanced. If you want to research the relationship between gender and attitudes to fast food then you will not be able to do so effectively if your sample consists of 99 men and 1 woman. If you want to contrast the opinions of school students with those of others you won't be able to do so if you conduct your interviews on a working day during a school term.

To make sure that you get a balanced sample from this sort of investigation use *quota sampling*. Suppose you want to make sure that a sample of 100 people is balanced by gender and whether or not the respondents are school students. You might decide to interview a quota of 25 male school students, a quota of 25 female school students, a quota of 25 adult males, and a quota of 25 adult females. This would mean that once you have interviewed the 25th male school student you don't bother interviewing any more male school students and so on.

10.2.2 Choosing the size of your sample

As well as deciding how you will select your sample you need to decide how large it should be. Basically the larger the sample the better, but also the larger the sample the more time and resources will be required to collect the data. There are two issues that you have to consider, the first is how much data you will need in order to use the techniques you would like to use to analyse it. The second issue is the proportion of inquiries that will be successful, the *response rate*.

Although we can say that the larger the sample, the better, we should add that the larger the sample the less the marginal advantage of a large sample tends to be. For instance, if you have a sample that consists of 30 elements you will be able to use the Standard Normal Distribution in any statistical decision making based on your sample data even if the sample doesn't come from a Normal population. So having a sample that consists of at least 30 elements is to your advantage. The extra advantage of having a sample much larger than 30, for instance 100, is not so great, in fact so little that it may be difficult to justify the extra time involved.

If you need to produce inference results to a particular degree of precision and level of confidence then you must calculate the minimum sample size you should use. Example 8.4 in Chapter 8 illustrates how this can be done.

If you plan to carry out contingency analysis on your sample data to test for association between characteristics, then you have to take into account the number of categories in each of the characteristics. Suppose you want to ask a sample of respondents from five different geographical regions their opinion of five different types of leisure activity, then the contingency table you will be using for your results will have five rows and five columns, making 25 cells in all. If your sample consists of 100 respondents then the sample data will be spread around these cells far too thinly. If you cannot reduce the number of categories you will have to increase the sample size as well as use cluster sampling to ensure that your results are substantial enough to make your conclusions valid.

You should also consider that the sample size is not necessarily the same as the number of people or organizations that you will need to approach for data. The reason is that some of them will be disinclined or unable to respond to your request. The proportion of responses that are successful is the response rate.

The response rate you achieve will depend partly on the method you use to collect your data and there are a number of things that you can do to make the response rate higher. We will look at these in the next section. However, when you are planning your data collection you need to build a figure for the response rate into your calculations.

Response rates vary widely, but in most investigations like the one you are undertaking a response rate of more than 40 per cent, which means that more than 40 per cent of requests made are successful, would be considered very good. A response rate of less than 20 per cent on the other hand, would be considered poor.

To make sure that you get enough responses to satisfy your sample size requirements multiply the sample size you need by a factor of three, or even four if your requests will be difficult for your respondents to fulfil. This means that if, for the purposes of your analysis, you need a sample of 30, then you should approach a sample of 90, or even 120.

10.2.3 Methods of collecting primary data

If the primary data that you need will be collected as a result of experiments you will be carrying out in laboratory-style conditions, planning the process of collection involves allocating your time and making sure you have access to the appropriate facilities when you need to use them. The process of collection is under your control. Allow sufficient time for conducting the experiments and, if you are wise, some extra margin of time in case something goes wrong. Even if things go badly wrong there is every chance that you will be able to reschedule your other work in order to complete your research in time to be able to use the data.

Although there are areas of research within the hospitality and tourism sectors that do involve this sort of work, for instance research into safe cooking times or catering ergonomics, it is much more likely that your project will involve seeking information from other people or organizations. If your project does involve collecting data from others, your planning needs to take into account that you do not control their actions. You will have to consider how and when to make your requests very carefully and allow time in your schedule for the organizations or people who will be asked for data to make their response.

You must start by being absolutely clear about the information you want from them. If you do not understand this, how can you expect them to understand your request? Probably the least effective approach that you could make is to write to them, tell them what your project is about and ask them if they can supply you with any relevant information. At the very best they will send you a leaflet about their business that will probably be of little value to you. Most likely they will not respond to your request at all. After all, if you don't take the trouble to be clear about your information needs why should they take the trouble to help you?

So, you have to be absolutely clear about what you want to know, who will be able to give you the information you need, and how you plan to ask them for it. You will have to be precise about your requirements, make sure you are approaching the right people and ask them for what you need in such a way that they will find it as easy as possible to help you.

If your respondents are individuals, make sure that you have the correct name and address for every one of them. If your respondents are people who hold certain types of posts within an organization, make sure you have the correct name, job title, and business address for every one of them. Getting these details right will improve your response rate. The fastest way that anything you send gets into the waste paper basket is if it isn't directed to a named individual.

Your request for information should be made in the form of a business letter. It must be word-processed and you should use appropriate opening and closing formalities, after all you are not writing to a friend. The letter should explain clearly to the recipient who you are, what research you are undertaking, and how they can help you. The final paragraph should thank them in anticipation of their help.

What you ask your respondents to do depends on the depth and breadth of the information that you are seeking. If you only want one or two pieces of data, then simply ask for this in your letter, making sure that you are as precise as possible about your requirements. For instance if you want a figure relating to a particular year or location, then say so.

If you need information in depth, such as opinion and comment on particular issues, then consider requesting an interview with each of your respondents. If you decide to do this, ask for an interview in your letter and explain in the letter what sort of issues you would like to ask them about. To make it easy to compare the results from the different respondents, conduct *structured interviews*, interviews that consist of the same framework of primary and supplementary questions.

If you need a broad range of information, then you will probably have to design and use a questionnaire. This is a standard document that consists of a series of questions and spaces for the respondent to provide a written response.

Before you start compiling a questionnaire, make sure that it is the most appropriate method of collecting the data you need. Good questionnaire research is not easy to conduct, so explore all other ways of assembling the data you need first.

Unfortunately, there are many final year students who have launched themselves straight into collecting data using questionnaires without thinking things through. One student studying the effectiveness of special hospitality events in boosting sales sent a questionnaire to every member of the marketing department of a multinational IT company. She asked each respondent to say how many new sales leads had come from special events over the previous year. The Administrative Officer in the marketing department had this information at her fingertips. In that case one well-directed letter would have produced better results more quickly than the 50 or so questionnaires she sent out.

However, if you want responses to many precise questions from many respondents, then a questionnaire is probably the best way of getting them. If you do it properly, questionnaire research will give you the data you need at relatively little expense. But done badly, questionnaire research can result in poor response rates and inappropriate data.

So, how can you undertake questionnaire research to maximize the chances of good results? The key is to design the questionnaire carefully and to test it before sending it out to all the respondents in your sample. If you make the effort to produce a questionnaire that is straightforward for your respondents to complete, you will get a higher response rate.

You should send the questionnaire out with the letter requesting help from your respondents. If you do not send it out with an accompanying letter, perhaps because you will be distributing it personally, insert a message at the top of the questionnaire thanking your respondents for their help. If you want your respondents to return the completed questionnaire by post, you can improve the chances of them doing so by enclosing a self-addressed envelope with the questionnaire.

Aim to restrict the length of the questionnaire to two sides. This will make the task of completing it feel less onerous for your respondents and make it easier for you to collate the results at a later stage.

The sequence in which you pose the questions needs careful thought. You may want to know some details about the respondents, such as the time they have worked in their current post, or their qualifications. It is probably best to ask these sorts of questions first, because they will be easy for your respondents to answer, and once they have started filling in your questionnaire they are more likely to finish it.

Sometimes researchers will put questions that seek personal information at the very end of the questionnaire. They do this because they are concerned that putting requests for personal information first makes the questionnaire seem too intrusive and respondents will be wary about completing it. This is a matter of judgement. Unless the questions you use to request personal information are invasive, it is probably better to put them first.

Arrange the questions that you want to put in your questionnaire in a logical sequence. Avoid jumping from one topic to another. You may find it useful to arrange the questionnaire in sections, with each section containing a set of questions about a particular topic or theme.

Design the questions so that they will be easy for your respondents to answer *and* so that the answers will be easy for you to collate. Avoid open-ended questions like 'What do you think about internet marketing?'. Many respondents will be deterred from answering questions like this because they feel they have to write a sentence or a paragraph to respond to them. You will find the responses difficult to analyse because there will probably be no obvious way of segregating and arranging them. At best you will only be able to put them into broad categories of response.

You will find the results far easier to analyse if you build appropriate categories into the questions. In some cases these categories are obvious, such as female and male for gender. In other cases you may need to establish the categories yourself, for instance types of holiday.

If you want to find what opinions your respondents have, you might use *rating scales*. One way of doing this is to make a statement and invite your respondents to express the strength of their agreement or disagreement with the statement using a numerical scale. For instance we might ask respondents to give their assessment of the statement:

'Internet marketing is vital for the future of our business.'

We could ask them to indicate their opinion by giving us a rating on a scale of 1 to 5, where 1 is strong agreement with the statement and 5 is strong disagreement with the statement.

The data we get from questions that use rating scales is often described as 'soft', to suggest that it is likely to be a little vague or erratic. The adjectives 'firm' or 'hard' data on the other hand describe data that is clear and consistent.

The reason that data collected by means of rating scales is likely to be soft is that the scales are subject to the interpretation of the respondents. Different respondents will have different perceptions of concepts like 'strong agreement'. Two people may have identical viewpoints but one may consider it to be 'strong agreement' and put a '1' whereas the other may consider it 'general agreement' and put a '2'. We would not have the same difficulty with a question like 'how many children do you have?' which would generate hard data.

It is better to ask questions that will provide hard data if you can. For instance, instead of the request for an opinion on a statement about internet marketing, it would be better to ask if the organization uses the internet in its marketing activities, how much business has been generated through it, and so on.

When you have designed your questionnaire it is absolutely vital that you try it out before you send it out to your respondents. You need to make sure that somebody who is reading it for the first time will understand it completely and be able to respond to the questions asked. This is something you simply cannot do yourself. You have written and designed it, so of course it makes sense to you, but the key question is, will it make sense to the people that you want to complete it?

Try to test or 'pilot' your questionnaire by asking a number of people to complete it. Ideally these people should be the same sort of people as the respondents in your sample, the same sort of age, occupation, etc. If you can't find such people then ask friends. Whoever you get to test the questionnaire for you, talk to them about it after they have completed it. You need to know which questions were difficult to understand, which ones difficult to answer, was the sequence right, and so on. If necessary modify the questionnaire in the light of their criticisms. Then test it again, preferably on different people. Keep testing it until it is as easy for respondents to use as possible, yet will still enable you to get the information you need.

Testing a questionnaire can be a tedious and annoying process, not least because *you* are convinced that *your* questionnaire is something that even a compete idiot can understand. The point is that it is not your assessment of the questionnaire that matters. It is whether the respondents who can provide you with the information you want will understand it. If they can't then the whole exercise will turn into a waste of time. So, be patient and learn from the people who test your questionnaire. Their advice can improve your response rate and the quality of information you get.

10.3 Presenting your analysis

When you have completed your investigations and analysed your results you will need to think about how you will incorporate your analysis into your report. The key editorial questions that you have to address are what to include, how to present it, and where to put it. You will have to think about these issues when you plan the structure of your final document.

If you have collected primary data you will need to explain how you collected it. You should do this in a section called 'Methodology' that ought to be located amongst the early sections of the report, probably after the introductory sections. Your reader should be able to find out from your methodology section how you selected you sample, and what process you used to gather your data.

You shouldn't need to include the raw data in your report. Your reader is unlikely to want to comb through a stack of letters, completed questionnaires, or record sheets. However, it may be wise to put a single example in an appendix, and make reference to that appendix in the methodology section, to help your reader understand how the data was collected.

Unless you have a very modest amount of data, use a suitable computer package to produce your analysis. If you have a set of completed questionnaires, make sure you number each one of them before you store data from them in the package, and put the data from questionnaire number one in row one of the worksheet or spreadsheet and so on. If you do this you will find it much easier to rectify any mistakes that you make when you enter your data. You will also find it convenient if you need to check specific responses when you come to examine the analysis.

The package you use to analyse your data may provide ways of saving you time when you enter your data. For instance, if you have data about UK holiday locations that consists of replies that are either 'England', 'Scotland' and 'Wales', typing these words into the package is laborious. If you use MINITAB you can use the coding facility to change labels like 'E' for England and 'S' for

Scotland, which are easy to enter, to the full name of the country. Select **Code** from the **Manip** menu then **Text to Text** from the sub-menu (or **Numeric to Text** if you use numeric labels). In the command window you will have to specify the location of the data you want to change, and where you want the changed data stored, as well as exactly how you want the data changed.

The results that you do include should be those that have proved useful. There may be data that you tried to collect, but were unable to. Perhaps your respondents simply didn't have the information, perhaps they supplied the wrong data. For a variety of reasons collecting primary data can produce disappointments.

If part of your data collection activity has not borne fruit, there is not a lot you can do about it. Don't be tempted to include inappropriate data purely because you have collected it. The results you include in the report should be the ones that have a part to play within your report, not ones for which you have to create an artificial role.

You may well need to discuss the reasons for the failure of part of your quest for information in your report, particularly if it relates to an important aspect of your project. Others could use your work and you will be making a valid contribution to knowledge if your unfortunate experience is something they can learn from.

The structural plan of your final report should help you decide what results you will need to include, but you will also have to decide how to present them. You need to remember that your reader will be looking at your final report without experiencing the process of carrying out the project. You will have to introduce the results to them gradually, starting with the more basic forms of presentation before showing them more elaborate types of analysis.

In the early parts of the discussion of your results you should explain the composition of your sample. You can do this effectively by using simple tables and diagrams. Further on you may want to show what your respondents said in response to the questions you asked them. Again there is scope here for using simple tables and diagrams. If the results you are reporting consist of quantitative data, use summary measures to give your reader an overview of them.

Later on in your report you will probably want to explore connections between the nature of your respondents, or the organizations they work for, and the facts or opinions they have provided. Here you can make use of bivariate techniques: contingency tables for qualitative data, and scatter diagrams, regression and correlation for quantitative data.

The techniques we have referred to so far in this section are descriptive methods, techniques we can use to show or describe data. Look back at the first few chapters of this book for more information about them.

At the heart of most good projects is at least one proposition or hypothesis that the project is designed to evaluate. You should be able to put your hypothesis to the test by using statistical decision-making techniques, the methods of statistical inference that feature in the later chapters of this book. These techniques will enable you to make judgements about the population, from which your sample is drawn, using your sample results.

For instance, suppose the proposition that your project is intended to assess is that growing travel companies use internet marketing. You could use a contingency test to test for association between whether or not companies use internet marketing and whether or not they recorded an increase in turnover during the last year. If your proposition is that hours worked in the hotel sector exceed those specified in working time regulations, you could produce an interval estimate for hours worked by all hotel workers.

If you want to produce estimates or test hypotheses and your results come from a sample taken from a small population you may need to make a small adjustment when you calculate the estimated standard error. You need to multiply it by the *finite population correction factor*. If we use n to represent the size of the sample and N to represent the size of the population, we can express the correction factor as:

$$(N - n)/N$$

Example 10.3

A sample of 40 hotels is taken at random from the 150 hotels in a town. The standard deviation of the number of staff in these 40 hotels is 25. Calculate the estimated standard error using the appropriate finite population correction factor.

Estimated standard error $= s/\sqrt{n} \times (N - n)/N$

$$= 25/\sqrt{40} \times (150 - 40)/150$$

$$= 3.953 \times 0.6$$

$$= 2.372$$

The adjustment is important if the sample constitutes a large proportion of a finite population, as in Example 10.3. However, if the sample is less than 5 per cent of the population then it is not necessary to make the adjustment.

Once you have decided which analysis you are going to include in your final report and the form in which you will present it, you must consider exactly where the various tables, diagrams and numerical results will be located within the report. You will have gone to a lot of trouble to collect your data and analyse it, so it is worth making sure that you use it in the most effective way.

Your guiding principle should be to make it as easy as possible for your reader to find the pieces of your analysis that you want them to consult. If the piece of analysis is a diagram or table you have two options: you can insert it within the text of your report or you can put it in an appendix. If the piece of analysis is a numerical result you have a third option, you can weave it into the text itself.

In order to decide where to put a piece of analysis, consider how important it is that your reader looks at it. If it is something that the reader has to look at, then it really should be inserted within the text. Avoid full-page inserts and make sure that the analysis is positioned as closely as possible to the section of the text that first refers to it. It will be very frustrating for your reader if they have to comb through the whole report to look for something that you refer to pages away from it. Every insert you place within the text must be labelled, for instance 'Figure 1' or 'Table 3', and you should always refer to it using the label.

If you have some analysis you consider your reader may want to refer to, but doesn't need to look at, put it into an appendix. Make sure that every appendix is numbered, and you use the appendix number whenever you refer to that analysis. Arrange your appendices so that the first one the reader finds referred to in your text is Appendix 1, and so on. Don't be tempted to use an appendix as a 'dustbin' for every piece of analysis that you have produced, whether you refer to it in your text or not. Any analysis that you do not refer to directly will be superfluous as far as your reader is concerned and may distract them from what you want them to concentrate on.

Single numerical results such as means and standard deviations can be reported directly as part of your text. However you may want to draw your reader's attention to the way in which the result was produced. If so, you can put the derivation of the result in an appendix and refer your reader to it. This is a good idea if you have had to adjust the procedure that your reader would expect you to use to produce such a result, for instance if you have to use the finite population correction factor that we looked at earlier in the chapter.

Allow yourself time in your schedule to read through your final report before submitting it. Make sure that all your inserts are labelled, all your appendices numbered, and all your sources are acknowledged. If you have time, ask a friend to read though just in case there are glitches that you have overlooked. Ask them how easy it was to find the inserts and appendices when they were referred to them.

Checking the draft and the final version can be tedious and time-consuming, but it is time and effort well spent. When your tutor reads it in order to assess it you want to make sure that the version they read is as polished and professional as possible.

Solutions to selected review questions

Chapter 1

1.1   (a) (v),   (b) (vi),   (c) (i),   (d) (ii),   (e) (iii),   (f) (iv)

1.2   (a) (iii),   (b) (v),   (c) (iv),   (d) (i),   (e) (ii)

1.3   (a) $\sum\limits_{i=1}^{n} x$ = £25.60

      (b) $\sum\limits_{i=2}^{4} x$ = £18.39, the total cost of the food items.

1.4   (a) 1740 hrs   (b) 1015 hrs

1.5   The coach used in Germany does 14.13 mpg, so choose the other one.

1.6 $\sqrt{175}$ = 13.23, so the paved area will be 13 m × 13 m.

1.7   Total cost = $73.92, which is £46.20.

1.8   £25.52 + £29.78 + £42.54 = £97.84

1.9   405

Chapter 2

2.1   (i) (d), (f)   (ii) (c), (e)   (iii) (a), (b)

2.10 (a) (v),   (b) (vi),   (c) (vii),   (d) (i),   (e) (iv),   (f) (iii),
      (g) (ii)

Chapter 3

3.1 (a) (v), (b) (iv), (c) (i), (d) (ii), (e) (vi), (f) (iii)

3.2 (a) 1
(b) Median = 3, Q1 = 1, Q3 = 4
(c) 2.92

3.3 (a) Median = (324 + 343)/2 = 333.5.
(b) Q1 = 257, Q3 = 403, SIQR = (403 − 257)/2 = 73

3.4 (a) Median = (500 + 512)/2 = 506.
(b) Q1 = 441, Q3 = 547, SIQR = (547 − 441)/2 = 53

3.5 (a) A Mean = 22.72.   B Mean = 19.50.
(b) A Standard deviation = 4.32
    B Standard deviation = 4.33

3.6 Silly Burger   Median = £14,196,   Mean = £14,500
    Car Burger Eater   Median = £21,590,   Mean = £21,000

3.7 Median = 11 minutes, Q1 = 8.5 minutes, Q3 = 16 minutes, SIQR = (16 − 8.5)/2 = 3.7 minutes

3.8 (a) False, (b) True, (c) True, (d) False, (e) True,
    (f) False, (g) True, (h) False

Chapter 4

4.1 (a) (viii), (b) (vi), (c) (v), (d) (vii), (e) (iv), (f) (i),
    (g) (ii), (h) (iii)

4.2 (a) positive, (b) negative, (c) positive, (d) positive,
    (e) negative, (f) positive

4.3 (a) −0.815, (b) Visits, (d) Visits = 15.7 − 0.323 Age,
    (e) 6 times, (f) under 18

4.4 (a) 1998 = 114.23, 1999 = 131.75
    (b) 1998 = 114.24, 1999 = 131.75

4.5

	1994	1995	1996	1997	1998
A	10.0	10.3	10.9	10.6	10.1
B	11.5	11.4	11.3	11.6	11.6

4.6 (a) Centred MAs

Summer Year 2	291.625
Autumn Year 2	296.125
Winter Year 3	305.625
Spring Year 3	314.75

(b) Seasonal components

Winter	243.56
Spring	−11.375
Summer	−88.19
Autumn	−150.88

4.7

Day 21	276.46
Day 22	371.92
Day 23	335.08
Day 24	411.04
Day 25	225.20

Chapter 5

5.1 (a) (ix), (b) (iii), (c) (vi), (d) (viii), (e) (i), (f) (iv), (g) (ii), (h) (x), (i) (vii), (j) (v)

5.2 (a) 0.216, (b) 0.256, (c) 0.464, (d) 0.572, (e) 0.100, (f) 0.116, (g) 0.093, (h) 0.481

5.4 (a) 0.158, (b) 0.433, (c) 0.736, (d) 0.050, (e) 0.182

5.5 0.7524

5.6 (a) 0.360, (b) 0.146, (c) 0.438, (d) 0.059, (e) 0.178

5.7 (a) 0.050, (b) 0.264, (c) 0.686

Chapter 6

6.1 (a) (iii), (b) (vi), (c) (iv), (d) (i), (e) (ii), (f) (v)
6.2 0.1869
6.3 0.2621
6.4 No. The expected number of tables with no English speaker is 15.726.
6.5 0.1912
6.6 (a) 0.1225, (b) 0.3797, (c) 0.4066, (d) 0.2275
6.7 (a) £500, (b) Yes
6.8 EMV (large order) = £1250, EMV (small order) = £200

Chapter 7

7.1 (a) (iv), (b) (vii), (c) (vi), (d) (i), (e) (viii), (f) (v), (g) (ii), (h) (iii)
7.2 (a) 0.9332, (b) 0.6915, (c) 0.3413, (d) 3.3355 hours, approximately 3 hours 20 minutes, (e) 3.56745 hours approximately 3 hours 34 minutes
7.3 (a) 0.0548, (b) 0.2696, (c) 8.08 per cent, (d) 34.46 per cent, (e) £436.50
7.4 (a) 0.6554, (b) 0.7881, (c) 0.5028, (d) 0.0446, (e) 58.4 years, (f) 18.7 years
7.5 (a) 0.0062, (b) 0.8351, (c) 71.72p, (d) 79.66p
7.6 (a) 0.0228, (b) 0.3821, (c) 0.0035
7.7 (a) 0.0062, (b) 0.8351, (c) 0.3085, (d) £9.16
7.8 (a) 0.0008, (b) 0.0017

Chapter 8

8.1 (a) (v), (b) (vi), (c) (vii), (d) (i), (e) (iv), (f) (iii), (g) (viii), (h) (ii)
8.2 (a) 1.633 to 2.037 hours, (b) 1.604 to 2.096 hours
8.3 (a) £27.50 to £32.30, (b) £27.05 to £32.75
8.4 (a) £59.07 to £65.69, (b) 200
8.5 0.187 to 0.331

8.6 Test statistic = 1.63, not significant at 5 per cent.

8.7 Test statistic = 5.97, very significant.

8.8 Test statistic = −1.56, not significant at 5 per cent.

8.9 Test statistic = −2.95, significant at 5 per cent.

8.10 Test statistic = 6.78, very significant.

Chapter 9

9.1 (a) (v), (b) (vii), (c) (viii), (d) (i), (e) (iv), (f) (iii), (g) (ii), (h) (vi)

9.2 Test statistic = 2.95, not significant

9.3 Test statistic = 7.89, significant

9.4 Test statistic = 9.25, significant

9.5 Test statistic = 14.06, significant

9.6 Test statistic = 2.26, significant

9.7 (a) r = 0.797, test statistic = 3.49, significant

(b) Audience = −1018 + 0.487 Cards, test statistic = 3.49, significant

9.8 (a) Inquiries = 247 − 8.94 Distance, test statistic = −5.14, very significant

(b) 75 to 151

(c) −0.8 to 226.8

9.9 (a) Profit = 142 + 1.00 Guests, test statistic = 4.93, very significant

(b) £339.10 to £545.20

(c) £138.50 to £745.50

9.10 (a) Sales = 52.5 − 24.5 Price, test statistic = −8.04, very significant

(b) (i) 7.006 to 12.340   (ii) −15.872 to −1.479

Index